This book responds in thoughtful and research-informed ways to ideas about education that position students as passive receivers of information embedded in the curriculum and transmitted by teachers. Manyukhina and Wyse draw on children's perspectives, as what Jean Rudduck referred to as 'expert witnesses' of their school experience, to systematically document the structures of contemporary schooling and specifically curriculum that both enable and constrain student agency. It provides sound evidence of what can be accomplished in schools when children's curiosities and interests are restored to the centre of teaching and learning, and as such is essential reading for educators navigating complex times and contexts.

– **Nicole Mockler**, *Professor of Education,*
Sydney School of Education and Social Work

This is an important and timely book, reflecting how international trends in national curricula are increasingly shaping a new paradigm for children's education. This new paradigm embraces a holistic view of the child and their educational experience, emphasizing not only what children learn but, importantly, how they learn and who they become through the learning process – recognizing the transformative role that education can play in the lives of children. The authors have done a superb job of capturing the importance and relevance of agency for education today, making this essential reading for anyone involved in building progressive education systems that embody contemporary values.

– **Tracy Curran**, *Director for Curriculum & Assessment with*
National Council for Curriculum and Assessment, Ireland

CHILDREN'S AGENCY IN THE NATIONAL CURRICULUM

How much say should children have in their own education? Through in-depth research in diverse primary schools, Manyukhina and Wyse explore how children's voices and choices shape their learning experiences – and why it matters. This groundbreaking text offers new insights into one of education's most pressing questions: how to balance children's agency with educational standards.

The 40-month research project that is at the heart of the book investigated how England's national curriculum, and other educational structures, affect children's agency. The authors report findings in three contrasting schools: an inner-city primary school, a suburban academy primary school, and an independent school. As a result of the in-depth longitudinal research, this book uncovers the details of how schools can enable or limit children's ability to shape their learning, from classroom choices and playground decisions to curriculum and School Councils.

Children's Agency in the National Curriculum engages with England's national curriculum in the context of curriculum studies and curriculum development internationally. The new findings arise from research that is 'close-to-practice', ensuring that the implications of the work are relevant for children, teachers, and policy makers alike.

Dr. Yana Manyukhina is Senior Researcher at the Helen Hamlyn Centre for Pedagogy (0–11 years) (HHCP) at the Institute of Education (IOE), University College London (UCL).

Dominic Wyse is Professor of Early Childhood and Primary Education at the Institute of Education (IOE), University College London (UCL). He is Founding Director of the Helen Hamlyn Centre for Pedagogy (0–11 Years) (HHCP). From 2019 to 2022 he was President of the British Educational Research Association (BERA). Dominic has also published *The Balancing Act: An Evidence-Based Approach to Teaching Phonics, Reading and Writing* (2024, Routledge), and *Teaching English, Language and Literacy 5th Edition* (2023, Routledge).

CHILDREN'S AGENCY IN THE NATIONAL CURRICULUM

The Promise of Structured Freedom

Yana Manyukhina and Dominic Wyse

Routledge
Taylor & Francis Group
LONDON AND NEW YORK

LEVERHULME
TRUST

UCL
Helen Hamlyn
Centre for Pedagogy

Designed cover image: © Sophia

First published 2025
by Routledge
4 Park Square, Milton Park, Abingdon, Oxon OX14 4RN

and by Routledge
605 Third Avenue, New York, NY 10158

Routledge is an imprint of the Taylor & Francis Group, an informa business

The research reported in this book was funded by a *Leverhulme Trust Research Project Grant*.

We are grateful to the Helen Hamlyn Trust for their support of the work of our research centre, *The Helen Hamlyn Centre for Pedagogy* (0 to 11 Years) (HHCP).

We are grateful to *University College London* (UCL) for providing funding to enable this book to be distributed as open access in digital form.

British Library Cataloguing-in-Publication Data
A catalogue record for this book is available from the British Library

ISBN: 978-1-032-13125-2 (hbk)
ISBN: 978-1-032-13124-5 (pbk)
ISBN: 978-1-003-22777-9 (ebk)

DOI: 10.4324/9781003227779

Typeset in Times New Roman
by Apex CoVantage, LLC

We dedicate this book to the children and teachers who inspired and informed our research, and to children everywhere – we hope your choices shape your world.

CONTENTS

Figures		*xiii*
Tables		*xiv*
Preface		*xv*
Acknowledgements		*xvii*
Acronyms and abbreviations		*xix*

1	Children and agency in the twenty-first century	1

Childhood globally 2
Children in the UK 3
What is 'agency'? 5
Primary education and the curriculum 6
Introduction to the book 7

2	Curriculum, pedagogy, and assessment	10

Knowledge and the curriculum 12
Agency, learning, and educational outcomes 13
National curricula internationally 15
National contexts 18
Redevelopment of the primary curriculum in Ireland 19
National curriculum in Hong Kong 21
National curricula in the UK 22
National curriculum in England from 2014 24

3   Agency and structure in education: A critical realist perspective   31

Defining agency 31
*Critical realism: a framework for understanding
    educational reality 33*
Dimensions of agency in educational settings 35
Sense and exercise of agency: a dual framework 36
Agency as a socially situated capacity to act 39

4   The methods of the CHANT project   43

Research approach and design 44
Critical discourse analysis and critical realism 44
Causality of texts 44
Contextual causality 45
Examining causality in the curriculum 46
The process of critical discourse analysis 46
Limitations of critical discourse analysis 47
Longitudinal in-depth qualitative inquiry 48
Data collection 50
Analyses 57

5   The schools and participants   61

South City Independent 61
    The teachers – 2021 to 2023 62
    The case study pupils 63
    The curriculum 65
    Mental health assembly 66
    School Council 67
    Lesson design 68
    Extracurricular activities 70
    Behaviour policy 71
South City State 72
    The teachers – 2021 to 2022 72
    The teachers – 2022 to 2023 74
    The case study pupils 75
    The curriculum 76
    Beyond the curriculum 79
    The School Council 80
    Lesson design 81
    Behaviour policy 82
    Reading champions 83

Northern City State 84
  School overview 84
  The teachers – 2021 to 2022 84
  The teachers – 2022 to 2023 86
  The case study pupils 87
  The curriculum 89
  The School Council 93
  Lesson design 94
  The reward system 95
  Behaviour policy 96

6 Children and their agency 99

*Talking about agency: our approach to introducing
  the term 99*
Children's agency and choice 100
  South City Independent 100
  South City State 107
  Northern City State 110
Children's agency and perceived subject hierarchies 114
  South City Independent 115
  South City State 116
  Northern City State 118
Children's agency and social dynamics 119
  South City Independent 119
  South City State 120
  Northern City State 121
Children's agency and School Councils 122
  South City Independent 123
  Northern City State 125
Conclusion 127

7 Education structures influencing children's agency 129

Curriculum, knowledge, and subject areas 129
  South City Independent 129
  South City State 133
  Northern City State 137
Assessment, accountability, and children's learning 142
  South City Independent 142
  South City State 144
  Northern City State 146

The school and society 147
   South City Independent 147
   South City State 149
   Northern City State 150

8   Children's agency and primary education   153

Children's choice and agency in primary schools 153
The impact of assessments and the implementation
   gap 155
The role of social dynamics in fostering agency 156
Interplay between structure and agency 158
Structured freedom 160
Implications for policy and practice 163
   Implications for policy 163
   Implications for practice 165
Conclusion 165

Index   *168*

FIGURES

4.1	My Learning Choice Diary	52
4.2a	My Agency Timeline	53
4.2b	My Agency Timeline	54
4.3	Feelings at School	55
5.1	A Pupil's Mathematics Exercise Book	69
5.2	Year 4 Knowledge Organiser	78
5.3	Termly Curriculum Map	90
6.1	Sonia's Learning Choice Diary (Wednesday)	101
6.2	Miriam's Learning Choice Diary (Wednesday)	108
6.3a	Dahlia's Agency Timeline	111
6.3b	Dahlia's Agency Timeline	112

TABLES

4.1   Themes and codes   58

PREFACE

For at least seven years, children's agency has been a key focus for our work and the work of our research centre, the Helen Hamlyn Centre for Pedagogy (0 to 11 Years) (HHCP) at the Institute of Education (IOE), University College London (UCL). The early ideas that ultimately led to the research reported in this book arose from our collaboration with Ireland's National Council for Curriculum and Assessment (NCCA). This initial project involved analysing national curriculum texts from regions performing well in international education comparisons to propose a definition of knowledge for a redeveloped primary curriculum.

Through this and subsequent work, we noted that the voices of key stakeholders in schooling – namely children – appeared to be absent from some national curriculum requirements, particularly England's. However, while national curriculum texts are one thing, we knew from other research that what happens in schools and classrooms can be quite different. This realisation led us to propose studying practices in schools in great depth.

The early realisations led us to grapple with a series of questions: if children are denied opportunities to develop and exercise agency during some of their most critical developmental years, what does this mean for their experiences and outcomes in school? Furthermore, what does it imply for their ability to shape their lives and the world around them in the future? In other words, if society and education do not raise agentic children, how can we expect them to become agentic adults? Such questions were a stimulus for the research project reported in this book: the Children's Agency in the National Curriculum Project (CHANT). Our work is inspired by a desire to deepen the understanding of children's agency in theory, practice, and policy in education and to outline possible ways in which education practitioners can recognise and support the development of children's agency in schools.

We collaborated on all aspects of the CHANT project, hence the order of names for this book is in alphabetical order. The writing of this book was also a collaboration. Yana's main contributions to the CHANT project were theorising agency, critical discourse analysis of the national curriculum, carrying out the research fieldwork, leading the analyses in relation to children, and leading the delivery of the book's manuscript to the publisher. Dominic's main contribution was as Principal Investigator for the CHANT grant application and research project; expertise in the content of researching curriculum, pedagogy and assessment, and in research methods; carrying out some fieldwork visits; leading the analyses in relation to education structures and education policies; and leading the proposal for this book.

We hope you will enjoy reading this book and be as inspired by the children's ideas as we are.

– Dominic Wyse and Yana Manyukhina

ACKNOWLEDGEMENTS

We are very grateful to the many people who supported our work on the CHANT project. In this acknowledgments section, we recognise those individuals who had specific roles.

Alice Bradbury, Professor of Sociology of Education at UCL Institute of Education (IOE) and Co-Director of the Helen Hamlyn Centre for Pedagogy (HHCP). Member of the CHANT Advisory Board.

Alison Foyle, Senior Publisher at Routledge, for her engagement with us over many years and particularly for commissioning this book.

Diane Reay, Emeritus Professor of Sociology of Education at the University of Cambridge, for her review and endorsement of our book.

Eleanore Hargreaves, Professor of Learning and Pedagogy, Department of Curriculum, Pedagogy and Assessment, UCL Institute of Education (IOE). Member of the CHANT Advisory Board.

Emily Ranken, Research Assistant, Helen Hamlyn Centre for Pedagogy, UCL Institute of Education (IOE), for contributing to the review of literature on children's agency.

Gemma Moss, Professor of Literacy and Director of the International Literacy Centre, UCL Institute of Education (IOE). Member of the CHANT Advisory Board.

Helen Bruckdorfer and Holly Churchill, Executive Head Teacher of the Brecknock and Torriano Schools Federation and Head of Torriano School respectively. We have worked with Helen and Holly on projects related to children's rights and agency.

John Carden, Doctoral Researcher, University of Sussex. John spent many hours with Yana theorising children's agency.

Jayati Tripathi, Editorial Assistant, Routledge, for her editorial assistance in publishing the book.

John O'Regan, Professor of Critical Applied Linguistics, Institute of Education (IOE), University College London (UCL). Member of the CHANT Advisory Board.

Louise Hayward, Professor Emeritus, University of Glasgow. Member of the CHANT Advisory Board. We are also grateful to Louise for her review of our research proposal.

Nicole Mockler, Professor of Education, Sydney School of Education and Social Work, for her review and endorsement of this book.

Phil Jones, Emeritus Professor of Children's Rights, Institute of Education (IOE), University College London (UCL). Member of the CHANT Advisory Board.

Richard Harrison, Chair of Governors, Brecknock and Torriano Schools Federation, UCL Institute of Education (IOE). We are grateful to Richard for introducing us to Brecknock and Torriano Schools.

Rupert Higham, Associate Professor, Institute of Education (IOE), University College London (UCL). Member of the CHANT Advisory Board.

Steven Higgins, Professor Emeritus, University of Durham. Member of the CHANT Advisory Board, for his support with our research proposal.

Tracy Curran, Director, National Council for Curriculum and Assessment (NCCA), Ireland, for her review and endorsement of our book.

We are immensely grateful to the children, teachers, and head teachers of the three schools that were part of our research. For reasons of research ethics, we have not named them here.

We are grateful to the Helen Hamlyn Trust for their support for the work of our research centre *The Helen Hamlyn Centre for Pedagogy (0 to 11 Years) (HHCP)*.

The research reported in this book was funded by a Leverhulme Trust Research Project Grant RPG-2020–361.

ACRONYMS AND ABBREVIATIONS

CDA – critical discourse analysis
CHAMP – Calmly and quietly, Hands to yourself, Aware of others, Move slowly, and Pass on the left
CRC – Convention on the Rights of the Child
DfE – Department for Education
D&T – design and technology
EEF – Education Endowment Foundation
HBAI – Households Below Average Income
HHCP – Helen Hamlyn Centre for Pedagogy
IAPS – Independent Association of Prep Schools
ICAPE – Independent Commission on Assessment in Primary Education
IOE – Institute of Education
INSET – in-service training
IPC – International Primary Curriculum
NCE – national curriculum for England
NCCA – National Council for Curriculum and Assessment
NCS – Northern City State
NFER – National Foundation for Educational Research
NQT – Newly Qualified Teacher
NPQ – National Professional Qualification
OECD – Organisation for Economic Cooperation and Development
OED – Oxford English Dictionary
P4C – Philosophy for Children
PE – physical education
PGCE – Postgraduate Certificate in Education
PISA – Programme for International Student Assessment

PRC – People's Republic of China
PSC – phonics screening check
RE – religious education
SAR – Special Administrative Region
SCI – South City Independent
SCS – South City State
SLT – senior leadership team
STEM – science, technology, engineering, and mathematics
TLR – Teaching and Learning Responsibility
UK – United Kingdom
UN – United Nations
UNCRC – United Nations Convention on the Rights of the Child
UNICEF – United Nations Children's Fund
USA – United States of America

1

CHILDREN AND AGENCY IN THE TWENTY-FIRST CENTURY

The metaphor of a factory where children are commodified as products who receive interventions from the education production line who will then emerge fully formed as citizens is a well-used one that takes us back through time to the beginnings of state-funded education in England. It is, however, a metaphor that should still cause us to reflect on the aims of education and how education could be more appropriate for all children. Perhaps a more telling metaphor for the twenty-first century is that of the ghost. Although there are thousands of well-meaning words written about what society thinks is in the best interests of children for their education, their health, their social conditions, and their lives in general, the influence of children themselves on these matters is rarely seen or heard. Much of education is done 'to' children rather than 'with' them. So, although children are clearly physically present in education, it may be that they are in some senses not really visible, or at least this is the case in relation to some education policies that render them ghost-like.

For those people who are involved with education it can be all too easy to lose sight of a holistic view of children and childhood because of what is in some countries an instrumental emphasis on education generated by state education policies and their technicalities. For example, national statutory tests of children's progress in reading, writing, and mathematics can dominate education and educational discourse and lead to a disconnect with children and their wider contexts, but also a neglect of their preferences, their emotions, and a more complete sense of learning and the learner.

One of the main priorities of this book is to explore children's views about education and, in so doing, make children visible, prominent, and seriously attended to.

DOI: 10.4324/9781003227779-1

Childhood globally

There are many factors that affect how we view children and childhood. Conceptions of children are related to histories of thinking, to geography and culture, and hence understanding children and childhood is a global phenomenon. Although progress has been made in education over time, for example in increasing the numbers of children who attend primary schools, there are still many questions about why more children are not thriving in education. A long-standing problem across the world has been children who do not attend school. As a result of not attending school, children miss out on what have been called foundational skills. The United Nations Children's Fund (UNICEF) has a vital role in monitoring trends in education, and coordinating activities, particularly for those children in most need globally. The stark reality is that even before the Covid-19 pandemic, 56% of children in middle-income and low-income countries could not read a simple text by age 10 (Valenza & Dreesen, 2022). In recent work UNICEF's 'Let Us Learn' (LUL) report (UNICEF, 2022) addressed both challenges and potential solutions, with particular emphasis on supporting children returning to school or entering for the first time.

Although foundational skills are essential for educational success, there is a risk that a curriculum can become dominated by these skills to the exclusion of other vital areas of education. One part of this, which has been recognised by UNICEF and hence included in its global monitoring, is the importance of learners' well-being and other social factors. Another vital area that is central to our concerns in this book is the extent to which education is centred on children themselves and includes consultations with children as part of their education. As part of the LUL initiative, in a target region in Bangladesh, parents reported that one of the reasons for their children missing school was that they did not enjoy school when they were there. As a result, teachers were trained in child-centred pedagogy so that they could plan engaging teaching. This new approach appealed to both children and parents. However, despite such promising advances internationally in relation to children's education, the role of children themselves in such developments is uncertain and not frequently documented, particularly not in significant depth or scale.

Another important global mechanism, which is used to monitor children's rights, is the Convention on the Rights of the Child (CRC) (United Nations, 1989). Along with many other countries, the UK was an early signatory and was quick to ratify the CRC (only the USA has still not ratified the CRC). All countries are required to submit regular reports on their progress towards meeting all the articles of the CRC. The reports are then considered by the UN Committee on the Rights of the Child. The most recent report included reflections on a long-standing issue for the UK: the extent to which the views of children are taken into account in all matters that affect them. The most recent feedback from the committee was as follows:

Respect for the views of the child

23. Noting with concern that children's views are not systematically taken into account in decisions affecting them and in national and local decision-making, and underscoring the importance of the availability of age-appropriate information to facilitate child participation, the Committee recommends that the State party:

    (a) Ensure the right of all children, including younger children, children with disabilities and children in care, to express their views and to have them taken into account in all decisions affecting them, including in courts and relevant judicial proceedings and regarding domestic violence, custody, placement in alternative care, health care, including mental health treatment, education, justice, migration and asylum;

    (b) Strengthen measures to promote the meaningful participation of children in family, community and school settings and in policymaking at the local and national levels, i43.5 pincluding on so-called reserved matters, and develop mechanisms to ensure that the outcomes of children's and youth parliaments are systematically fed into public decision-making;

    (c) Ensure that all relevant professionals working with and for children systematically receive appropriate training on the right of the child to be heard and to have his or her opinions taken into account;

    (d) Consider holding consultations with children and civil society organizations in England and Northern Ireland on lowering the voting age to 16 years.

    (United Nations Committee on the
    Rights of the Child, 2023, paragraph 23)

Schools are important places where children's views should be taken into account, but this requires education policies that explicitly require schools and teachers to seek children's views and seriously attend to them. Such policies also require teacher education and professional development that builds on a holistic view of children and childhood, and which addresses effective strategies to consult with all children in schools.

In global terms, the inequality caused by financial disparities is long-standing and of great concern. However, the detrimental results of poverty are not unique to low-income and middle-income countries: poverty and inequity is a long-standing characteristic within high-income countries as well.

Children in the UK

Many readers of this book are likely to be people who work with children and/or who have a professional interest in children. As a result of being professionally employed they are likely to have succeeded in their education, and have a job that is relatively well paid in relation to people who live in poverty. The experience of childhood for the majority of people in high-income regions is, in general, a happy, secure, and well-supported time, so it can be hard to imagine how different some children's lives are. In 2024, a UK government report revealed data about households living on incomes below the national average. The Households Below Average Income (HBAI) report data (Department for Work and Pensions, 2024) is also known as the 'poverty statistics'. The 2024 report described robust data on the ways in which incomes were distributed between the year-ends 1995 and 2023. Most concerning of all was the finding that 'the largest increases in low-income measures are seen for children, with absolute measures showing the most increase' (p. 1). This also meant that compared to the overall population in the UK, children, the largest group of vulnerable people in the UK, were more likely to live in poverty.

One of the most basic requirements for children is that they have sufficient healthy food to thrive. However, a review of food and nutrition that looked in detail at the issues of children's food, and which reviewed data and policies from 2019 to 2020, presented some very worrying statistics (The Food Foundation, 2020) – 4.2 million children were living in poverty, and 3.7 million children were living in households that would have to spend more than 40% of their income on food, after housing had been paid for. Obesity rates for children from disadvantaged backgrounds were rising, whereas they were falling for children in the wealthiest backgrounds. Such health equalities had risen every year for a decade.

One of the many consequences of UK governments' failures to alleviate child poverty, including failing to ensure that all children have sufficient nutritious food, was that schools felt the need to provide some help in the form of food banks located in schools. Research in our research centre the Helen Hamlyn Centre for Pedagogy (HHCP) included work to look at the practices of food banks in schools (Bradbury & Vince, 2025). It was found that some of the functions traditionally expected of the state were no longer effective, resulting in schools having to shoulder the burden of addressing these gaps. Teachers and other education professionals understood that children arriving at school hungry were unlikely to be in the right frame of mind for learning, which led many schools to feel compelled to take action themselves.

Children's lives in primary schools are affected by the conditions in the society that they live in. These conditions are the background to children's day-to-day experiences in primary school classrooms, and hence were in our minds throughout the process of carrying out the research reported in this book, and as part of other projects in our research centre. More practically, our concerns about children influenced our decision to include children situated in areas of severe poverty as part of our strategy to select contrasting socio-economic contexts for the schools that were part of our research.

One of the most significant determinants of children's experiences in school, and to some degree out of school through homework, is the curriculum. In schools, the particular activities and experiences that are the curriculum – and the associated phenomena of pedagogy and assessment – are determined at national, community, school, and classroom levels. This book is about children and their experiences of a vital phase in their lives: primary education, which in England typically means children aged from 5 to 11. More particularly, the research project that is the main focus of the book was about the curriculum in primary education, and the place of children's 'agency' in the curriculum. The remainder of this chapter addresses our starting points for understanding agency, then the chapter turns to some of the main topics that characterise how we think about the curriculum in primary education.

What is 'agency'?

The most straightforward definition of the term agency is 'the capacity to act' (Oxford English Dictionary [OED], n.d.). Humans all have agency, as a capacity, but the extent to which humans can exercise agency varies a great deal. This variation is primarily caused by aspects in people's lives that affect agency. For example, when in school, children may feel a sense of their agency but find that the rules of the classroom and school restrict their ability to exercise it. And there may well be some good reasons for constraining a person's agency, for example if a child's actions might unreasonably impact in a negative way on other children. Adults also have agency which is sometimes constrained by the structures that are the contexts for their lives and work. For example, teachers may wish to exercise their agency by selecting an approach to teaching that they deem to be effective, but a high stakes statutory assessment such as a test, and associated government guidance, may require them to use an approach to teaching that is counter to their preference. In Chapter 3, we provide a more nuanced and theoretically grounded definition of agency, explaining why this deeper conceptualisation matters for understanding children's experiences in education.

There are three compelling reasons why agency is an important concept in terms of education. The first reason is based on moral values and rights: it is to do with what we value in people and, therefore, what we want from our education systems. Children have fundamental rights, as outlined in the UN Convention on the Rights of the Child (UN, 1989), to have their views taken into account in all matters that affect them. Education that fails to consider children's agency risks violating these basic rights and undermining children's dignity as human beings capable of making meaningful choices about their lives.

The second reason centres on engagement and motivation in learning. If children's agency is supported through their education, they can feel a sense of empowerment and responsibility in their lives. Picture yourself as a learner. How does it feel if you are encouraged to make choices as part of your learning? For example, the first time you were able to choose which subjects to study, and just as important which subjects you chose *not* to study anymore. To take another example, can you remember a time from your primary education when you were encouraged to choose a topic to learn about more independently? Perhaps on these occasions when you were given some choice, and agency, you felt more connected to your education, and more motivated to learn. If children's agency is not supported, then education is likely to be less engaging.

The third reason relates to educational outcomes. There is growing evidence that supporting children's agency can lead to improved well-being and potentially better academic outcomes. While we will examine this evidence more closely in Chapter 2, particularly in relation to curriculum design and implementation, it is worth noting that agency appears to contribute to both psychological well-being and learning success. This suggests that agency is not just morally right or motivationally beneficial but may also enhance fundamental goals of education.

An education system that has a main emphasis on feeding learners' knowledge and which then requires them to regurgitate that knowledge through test answers (the factory model of education), is one where children's agency is not at the forefront, to put it mildly. This is, we think, a less engaging and less beneficial way of educating people. What's more, as we have already begun to discuss in this chapter, children have rights to control their own lives, to be empowered, to be part of an inclusive and respectful society. It is difficult to see how such a society can truly exist if all its citizens are not afforded agency.

In the earlier part of this chapter, we raised the issue of children in poverty. The worrying conditions that many children face in the twenty-first century in a wealthy nation such as England seem even more shocking when we remember that state education in England first emerged from societal concerns about children's lives, which for the poor were dangerous and unhealthy. The Education Act of 1880 that established the idea of compulsory education for all children between the ages of five and ten in England emerged from a series of largely unsuccessful attempts to improve the conditions in poor children's lives. Histories of children and childhood have been part of what has been called *the sociology of childhood*, an academic focus in universities that gained momentum in the 1980s.

In a more recent account of the study of children and childhood Spyrou, Rosen and Cook (2018) noted the importance of the focus of the sociology of childhood on ontological questions such as 'what is a child?', and hence 'what is childhood?', including considerations of social and cultural norms in relation to childhood. They also argued that the field of childhood studies had failed to move sufficiently beyond the concept of 'the agentic child'. Spyrou, Rosen, and Cook argued that what is required is to move beyond thinking about children only as individuals, or independent units of analysis, towards thinking about the ways in which children affect and are affected by the contexts they find themselves in. Ironically, this requires overcoming what they saw as the tendency of an inward-looking gaze of child-centredness by some scholars. Instead, what is required of research into children and childhood is to examine the 'entangled relations which materialise, surround, and exceed children as entities' (Spyrou, Rosen & Cook, 2018, p. 8). The research reported in this book addressed the issue of children's agency in the curriculum in this way.

Primary education and the curriculum

The curriculum in primary education is represented in various ways. One representation of the curriculum is the learning activities that primary schools plan for the children in the classes of the school. Another representation of school curricula is through education policies at a national level which often include a national or state level curriculum that, to varying degrees, require schools and teachers to deliver specified knowledge, skills, and understanding. A key consideration for us is the extent to which children are consulted and involved in the curricula that they experience.

The history of the development of England's national curriculum that was established in 1988 as a result of the Education Reform Act is a history of, at most, superficial consultation with children about their primary education. In 2014 a research report from the Cambridge Primary Review summarised the evidence by noting that although there was interest by teachers and school leaders in consulting pupils, in practice there was a substantial lack of research reporting the outcomes of such consultations (Robinson, 2014). We would add that significant breadth and depth of systematic consultations with primary children had not happened.

The development of England's 2014 national curriculum lacked any systematic consultation with primary-age children. Furthermore, the curriculum's text contained no explicit encouragement for children's agency. Through critical discourse analysis of England's national curriculum text, Yana demonstrated how children's agency was minimally present, due in large part to the knowledge-based theory underlying the curriculum (Manyukhina, 2022). While the language of the curriculum text implied children's agency in certain instances, it failed to explicitly integrate this agency into the subject-specific programmes of study. For instance, the English subject preamble emphasised children's confident use of language as essential to prevent societal disenfranchisement. However, the English programmes of study themselves included no requirements for schools to seek pupils' views, encourage their choices, or involve them in decisions about this vital aspect of their social lives. Ultimately, the national curriculum text positioned children as passive rather than active learners.

As we were doing the final edits of this book, England was in the middle of a review of its national curriculum, and the interim report was due. The only consultation about possible curriculum changes with children and young people up to that point was via the 'Youth Shadow Panel'. The report from the Youth Shadow Panel included a recommendation that the curriculum should have less emphasis on exams and tests, and more emphasis on practical, creative, and interactive learning (Youth Shadow Panel, 2025). Unfortunately, although 554 children and young people responded to a survey initiated by the Youth Shadow Panel, only 14 of these were primary-age children.

Introduction to the book

As you have learned in this introduction chapter so far, the focus of the book is on children's agency and the curriculum in primary education. The book and its analyses are written first and foremost from the perspectives of children and their agency. But a robust consideration of agency necessarily has to take into account the structures that impact on the extent to which any person, child or adult, can exercise their agency. For this reason, the book also has a clear focus on the work of teachers, education leaders, and education policies because they act as a structural dimension that impacts children's agency. What is more, if the evidence shows that children would benefit from more agency in a given education context, then teachers and other educators, including parents, are an important part of how that agency might be realised.

This book reports the first externally funded[1] in-depth qualitative research study of children's agency in the national curriculum in England: it makes an original contribution to understanding a vital aspect of primary education, and children's lives in the twenty-first century, through its very close examination of children's views of their primary education in three very different kinds of primary schools.

In Chapter 2 we expand on the main focus of our research and this book: curriculum and the ways in which curriculum has been studied. We are particularly interested in the ways that national curricula are enacted in schools and classrooms, and the ways in which children and teachers navigate such curricula.

Chapter 3 addresses the theory of agency that has underpinned our research. The chapter begins with a detailed review of what agency means and how we defined agency for our study. Agency is a complex concept, and the way researchers use the word 'agency' often prompts questions from those involved in educational practice, in schools and in governments, about its meaning and practical application. Hence, we devote considerable time to exploring the concept of agency. We also explain how *critical realism* has provided a powerful theoretical framework that informs our thinking about children's agency in the curriculum.

Chapter 4 provides a detailed account of our research methods and explains the rationale behind key decisions, such as our selection of schools, teachers, and children participants. These methodological aspects come alive in Chapter 5 through detailed descriptions of all research participants. As our research employs in-depth qualitative enquiry, we aim for this chapter to give readers a rich understanding of both our participants and their working environments.

The research findings form the core of this book, presented across two major chapters. Chapter 6 concentrates on the children's perspectives and agency, drawing from our analysis of extensive datasets gathered during the research. Chapter 7 primarily examines structures, including how Head Teachers, teachers, and schools approach curriculum planning, while also exploring their reflections on governmental influence, the national curriculum, and related frameworks such as national assessments and the inspectorate.

The book's final chapter further refines and focuses our research outcomes, particularly concluding with our new theory of 'structured freedom' as a way to operationalise the concept of agency and lay a foundation for meaningful change in children's education and lives. Such change cannot be achieved without significant new thinking from politicians, policy makers, and those with expertise in national curricula development. We hope you will find the book compelling and agree with our argument for transforming primary education to prioritise children's agency as a standard requirement at classroom, school, regional, and national levels.

Having placed our research within the broader context of children and childhood in the twenty-first century – including their rights, well-being, and the importance of their agency in education – Chapter 2 examines curriculum, pedagogy, and assessment in detail. These three fundamental aspects of education create the structural framework within which children's agency is understood and enhanced. As the chapter demonstrates, how curriculum is conceived and enacted profoundly affects the extent to which children can exercise meaningful agency in their education.

Note

1 We are grateful to the Leverhulme Trust for the research grant that funded our research. We are also grately to the Helen Hamlyn Trust who fund our research centre for which children's agency is one of its main themes of work.

References

Bradbury, A., & Vince, S. (2025). *Food banks in schools and nurseries: The education sector's responses to the cost-of-living crisis*. Policy Press.

Department for Work and Pensions. (2024). *Households below average income: An analysis of the income distribution FYE 1995 to FYE 2023*. https://www.gov.uk/government/statistics/households-below-average-income-2022-to-2023

The Food Foundation. (2020). *A year of children's food: A progress review of policy on children's food and nutrition across the four UK nations 2019–2020*. https://foodfoundation.org.uk/publication/childrens-right-2food-charter

Manyukhina, Y. (2022). Children's agency in the national curriculum for England: A critical discourse analysis. *Education 3–13, 50*(4), 506–520.

Oxford English Dictionary. (n.d.). Agency. In *Oxford English dictionary*. Oxford University Press. Retrieved December 2, 2024, from https://www.oed.com/dictionary/agency_n1

Robinson, C. (2014). *Children, their voices and their experiences of school: What does the evidence tell us?* (CPRT Research Survey 2). Cambridge Primary Review Trust.

Spyrou, S., Rosen, R., & Cook, D. T. (Eds.). (2018). *Reimagining childhood studies*. Bloomsbury Academic.

United Nations. (1989). Convention on the rights of the child. *United Nations Treaty Series, 1577*, 3–178.

United Nations Children's Fund. (2022). *Let us learn: Learning together to create a gender equal future*. https://www.unicef.org/innocenti/media/4616/file/UNICEF-Let-Us-Learn-Report-2022.pdf

United Nations Committee on the Rights of the Child. (2023, June 22). Concluding observations on the combined sixth and seventh periodic reports of the United Kingdom of Great Britain and Northern Ireland (CRC/C/GBR/CO/6-7). https://www.ohchr.org/en/documents/concluding-observations/crccgbrco5-7-concluding-observations-combined-sixth-and-seventh

Valenza, M., & Dreesen, T. (2022). *Let us learn: Making education work for the most vulnerable in Afghanistan, Bangladesh, Liberia, Madagascar and Nepal*. UNICEF Office of Research – Innocenti.

Youth Shadow Panel. (2025). *School curriculum and assessment review. Interim report. Summarising our youth-led call for evidence*. https://shadowpanel.uk/about/interim-report

2

CURRICULUM, PEDAGOGY, AND ASSESSMENT

In Chapter 1, we established the central importance of children's agency and voice in education, set against the backdrop of children's lives in the twenty-first century. We saw how children's rights and well-being are increasingly recognised globally, yet their agency in specific educational settings, at country, region, and local levels, often remains limited. To understand why this contradiction exists and how it might be addressed, we examine the fundamental structures that shape children's educational experiences – particularly curriculum, pedagogy, and assessment. These elements form both the potential constraints on children's agency and the possible pathways through which their agency might be enhanced.

Curriculum is a fundamental part of learning and teaching: it is what children and teachers experience during lessons in school, and to some degree out of school if we include school homework. From a child's point of view, curriculum is particularly important because of its direct role in the activities they will encounter every day. A curriculum organises children's learning experiences into the days and times of the school week, intended learning focuses, and expected learning outcomes. Academic definitions of curriculum differ according to the disciplinary context, and by the scope and scale of the conception of curriculum. For example, from a sociological perspective, curriculum has been defined as 'the principle by which units of time and their contents are brought into special relationship with each other' (Bernstein, 1971, p. 48). From an educational perspective, curriculum has been described as 'what is intended to be taught and learned overall (the planned curriculum); what is taught (the curriculum as enacted); what is learned (the curriculum as experienced)' (Alexander, 2010, p. 250). The definition of curriculum that we use in this book is 'planned human activity intended to achieve learning in formal educational settings' (Wyse, Hayward & Pandya, 2016, p. 4). The sociologist Basil Bernstein (1975, p. 199) identified curriculum, pedagogy, and evaluation

DOI: 10.4324/9781003227779-2

as three message systems that work to make education 'an agency of socialization and allocation'. In other words, systems that enable pupils to become socialised, and ultimately allow for people to take up different roles in their later lives. According to Bernstein, curriculum constituted valid knowledge, pedagogy represented its valid transmission, and evaluation measured its valid realisation.

If, put more simply, curriculum is the 'what', then *pedagogy* is the 'how'. Pedagogy means the ways in which the curriculum is taught and learned within the social contexts for learning. If people believe that the main emphasis of curriculum is the knowledge to be learned, they might argue that the pedagogy of 'chalk and talk', or 'transmission teaching', where in general children sit in rows facing the front of the class and the teacher explains to the children what is to be learned, is the most appropriate pedagogy. This pedagogy influences the curriculum to be covered because the materials selected for learning have to be suited to the style of teaching, typically amenable to information displayed on a board (digital or black/whiteboard) followed by worksheets or workbooks for pupils to practice and consolidate their learning. However, if people believe that children learn best mainly through hands-on experience, or experiential *learning* (Ranken et al., 2024), including by trial and error, supported by teachers as facilitators of learning, then the resources for learning would focus more on the activities that children would undertake, and the processes of learning that the children go through while doing the activities. The distinction drawn between these two pedagogical approaches – chalk and talk versus experiential learning – is somewhat artificial, as most teachers actually employ a range of methods depending on the lesson. However, this distinction remains significant, as the history of primary education demonstrates that these different assumptions about learning have been central to fundamental debates about the nature of children's education and have shaped educational policy.

In addition to curriculum and pedagogy, another vital aspect of education is assessment. Assessment is important because we need to know if children have learned what we intended them to learn. Teachers' moment-by-moment interaction with children as they engage with the curriculum is one opportunity for assessing learning in an ongoing way: this is known as *formative assessment*. Another main type of assessment is *summative assessment*, where the outcomes of assessments give information about children's learning at a point in time compared to their peers.

Summative assessments are also used to determine if teaching has been effective, although great care has to be taken to separate the functions of assessment for children's learning from the functions of governments using assessments to hold teachers and schools to account (Wyse, Bradbury & Trollope, 2022). There is a long history of research showing how assessments used for accountability purposes influence the curriculum, often in negative ways (e.g. Harlen & Deakin Crick, 2002). When governments mandate summative assessments through statutory testing in primary education and use these results to hold schools and teachers accountable, teachers inevitably adapt their classroom curriculum to ensure their pupils' success – which in turn demonstrates the teacher's and school's success.

The curriculum children experience, particularly around key assessment periods, can become dominated by test preparation. This narrows the curriculum to the limited scope of testable content, contradicting the principle of a *broad and balanced curriculum*. Thus, *high-stakes assessment* – so named because teachers and schools face serious consequences if their children do not achieve sufficient test success – transforms both pedagogy and curriculum.

Curriculum planning includes the organisation of material into areas of learning, for example the division of the curriculum into subject areas such as, history, science, or music. Curriculum planning also includes a distinction between cross-curricular areas of learning, such as oral language, reading, and writing which are relevant in all areas of the curriculum, versus single-subject focuses such as mathematics. However, even in a subject such as mathematics there are aspects that cross into other subjects. Counting and numbers are fundamental to many areas, not least in science subjects; concepts such as shape and space can be seen in geography and the arts; and equations can even be seen in some kinds of philosophical argument. The idea of knowledge being multidisciplinary and cross-curricula is a first challenge to those who argue strongly for curriculum to be organised and taught as traditional school subjects.

Knowledge and the curriculum

Knowledge is often seen as a prime focus for study of the curriculum, but too often it is equated with knowledge of curriculum content. From a philosophical point of view knowledge has been described in three main ways. 'Acquaintance knowledge', 'knowledge-that', and 'knowledge-how' (Pavese, 2022). Acquaintance knowledge is knowledge acquired through daily life through acquaintance with people and objects. Knowledge-that, also called propositional knowledge, is knowledge of facts. Knowing-how is knowledge that would include the ability to play a musical instrument.

The most persuasive seminal philosophical account of the curriculum and knowledge, with clear relevance for primary education, was written by John Dewey. Dewey's theory was underpinned by his conception of children in relation to the knowledge to be learned. More particularly he saw education as the reconciling of children's conceptions in relation to the knowledge that teachers and society hoped to help children learn. This reconciliation he called interaction: 'education' is the interaction between learners' experiences and motivations in relation to the knowledge that teachers and society deem necessary to be learned.

One of the problems that Dewey identified was the insistence that categorisations such as school subjects are natural. In Dewey's view these categorisations of knowledge appear to the child as torn away from a natural context. He also recognised that as well as being a practical problem of teaching and learning, subjects as categories of knowledge were the stimulus for 'sects': on one side the sect of those who believe that knowledge should drive teaching and learning, and on the other side those who believe that the child and their motivations and needs should be at the centre of learning and teaching.

Historically the tensions between emphases on knowledge or on children have been linked with phrases such as knowledge-based curricula and 'powerful knowledge' (Young, 2014), or 'cultural literacy' in the USA (Hirsch, 1988), versus child-centred education (Dewey, 1902). Child-centred education has been criticised for the erroneous suggestion that it means children learning without any teaching at all, and requiring only the appropriate stimuli for children to learn. Dewey was quite clear that this idea was as false as the idea that all children need undue pressure to acquire pre-determined knowledge.

> To interpret the fact is to see it in its vital movement, to see it in its relation to growth. But to view it as a part of a normal growth is to secure the basis for guiding it. *Guidance [from the teacher] is not external imposition. It is freeing the life-process for its own most adequate fulfilment.* What was said about disregard of the child's present experience because of its remoteness from mature experience; and of the sentimental idealization of the child's naive caprices and performances, may be repeated here with slightly altered phrase.
>
> *(Dewey, 1902, p. 17, italics in original)*

National curricula that unduly impose particular kinds of knowledge, and even specify approaches to teaching represent, in Dewey's terms, external imposition. They also restrict teachers' freedom to ensure that teaching is carefully matched with children's development and experience through a respectful and deep appreciation of the child's life inside and outside school.

Dewey's views have been seen as extreme by some, and labelled as 'progressive' in a pejorative sense, but Dewey could better be described as taking a balanced view. And yet we would argue that in terms of children's agency Dewey was not progressive enough. Although Dewey recognised the vital element of children's experience as part of education, this was conceived in relation to the knowledge that society hoped for children to acquire. This conception of children is different from systematically giving children some choice over the knowledge that they are interested in acquiring, which would be one important way of supporting their agency.

Our conception of children's agency is not a kind of Rousseauian romantic view of children's education, nor an education where teachers and society have no role in fashioning the curriculum. Giving children agency over the curriculum can result in teachers having a better understanding of children's motivations, their interests, and therefore better able to plan teaching that will both engage children more but also be a closer match with their level of development.

Agency, learning, and educational outcomes

The relationship between agency and educational outcomes has been examined through many types of research, providing compelling evidence for why agency should be central to curriculum design and implementation. This evidence spans both teacher agency and children's agency, suggesting that when either is supported through curriculum structures, learning outcomes are likely to improve.

The impact of teacher agency on children's learning has been well documented. A systematic review and meta-analysis by Shen et al. (2020) identified 'collective agency' as a defining feature of effective teaching, particularly through what they termed 'teacher leadership'. Their analysis revealed positive correlations between teacher leadership and student achievement (as assessed in standardised tests) in both mathematics (r = .24[1]) and reading (.18). Most significantly for curriculum development, the strongest relationships with student achievement were found in two key dimensions: teachers 'facilitating improvements in curriculum, instruction, and assessment' (.21) and 'promoting teacher professional development' (r = .19). This evidence suggests that when teachers have agency to shape and adapt curriculum implementation, student learning benefits.

A systematic review by Kaya and Erdem (2021) examined the relationship between students' well-being, focussing particularly on student autonomy, and students' academic achievement. Student autonomy is a vital aspect of agency and plays a crucial role in pupils' psychological well-being. Kaya and Erdem's analysis found a positive effect size of .17 for the overall relationship between students' well-being and academic achievement. Notably, this effect was strongest (.24) for primary/elementary education compared to other levels of schooling. More recent single research studies provide further relevant evidence. Jinling and Ke (2023) conducted an analysis of approximately 580 students across grades four, five, and six in a Beijing primary school, demonstrating significant positive correlations between students' sense of agency scores and their academic performance.

Research suggests that learners benefit most when their freedom to make choices is balanced with appropriate support and guidance. Tam, Chu and Tsang's (2023) study of 1,425 Hong Kong primary school students examined how structured opportunities for exercising personal agency affected students' self-perceptions. Students were allowed to independently choose and direct their own leisure activities during a homework-free holiday period. This freedom was supported by specific structures: an orientation workshop on goal-setting and self-regulation skills, a project diary for tracking daily activities and progress, and post-holiday debriefing sessions for sharing experiences. The intervention enhanced two key aspects of students' self-perception: their sense of agency (termed 'agency thinking' by the authors), measured as their belief in their ability to achieve self-chosen goals, and their sense of academic competence, measured through their self-reported beliefs about their academic performance and ability to manage learning. These improvements in self-perception were particularly pronounced among students who participated for a second year. This suggests that when children are given meaningful opportunities to make independent choices about their activities, with appropriate support structures, they develop stronger beliefs in both their capacity for goal achievement and their academic abilities.

The impact of agency is evident in cross curricular areas, and in curriculum subjects, such as in literacy development. For example, Dong et al.'s (2021) large-scale experimental study with 608 fourth-grade Chinese students demonstrated the effectiveness of a self-agency learning mode (where students independently identified word meanings from contextual sentences rather than receiving direct instruction) in improving reading comprehension abilities, with struggling readers ultimately achieving performance levels similar to typical readers. The researchers suggested this success might be partly due to increased student interest from self-directed learning. These findings are complemented by Reedy and De Carvalho's (2021) qualitative research with 60 Year 5 students, which showed that children's agency and choice in reading material was one of the main factors in their enjoyment of reading.

In science education, Siry, Wilmes and Frisch (2024), though a qualitative study with 17 four- to six-year-olds, demonstrated how creating room for children's agency through flexibility in what and how children investigated supported their science engagement and meaning-making. Lee et al. (2020), in their symposium synthesising empirical findings from four studies, highlight the importance of creating playful, agency-supporting environments for engaging learners in broader and meaningful mathematics learning. The authors argue that mathematics classrooms often lack enjoyment and agency, which has significant implications for students' sense of competence, participation, and their identities. The four studies explore different contexts, both in-school and out-of-school, to demonstrate how playful, open-ended, agency-supportive approaches can enable more engaging and meaningful mathematics learning.

Despite this growing evidence supporting children's agency, one of the challenges is to translate these insights into appropriate curriculum frameworks and policies for teaching and learning. As we will see in our examination of national curricula internationally, different education systems have approached this challenge in varying ways, with some explicitly incorporating agency into their curriculum design while others maintain more restrictive approaches. The tension between evidence supporting agency and political pressures for standardisation and control creates particular challenges for curriculum development. This tension, and how it might be resolved through the concept of structured freedom, will be explored more fully in Chapter 8.

National curricula internationally

In the twenty-first century, countries, states, and other regions have strengthened control over education through the development of national curricula and associated national systems of assessment in schools. National curricula are presented in texts, sometimes single documents, and increasingly as web-based sources. National curriculum texts are aspirational: they represent what governments say they want for their future citizens. However, a national curriculum text is just that, a text. The extent to which such texts affect practice and influence what children experience in their lessons in schools varies according to national and local contexts for their implementation. Nevertheless, the formality, aspirational nature, and varying statutory force of such texts means that they are an important source for analysis to understand curriculum internationally.

When we examine national curriculum texts, one of our questions is, 'to what extent and in what ways is children's agency present in national curriculum texts?' National curriculum texts can be divided into three broad types in relation to children's agency: a) explicit attention to children's agency, where the word agency is used in the text, and/or some other ways of representing children's capacity and right to act; b) some implicit attention to children's agency, for example a requirement for schools to support children to make choices in various aspects of learning; c) no explicit attention to children's agency in the text.

Analysis of national curricula begins with their overall aims, as children's agency is a concept that should permeate the entire curriculum. Therefore, if a nation or state is committed to children's agency, this commitment should be reflected in its national curriculum aims. Consideration of national curriculum aims leads to two further questions we are interested in when analysing national curriculum texts: a) is agency consistently and explicitly present in the programmes of study in all areas and subjects of the curriculum; and ultimately, b) do children exercise agency in school? The second question was at the heart of the fieldwork we did for the research we report in this book.

National, federal, or state curricula are requirements for all schools in a given region. These are developed at governmental level, with varying degrees of public consultation, to put forward a vision for education systems. To some degree these curricula are democratically constructed statements of intent for pupils, teachers, schools, and other relevant education settings. But increasingly over many decades politicians have been influenced by international comparisons and policy borrowing from other countries and regions, sometimes at the expense of democratically derived curricula.

One of the international influences on curricula is the Organisation for Economic Cooperation and Development (OECD). The importance of education systems that can foster the development of well-rounded individuals has been recognised by the OECD, for example through the Future of Education and Skills 2030 project (OECD, 2018). This project aims to shape the future of education by identifying the knowledge, skills, attitudes, and values that students require to successfully navigate a rapidly evolving global world. One of the key frameworks within the Future of Education and Skills 2030 project particularly reinforces the significance of learner-centred educational systems. It is known as 'Learning Compass 2030', which places a specific focus on the role of agency in children's education and overall lives.

The OECD's Learning Compass 2030 framework represents a significant milestone in the global discourse surrounding the objectives of a twenty-first century curriculum, notwithstanding the issues that surround the conflicting interpretation and misinterpretation of the international comparative testing, such as the OECD's

PISA outcomes, by politicians. The Learning Compass not only delineates the aspirations a modern curriculum should strive to achieve but also identifies the fundamental elements that should constitute its core. Moreover, the framework acknowledges a crucial aspect that has often been overlooked in traditional curriculum development – the inclusion of children as key stakeholders in shaping educational practices.

The framework aims to provide guidance to education leaders in creating nurturing relationships and learning environments that enable children's agency, which is considered a key future-oriented competency. A significant aspect of the framework is the connection it establishes between the curriculum and children's agency. It asserts that the curriculum should be designed in a manner that motivates children and acknowledges their prior knowledge, skills, attitudes, and values, elements that are seen as part of agency. By recognising and capitalising upon children's existing strengths and interests, the curriculum can effectively engage and empower learners.

As part of the project, the OECD conducted an analysis of curriculum content and pedagogical approaches across various countries. This research generated comparative data on curriculum content, providing insights into the priorities and approaches adopted by different countries. The findings emphasised the need to ensure the development of learners' competencies beyond traditional academic knowledge, highlighting the importance of integrating core foundations, knowledge, skills, attitudes, values, and transformative competencies into education. The OECD's Future of Education and Skills 2030 curriculum analysis reports have numerous references to approaches such as experiential learning, project-based learning, inquiry-based learning, and service learning. The OECD identifies these approaches as examples of good practice, highlighting their effectiveness as learner-centred pedagogies that promote active engagement, curiosity, independent learning skills, and civic engagement, empathy, and social responsibility.

The inclusion of pupils in decisions about curriculum necessarily brings us back to the realm of pedagogy. Revisiting Wyse, Hayward and Pandya's (2016) conceptualisation, we see pedagogy as the ways in which educators seek to support the development of an individual through their teaching. This teaching is informed to varying degrees by the history, values, and ideas of the culture in which the teaching is enacted. From the late eighteenth century until the early nineteenth century, pedagogy in schools in the UK and the US was linked to a view of learners as passive recipients of knowledge in education systems designed to socialise citizens and reduce crime. Pedagogy was strongly linked to discipline. More than 200 years later, understandings of pedagogy are more complex and more nuanced, although pupils are still too often viewed as passive recipients of their education. The task of engaging children, and supporting their agency, requires teachers and schools to enact types of pedagogy that are different from the traditional model of the teacher as someone whose overriding role is to teach children pre-specified knowledge that they are required to learn. The starting point for a different pedagogy is the belief that engaging with children's prior experiences and interests is worthwhile and necessary.

National contexts

The globalisation represented in international frameworks such as those of the OECD influence policy makers in countries and other regions worldwide (Lingard, 2021). Policy makers also seek to reflect their ideologies in the development of national curricula. National curricula are, as we have said, aspirational in character. Through varying processes of consultation and engagement, national curriculum texts are constructed. The hope of policy makers is that curricula will then be implemented by teachers in the ways intended. However, it has been argued for a long time that schools and teachers mediate curriculum policies in particular ways. As Priestley et al. (2021, p. 6) argued, 'teachers do not implement policy; they enact, translate, mediate it (e.g. Braun et al., 2011), through a process of iterative refraction (Supovitz, 2008), filtered via existing professional knowledge, dispositions and beliefs'. Summarising a series of chapters about *curriculum making* in countries in Europe, Priestley et al. (2021) noted a trend towards learner-centred curricula related to twenty-first century skills, but also a trend of tensions between regulation and deregulation in the context of the expansion of performance-based accountability regimes as part of national curricula. However very few empirical research projects have directly investigated the extent to which curricula are centred on primary age learners and their agency, fewer still have sought in-depth accounts of children's views about their education. The research reported in this book uses its empirical data to interrogate the nature of such trends. One of the original features that we bring is to understand curriculum making not only from the perspectives of schools and teachers but, crucially, from the perspective of primary children and their views of their education.

While it is, in general, true that teachers mediate national curricula, our hypothesis is that the extent of mediation that teachers undertake will depend on the types of policy levers that are used to support the desired implementation of a national curriculum. Key aspects of a national curriculum are subject to more pressure to conform than other aspects, as our reflections on the development of curriculum and pedagogy show later.

In order to reflect further on the nature of globalisation, national curricula, and trends in thinking, we end this chapter by focussing on three regions: Ireland, Hong Kong, and the countries of the UK. The selection of these countries was in part driven by a project in which we proposed how knowledge might be defined in a redeveloped primary curriculum in Ireland (Wyse & Manyukhina, 2018). The work involved analysing the place of knowledge in the curriculum in a selection of regions performing highly in international comparative studies such as PISA. We proposed three kinds of national curricula that dealt with knowledge in different ways: knowledge-based, skills-oriented, and learner-centred. Although, like any model, they are not mutually exclusive, they each represent important different ways of conceptualising and enacting national curricula. Children's agency was an important theoretical frame for understanding learner-centred curricula, and it was this connection between curriculum and children's agency that finally brought us to propose to the Leverhulme Trust the research project reported in this book.

Redevelopment of the primary curriculum in Ireland

From 2019 onwards Ireland embarked on the redevelopment of its primary curriculum, something that had not previously taken place since 1999. Three elements of this development process were particularly noteworthy: a) newly commissioned studies and reviews of existing research were a central part of the process of development; b) the review was undertaken in its first phase over a period of four years; and c) the views of children and all stakeholders were a key component in the development of the primary national curriculum in Ireland.

One example of the attention to new and existing research, and a serious intent to consult children, was the establishment of a new national longitudinal cohort research study of primary schooling in Ireland. This innovative research included significant attention to children's voice and agency in their primary schooling. One of the key findings of the research was that although children often felt that they were listened to by their teachers, and teachers said that they recognised the importance of children's agency in education, the children did not feel that they were included in decision-making as much as they would like to have been. More than 74% of children who were asked about agency said that they felt that they were listened to in school, but only just under half agreed that their ideas were then used to change things in school (Devine et al., 2023). In responding to children's views, teachers were more likely to prioritise children's views about rules and behaviour, and were less likely to do so in relation to decisions about learning and teaching. The views of younger children were sought more often than older children in primary schools.

Since our first project to analyse the nature of knowledge in the curriculum, Dominic continued as one of four members of an Advisory Panel for the redevelopment of Ireland's national curriculum, work led by Ireland's National Council for Curriculum and Assessment (NCCA). The other panel members were Louise Hayward (University of Glasgow), James Spillane (Northwestern University USA), and Thomas Walsh (Maynooth University). The report from the Advisory Panel included a section devoted to agency that noted the vision of agency that was summarised as the result of discussions at one of the consultation seminars, called Leading Out Seminars:

> The Draft Primary Curriculum Framework views the child as a capable actor who shares power and agency with the adult. Curriculum for the agentic child is co-constructed through adult-child collaboration. Adults guide the learning process, based on their learning, life experiences and resources. Pedagogy that encapsulates observation, recording of children's language, ideas and interests, and discussion of learning with children is indicative of the child's agency.
>
> *(National Council for Curriculum and Assessment, 2022, p. 18)*

This powerful statement about agency influenced the final version of the curriculum framework and is an exciting prospect for which new research will need to be undertaken to investigate the reality of children's agency on the ground in schools and other education settings once the new curriculum begins to be implemented.

Ireland's Primary Curriculum Framework was launched in 2023. Children's agency and teachers' agency are central to the framework. One of the Principles of Learning, Teaching and Assessment that structure the approach to all subjects in the curriculum states:

Engagement & Participation

Children are active and demonstrate agency as the capacity to act independently and to make choices about and in their learning. Curriculum experiences provide them with opportunities for decision-making, creativity, and collaboration.
(National Council for Curriculum and Assessment, n.d., p. 6)

At the time of writing this book, work was ongoing to complete the programmes of study for the different subject areas of Ireland's curriculum. Work was also being done to plan professional development for schools and teachers, including attending to what children's and teachers' agency might look like in practice.

Another of the unique elements of the processes of curriculum development in Ireland was timescales. Historically significant revision of the primary curriculum had only previously happened in 1922, 1971, and 1999 (Walsh et al., 2024). In addition to the relatively infrequent major revisions of the national primary curriculum, the timeline for the process of developing the new framework began in 2020 and was to continue for at least five years. Indeed the idea of having a framework rather than a more prescriptive curriculum structure was itself a new departure for Ireland.

Ireland had historically performed highly in the international comparative assessments such as PISA and PIRLS. However, this did not make Ireland immune from the political influences of what has been called 'PISA shock'. Ireland's overall scores for children's reading in 2006 was 517, then in 2009 it dropped to 496. This drop in score was regarded with concern by ministers who, from 2011, implemented a national strategy to improve literacy and numeracy. In 2012 Ireland's PISA score was 528. The national strategy could not have been the reason for the improved score in 2012, and it is not clear why this unusual pattern of scores happened. A national strategy for aspects such as literacy, numeracy, and digital literacy has continued with the latest for the period 2024 to 2033. These strategies are published by the Government of Ireland, unlike the national curriculum frameworks which are published by the NCCA, a context which represents the competing influence of politics, international comparative testing, and ultimately some of what happens in classrooms.

Ireland's primary curriculum development is unique for a number of reasons. For example, in addition to the use of an advisory panel who were all working in universities, research was an important influence at all stages in a variety of ways. Early work included the commissioning of multiple research projects to examine fundamental aspects of curriculum including the work we did on defining knowledge in the curriculum. The NCCA also carried out their own research throughout the process of curriculum development, in a variety of ways, to aid their consultations with a range of stakeholders about the proposed developments. Children were actively involved in some of this research, including being present at an event that brought together a wide range of stakeholders. And most of all children's agency, and teachers' agency, are explicitly part of the primary curriculum framework which is a good starting point for the potential for children's agency to be part of their daily lives in schools.

National curriculum in Hong Kong

Our initial research comparing the national curricula of some high performing regions included Hong Kong, in comparison with Ontario, Canada; Australia; and England. At the time we categorised Hong Kong's national curriculum as a learner-centred curriculum. Evidence for this view came from our content analysis of the four curricula. Contrary to the strongly knowledge-based curriculum in England, and even the skills-oriented curricula of Ontario and Australia, Hong Kong's curriculum included statements that explicitly warned against teachers and schools introducing a bias towards, and emphasis on, knowledge. Instead the emphasis of the curriculum was on the holistic development of children as people, through life-long learning, 'In addition to acquiring knowledge in class, students are expected to develop learning to learn capabilities as well as positive values and attitudes for achieving the educational aims of whole-person development and life-long learning' (BECG, Preamble, p. 1). There were also statements emphasising the importance of learners increasing their 'intrinsic motivation' and 'curiosity' for learning.

Both Hong Kong and China have performed highly in all PISA reporting rounds, so PISA was not a particular influence on the politics of curriculum development in those regions. Much more important was a wider politics, in particular Hong Kong being returned to control by the People's Republic of China (PRC) in 1997 having been under the control of Britan until then. At this point Hong Kong became renamed as the Hong Kong Special Administrative Region (SAR), and the China policy of 'one country two systems' increasingly became the source of protest by people in Hong Kong.

One of the ways that China sought control over the curriculum was through the censorship of certain ideas as published in school textbooks (Ho, 2020). The promotion of national Chinese identity became central to curriculum development in Hong Kong from the transfer of sovereignty onwards. In 2024 a Circular from the Chinese Government Education Bureau was released. This circular announced the release of the Primary Education Curriculum Guide 2024 which at the time of writing was only available in Chinese language format. One of the major developments was the additions to the list of 'Priority Values and Attitudes' of 'National Identity', 'Benevolence', 'Filial Piety', and 'Unity'. The following paragraph taken from the recent circular suggests that children's agency and teachers' agency may not be such a strong feature of the national curriculum in Hong Kong going forward:

> Promoting Patriotic Education: Echoing the announcement in the 'Chief Executive's 2023 Policy Address' to promote patriotic education on and off campus, enhancing education on our country's history, culture and current affairs on different fronts as well as promoting patriotism, the PECG (2024) enriches relevant suggestions related to patriotic education. School examples are provided in different chapters [of the new curriculum guidance] illustrating how national education and national security education that incorporated elements and spirit of patriotic education can be promoted inside and outside the classroom, so as to cultivate students' proper values and attitudes, strengthen their cultural confidence, sense of national identity and patriotism.
>
> *(Education Bureau, 2022, Paragraph 6)*

While government politics play an increasingly important part in influencing national curricula, and hence activities in schools, the relationships between policy and education on the ground are complex and unique to each region. Due to an invitation to give a talk at a conference in Shenzhen, China, which is very close to Hong Kong, Dominic witnessed firsthand some of the complexities. The trip provided the source for some anecdotal observations. A visit to a private early-years setting revealed education that was explicitly based on England's Early Years Foundation Stage curriculum. In some ways the practices seemed to reflect a stronger commitment to play and child-centred learning than was present in some early-years settings in England, not least due to pressures to ensure children are 'school ready' for their Reception class year in their primary school. A visit to a primary school revealed the importance that state education in China attributes to the learning of the English language, which is a compulsory requirement in the national curriculum. And the learning of the English language in China includes the need for pupils to learn something of the cultural context in England and the UK. However, perhaps akin to the challenges of helping primary and secondary pupils in England learn a European language, it was reported that pupils in China often do not see a positive purpose behind them learning English despite parents' encouragement for them to do so. The complexities reported so far in this chapter, and that are part of the national curricula in the UK, are one of the main reasons that longitudinal qualitative work in schools to compare intended curricula with curricula as implemented is so important.

National curricula in the UK

Prior to 1988 England did not have a national curriculum, and England and other parts of the UK were regarded internationally as beacons of exciting progressive primary education (Hennessey, 2010). The Education Reform Act 1988 gave power for the first time to the Secretary of State for Education to implement a national curriculum and associated assessment system. In 1994 a review of the curriculum was undertaken by Sir Ron Dearing, who recommended a reduction in the content, but problems with too much content continued. In 1999 a new skills-oriented national curriculum was implemented by the Labour government, then in 2014 the Conservative government implemented their knowledge-based curriculum.

An important modern historical development in the UK was the devolution of political power to Northern Ireland, Scotland, and Wales in the 1990s. The National Assembly for Wales had its first elections in 1999. From 1988 to 2008 schools in Wales followed England's national curriculum. In 2008 Wales developed its first Foundation Stage curriculum (for children aged three to seven), and in 2022 Wales introduced a new skills-oriented curriculum. Education in Scotland had always been more independent from England than the other countries in the UK, although elections to the Scottish Parliament did not take place until 1999. In 1992 Scotland introduced its 5–14 curriculum framework, then in 2004 Scotland launched its Curriculum for Excellence. Northern Ireland's Northern Ireland Assembly was established in 1998, and its national curriculum has been in place since 1992.

This political devolution brought significant differences in the attention to children's agency as part of their education. Wales' national curriculum stresses that the guidance is designed to help schools to develop their own curriculum in line with four purposes for education in Wales. The curriculum is explicitly oriented around the UN Convention on the Rights of the Child, including children's right to be consulted on their views in all matters that affect them commensurate with their stage of development. As part of the requirements for schools to develop their vision and curriculum, they are required to draw on learners' voice and respond to their needs, experiences, and input.

In Scotland, the Curriculum for Excellence included an explicit strand requiring teachers to support children to make choices in their learning. In 2019, Scotland produced guidance that refreshed some aspects of this curriculum. In a section about 'what matters?' and 'how we do it', the process of curriculum making explicitly mentions agency as part of 'understanding learners' through empowering them to have agency in their learning with opportunities for personalisation. Agency is defined as 'the capacity of individuals to act independently and to make their own free choices' (Education Scotland, 2024).

Northern Ireland seems to have a little less explicit attention to children's agency than Scotland. The curriculum does have an emphasis on equality of opportunity and access for all, and within this the need for teachers to teach in ways that suit individual pupils' abilities. The overall aim of the curriculum is to empower young people to develop their potential and to make informed and responsible choices. However, it is not until a section of approaches to learning and teaching that the idea of children having opportunities to make choices about their learning in the context of increasing their motivation for learning is explicitly mentioned. At the time of writing, Northern Ireland had just embarked on reviewing its national curriculum.

Although the changes to national curricula historically that we have outlined each caused a wide range of changes to education, the biggest impacts on children and teachers have perhaps been as a result of the tensions between what are known as the core subjects versus the foundation subjects (Alexander, 2010). The core subjects in England's national curriculum of 2014 were English (reading and writing and, to a lesser degree, oral language), mathematics, and science, although science had not received the attention that literacy and mathematics had received as a result of statutory testing. The foundation subjects were art and design, citizenship, computing, design and technology, languages, geography, history, music, and physical education. As a result of some of the political levers used to control pedagogy, reading, writing, and mathematics became de facto the core subjects. While we agree that oral language(s), reading and writing, and mathematics are fundamental areas of the curriculum not least because, as we have said, they are also cross-curricula elements, we see the binary category of core and foundation subjects to be lacking a credible rationale as well as detrimental to children's perceptions and experiences of learning in schools.

National curriculum in England from 2014

From 2014 onwards, an already-low baseline for children's and teachers' agency over the curriculum in England (due to the increase in control of the curriculum by the Labour government from 1997 onwards) was to diminish to an extent never seen in 100 years of education (Wyse & Bradbury, 2022). The reason for the further retrenchment of agency was due to the ideology of Secretary of State for Education Michael Gove and the Minister for Schools Nick Gibb. From the very start of the development of the new national curriculum prior to its implementation from in 2014, many people with expertise in curriculum were disenfranchised from the process. For example, three of the four academic advisors to Gove resigned because they felt that key aspects of their advice were not being acted on (James, 2012). We could find no record of any children or young people being consulted about the 2014 national curriculum.

The impact of this curriculum narrowing on children was profound, particularly for some lower-attaining pupils. A five-year longitudinal study by Hargreaves, Quick and Buchanan (2023) following 23 lower-attaining primary school children found that the emphasis on mathematics and English over other subjects significantly undermined these children's well-being and opportunities for engaged learning. Their research revealed how children experienced distress and disengagement when forced to spend large portions of their school day on subjects they found most challenging, while having reduced access to areas where they might experience success and build confidence. This provided empirical evidence of how the 2014 curriculum's narrow focus constrained children's agency and contradicted stated aims about inspiring all learners.

A critical discourse analysis of the 2014 national curriculum for England, which constituted the first stage of the CHANT study, revealed significant patterns in how children's agency was conceptualised and constrained within the curriculum text (Manyukhina, 2022). The analysis examined how the curriculum positioned children in relation to their learning and identified five key patterns that demonstrated how the curriculum systematically constrained children's agency.

First, while children's agency was implicit in many learning goals, it was not explicitly acknowledged in the curriculum text. The development of agentic capacity was only referenced indirectly through concepts like efficiency, independence, motivation, and confidence. Even these indirect references to agency were narrowly confined to academic competencies in specific subjects, such as writing efficiency or confidence in numeracy, rather than supporting children's development as independent agents in their broader learning and lives. Second, while the curriculum occasionally acknowledged the importance of children's views and feelings, this was limited to the section outlining statutory requirements for English, for example: 'A high-quality education in English will teach pupils to speak and write fluently so that they can communicate their ideas and emotions to others' (DfE, 2013, p. 13). Children's individual views and preferences were notably absent from discussions of curriculum design, delivery, and assessment approaches. Third, children's enjoyment of learning received minimal attention, with references to motivation almost exclusively limited to reading. For example, the curriculum stated that pupils 'should be reading widely and frequently, outside as well as in school, for pleasure and information' (DfE, 2013, p. 41), but failed to extend this emphasis on enjoyment to other subjects or learning activities. This suggested little intention to account for children's right to exercise agency across all aspects of their learning experience. Fourth, the curriculum text consistently positioned children as passive recipients rather than active agents of learning. This was evident in the phrasing of learning outcomes and goals, which typically applied passive rather than active voice when referring to pupils. Finally, responsibility for learning progress was predominantly attributed to teachers and schools, with children rarely positioned as capable of taking ownership of their learning.

These patterns revealed how the curriculum's approach to children's agency was fundamentally constrained. By failing to provide opportunities for children to contribute more fully to the nature of their curriculum, the text prevented children from becoming genuine co-participants in their learning process. This has the potential to inhibit both children's sense of agency and their opportunity to exercise agency in school. The analysis suggested that the 2014 national curriculum failed to provide the foundation for a personally relevant school experience with consistent opportunities for children to develop and exercise agency in learning.

The analysis of England's national curriculum also revealed particular tensions around language and literacy, where the constraining of agency was pronounced. This was most evident in the treatment of oral language, reading and writing – areas that are not only fundamental to any curriculum because of their place in all subjects but also because they act as a bridge between learners' identity and the education they encounter in schools. The focus on oral language was not only much reduced in comparison with the national curricula prior to 2014, but there was also the problem of a particular emphasis on, and inaccurate conception of, 'standard English'. The idea that 'standard English . . . is the variety of English which is used, with only minor variation, as a major world language' (DfE, 2013, p. 95) is not tenable. Oral language use of English shows astonishing variation in every part of the world that it is used, including in the British Isles (Kerswill, 2007). And even in relation to written English, significant variations are present, for example represented in the different dictionaries that represent global variations of the English language.

The poor conception of, and disproportionate emphasis on, a monolithic, old-fashioned, elitist conception of standard English also failed to explicitly accommodate the multiple languages and dialects that are central to children's identities (Snell & Cushing, 2022). In 2023, 30.4% of children aged 3 to 4 in state-funded nursery settings in England spoke a language that was known or believed to be different from English (Gov.uk, 2023). At the very least, explicit statements in the national curriculum that acknowledged the reality of language variety were needed, not least the idea that supporting home languages helps the development of the English language, and that full support for multiple languages promises greatly improved outcomes for children (Wei, 2018).

An important aspect of agency is the ability to make choices about education and learning. Some choices are profound, for example the point when children and young people first get a choice over which subjects they want to continue to study. Other choices may be less profound but are nonetheless important. For example, the right to choose which books to read is a vital part of citizens' rights. The consequences of denying citizens choice over texts have been most severe when books face censorship or destruction due to their content. Our Hong Kong example highlighted academic research documenting textbook censorship. In England, children's lack of choice over their reading materials was caused by the implementation of government prescriptions about an approach to teaching reading called *synthetic phonics* forcefully driven by Nick Gibb, the Minister for Schools, for more than a decade, something that he conceded was his 'obsession' (Wyse, 2023).

A series of political levers were enacted in England to ensure teachers', and hence children's, compliance with the synthetic phonics approach. These political levers represented the biggest incursion into teachers' professional lives, and their agency, ever seen in England, particularly because not only was the curriculum content statutory, but de facto so was the pedagogy of teaching reading. Probably the strongest political lever was the introduction of the national assessment called the phonics screening check (PSC), a test required to be taken by all children aged 6 in England, then again when they were 7 if they failed the test. Teachers teaching to the test naturally followed the introduction of the PSC. Alongside the PSC the government introduced for the first time a vetting system to determine which commercial synthetic phonics teaching resources were allowed to be used by schools. These schemes had to have a main focus on 'decodable books', which are books that are restricted to use words that contain the phonemes (sounds) that children will have been taught up to that point according to the scheme being used. It was not uncommon for the schemes to recommend that children be restricted access to any other books apart from decodable books at certain points in the programme of synthetic phonics teaching. And so, children's agency to select books to read was curtailed.

Internationally the debates about teaching children to read also shed light on a new twist in globalisation and policy borrowing that impacted directly on children's agency through an unexpected focus on children's rights. An entity called the Ontario Human Rights Commission published a report alleging that children's rights were being breached in schools in Ontario because they were not being taught using the methods of 'the science of reading' by which they meant systematic phonics. The use of a children's rights argument to lobby for the pedagogy of systematic phonics was a new twist in the long-standing debates about teaching reading that are sometimes called 'the reading wars'. It is true that children have a right to a good education, and being taught to read is one important part of such education. However, it is a very different thing to then claim that there is a particular teaching method that must be used. What was worse was that the review of research to back up the claim, that was a chapter in the report about curriculum, was unduly partial and, on some issues, was simply not accurate (Wyse & Hacking, 2024).

In 2024 a Labour government was elected in England for only the seventh time since 1900. The government committed to a review of the national curriculum. At the time of writing this book, a call for evidence had been released. Our research centre, the HHCP, submitted a response to the curriculum as did many other organisations and individuals. The response was informed by a briefing paper that we had released some weeks prior to the call for evidence (Wyse et al., 2024). The HHCP view, based on the research evidence in the project reported in this book, was that children's agency, and teachers' agency, needed much more recognition in any national curriculum review, in addition to a series of other changes needed to curriculum, pedagogy, and assessment in primary education.

This chapter has shown how curriculum frameworks, pedagogical approaches, and assessment systems create the structural conditions within which education operates. We have seen how these structures can either enable or constrain children's and teachers' agency through various mechanisms, from curriculum content, to teaching methods, to assessment practices. However, to fully understand how agency operates within these structures, we need a theoretical framework that helps to conceptualise the relationship between structural conditions and children's capacity for meaningful action. Chapter 3 addresses this need by examining the complex relationship between structure and agency through the theory of *critical realism*, providing theoretical tools to understand how children's agency emerges from and operates within educational contexts. This theoretical foundation helped us to examine how national curriculum structures shape children's educational experiences while also recognising children's capacity to influence and sometimes transform these structures.

Note

1 "r" represents what are called 'effect sizes' in quantitative analyses. Effect sizes are a statistical estimate, based on outcomes data, of the amount of progress that students in intervention groups made as a result of the intervention.

References

Alexander, R. J. (2010). *Children, their world, their education: Final report and recommendations of the Cambridge Primary Review*. Routledge.

Bernstein, B. (1971). On the classification and framing of educational knowledge. In M. F. D. Young (Ed.), *Knowledge and control: New directions for the sociology of education* (pp. 47–69). Collier-Macmillan.

Bernstein, B. (1975). *Class, codes and control: Volume 3 – Towards a theory of educational transmissions*. Routledge & Kegan Paul.

Department for Education. (2013). *The national curriculum in England: Key stages 1 and 2 framework document*. Department for Education. https://www.gov.uk/government/publications/national-curriculum-in-england-primary-curriculum

Devine, D., Martinez Sainz, G., Symonds, J., Sloan, S., Moore, B., Crean, M., Barrow, N., Grieves, M., Donegan, A., Samonova, E., Davies A., Farrell, E., O'Giobuin, R., & Farrell, J. (2023). Primary pedagogies: Children and teachers' experiences of pedagogical practices in primary schools in Ireland 2019–2022. University College Dublin.

Dewey, J. (1902). *The child and the curriculum*. University of Chicago Press.

Dong, Y., Chow, B. W. Y., Wu, S. X. Y., Zhou, J. D., & Zhao, Y. M. (2021). Enhancing poor readers' reading comprehension ability through word semantic knowledge training. *Reading & Writing Quarterly*, 37(4), 348–364.

Education Bureau. (2022). *Ongoing renewal of the school curriculum: The primary education curriculum guide*. Education Bureau, The Government of the Hong Kong Special Administrative Region. https://www.edb.gov.hk/en/curriculum-development/renewal/guides.html

Education Scotland. (2024). *Scotland's curriculum*. https://scotlandscurriculum.scot/4/

Gov.uk. (2023). *Academic year 2022/23: Schools, pupils and their characteristics*. https://explore-education-statistics.service.gov.uk/find-statistics/school-pupils-and-their-characteristics

Hargreaves, E., Quick, L., & Buchanan, D. (2023). National curriculum and assessment in England and the continuing narrowed experiences of lower-attainers in primary schools. *Journal of Curriculum Studies*, 55(5), 545–561.

Harlen, W., & Deakin Crick, R. (2002). A systematic review of the impact of summative assessment and tests on students' motivation for learning. *EPPI-Centre Review Version 1.1.*

Hennessey, B. (2010). Intrinsic motivation and creativity in the classroom: Have we come full circle? In R. A. Beghetto & J. C. Kaufman (Eds.), *Nurturing creativity in the classroom* (pp. 342–365). Cambridge University Press.

Hirsch, E. D. (1988). *Cultural literacy: What every American needs to know*. Random House.

Ho, W. C. (2020). The influence of politics in Hong Kong's education system 23 years after its handover from the United Kingdom to China. *The International Education Journal: Comparative Perspectives*, 19(2), 36–53.

James, M. (2012). *Background to Michael Gove's response to the report of the expert panel for the national curriculum review in England*. British Educational Research Association.

Jinling, S., & Ke, Z. (2023). Classification model of the impact of psychological factors on children's academic performance based on machine learning. In *2023 IEEE 3rd International Conference on Social Sciences and Intelligence Management* (pp. 64–68). IEEE.

Kaya, M., & Erdem, C. (2021). Students' well-being and academic achievement: A meta-analysis study. *Child Indicators Research*, 14(5), 1743–1767.

Kerswill, P. (2007). Standard and non-standard English. In D. Britain (Ed.), *Language in the British Isles* (pp. 34–51). Cambridge University Press.

Lee, C., Wongkamalasai, M., Thompson, N., Jasien, L., & Rubin, A. (2020). Designing playful mathematics learning environments: Synthesizing empirical research across contexts. In *Computer-Supported Collaborative Learning Conference*. International Society of the Learning Sciences.

Lingard, B. (2021). Globalisation and education: Theorising and researching changing imbrications in education policy In B. Lingard (Ed.), *Globalisation and education* (pp. 1–27). Routledge.

Manyukhina, Y. (2022). Children's agency in the national curriculum for England: A critical discourse analysis. *Education 3–13, 50*(4), 506–520.

National Council for Curriculum and Assessment. (2022). *From purpose to practice – Primary curriculum developments in Ireland*. National Council for Curriculum and Assessment. https://ncca.ie/media/5683/primary-curriculum-developments-in-ireland-april-2022.pdf

Organisation for Economic Co-operation and Development. (2018). *The future of education and skills: Education 2030*. OECD Publishing. https://www.oecd.org/education/2030/E2030%20Position%20Paper%20(05.04.2018).pdf

Pavese, C. (2022). Knowledge how. In E. Zalta & U. Nodelman (Eds.), *The Stanford Encyclopedia of Philosophy*. Stanford University. https://plato.stanford.edu/entries/knowledge-how/

Priestley, M., Philippou, S., Alvunger, D., & Soini, T. (2021). *Curriculum making in Europe: Policy and practice within and across diverse contexts*. Emerald.

Ranken, E., Wyse, D., Manyukhina, Y., & Bradbury, A. (2024). The effect of experiential learning on academic achievement of children aged 4–14: A rapid evidence assessment. *The Curriculum Journal, 00*, 1–18. https://doi.org/10.1002/curj.304

Reedy, A., & De Carvalho, R. (2021). Children's perspectives on reading, agency and their environment: What can we learn about reading for pleasure from an East London primary school? *Education 3–13, 49*(2), 134–147.

Shen, J., Wu, H., Reeves, P., Zheng, Y., Ryan, L., & Anderson, D. (2020). The association between teacher leadership and student achievement: A meta-analysis. *Educational Research Review, 31*, 100357.

Siry, C., Wilmes, S. E., & Frisch, R. (2024). Agentic student science engagement: Highlighting open-ended pedagogical structures in a plurilingual classroom. *International Journal of Educational Research, 127*, 102357.

Snell, J., & Cushing, I. (2022). 'A lot of them write how they speak': Policy, pedagogy and the policing of 'nonstandard' English. *Literacy, 56*(3), 199–211.

Tam, V. C., Chu, P., & Tsang, V. (2023). Engaging in self-directed leisure activities during a homework-free holiday: Impacts on primary school children in Hong Kong. *Journal of Global Education and Research, 7*(1), 64–80.

Walsh, T., Wyse, D., Spillane, J., & Hayward, L. (2024). The primary curriculum framework: Heralding a new era for primary and special school education in Ireland. In B. Mooney (Ed.), *Ireland's education yearbook 2023* (pp. 124–129). Education Matters.

Wei, L. (2018). Translanguaging as a practical theory of language. *Applied Linguistics, 39*(1), 9–30.

Wyse, D. (2023). Teaching synthetic phonics and reading: PIRLS of wisdom? *IOE Blog*.

Wyse, D., & Bradbury, A. (2022). Reading wars or reading reconciliation?: A critical examination of robust research evidence, curriculum policy, and teachers' practices for teaching phonics and reading. *Review of Education, 10*(1), 1–53.

Wyse, D., Bradbury, A., Manyukhina, Y., & Ranken, E. (2024). *Briefing paper: The future of primary education in England – In the hands of a new government*. Helen Hamlyn Centre for Pedagogy (HHCP), IOE, UCL's Faculty of Education and Society. https://discovery.ucl.ac.uk/id/eprint/10193078/

Wyse, D., Bradbury, A., & Trollope, R. (2022). *Assessment for children's learning: A new future for primary education. The Independent Commission on Assessment in Primary Education (ICAPE): Final report.* https://www.icape.org.uk

Wyse, D., & Hacking, C. (2024). *The balancing act: An evidence-based approach to teaching phonics, reading and writing.* Routledge.

Wyse, D., Hayward, L., & Pandya, J. (2016). Introduction: Curriculum and its message systems: From crisis to rapprochement. In D. Wyse, L. Hayward, & J. Pandya (Eds.), *The Sage handbook of curriculum, pedagogy and assessment* (pp. 1–27). SAGE Publications.

Wyse, D., & Manyukhina, Y. (2018). *The place of knowledge in curricula: A research-informed analysis.* National Council for Curriculum and Assessment. https://ncca.ie/media/3502/seminar_two_wyse_paper.pdf

Young, M. (2014). What is a curriculum and what can it do? *Curriculum Journal, 25*(1), 7–13.

3

AGENCY AND STRUCTURE IN EDUCATION

A critical realist perspective

We started this book by discussing how contemporary children's lives are shaped by various social, economic, and educational factors, emphasising the importance of considering their voices and experiences in education. Building on our earlier examination of how curriculum, pedagogy, and assessment create the structural framework within which education operates, this chapter brings these threads together by exploring the complex relationship between educational structures and children's capacity to act within them – their agency. The chapter begins by establishing our understanding of agency as a socially situated capacity to act, introducing the fundamental debate between structure and agency in social theory. We then present critical realism as a theoretical framework that helps us understand how these elements interact in educational settings. We explore how three domains – *the real, the actual, and the empirical* – manifest in educational contexts, paying particular attention to how absences can be as influential as what is present in shaping children's educational experiences. The chapter then moves to examine how agency operates in practice, drawing on empirical research to illuminate the distinction between children's sense of agency and how they may exercise their agency. We consider how educational structures can either support or constrain these aspects of agency, using evidence from classroom research to illustrate the dynamics. The discussion also explores the various dimensions through which agency develops and manifests, considering contextual, personal, and social factors. We conclude by considering the implications of this theoretical framework.

Defining agency

Agency is a 'socially situated capacity to act' – one that emerges from the complex interplay between individuals and their social contexts. Most well-accepted theories of agency (Emirbayer & Mische, 1998; Biesta & Tedder, 2007; Priestley,

DOI: 10.4324/9781003227779-3

Biesta & Robinson, 2015) acknowledge that agency is not merely about individuals' will and capacity to act, but that people act within particular circumstances, which range from immediate environments to broader societal structures, each playing a crucial role in shaping how agency manifests and develops. Our emphasis on 'socially situated' explicitly builds this understanding into our definition. Given that agency emerges from social contexts, we must examine how social structures enable or constrain this capacity to act. This leads us to a fundamental theoretical debate: the relationship between structure and agency.

Structure refers to social contexts, institutions, norms, and practices shaping society. These structures influence individual actions by providing frameworks within which people operate, often setting boundaries on what is possible or permissible. For instance, educational institutions, with their established curricula, rules, and norms, create specific contexts for children to learn and develop. These contexts can either enable or inhibit a child's ability to act agentically. The relatively long-standing debates about structure and agency hinge on a critical question: to what extent are individuals autonomous agents who shape their social realities versus being shaped by the very structures within which they exist? Those who take a structural determinist view argue that social structures and contexts overwhelmingly dictate individual behaviour and opportunities. The assertion here is that individuals' actions and decisions are significantly constrained by their social, economic, and cultural environments. They point to persistent patterns of educational inequality, where socio-economic background continues to predict educational outcomes, as evidence of structural determination.

Conversely, some proponents of agency argue that individuals possess the power to transcend these constraints and enact meaningful change in their lives and broader social systems. This perspective emphasises the role of personal agency in innovation, resistance, and social transformation. Historical examples abound, from social movements that have transformed educational access and equity, such as the first female students to enrol in universities, to individual stories of students who have overcome significant structural barriers through determination and strategic action. Malala Yousafzai exemplifies this power of individual agency: despite facing life-threatening opposition from the Taliban for advocating girls' education in Pakistan, she continued her activism, becoming a global symbol of resilience and change (Yousafzai & Lamb, 2013). Her efforts have inspired educational reforms worldwide, demonstrating how one individual's agency can challenge and shift deeply rooted social structures.

Various social theorists have attempted to move beyond seeing structure and agency as opposing forces, instead proposing more integrative approaches (e.g. Giddens, 1984; Bourdieu, 1984). However, as Archer (2007) pointed out, these attempts at integration can lead to 'central conflation', a theoretical stance where the distinct properties and effects of structures and agents become indistinguishable. This conflation obscures the analytical distinction necessary to explore how structures and agents interact and influence one another. When we fail to maintain this analytical separation, we lose the ability to examine how structural conditions enable or constrain agency, and how agents might successfully challenge or transform existing structures. In educational settings, this distinction becomes particularly crucial for understanding how institutional practices affect children's agency while acknowledging children's capacity to resist or reshape these practices. To resolve this tension between structural influence and individual agency, we turn to critical realism, which offers a robust theoretical framework for understanding their interaction.

Critical realism: a framework for understanding educational reality

Critical realism offers a robust alternative to oversimplified approaches to structure and agency. Emerging in the 1970s through philosopher Roy Bhaskar's work, critical realism bridges two different approaches to studying the social world: one focussed on observable facts (positivism), and another emphasising how people interpret their experiences (interpretivism). At its core, critical realism proposes that while a real world exists, our understanding of it is always shaped by our social experiences, and is inherently incomplete. This theoretical framework proves particularly valuable for understanding education because it illuminates how education systems and children's capacity for choice interact. It avoids two common problems: an excessive focus on systems that neglects children's agency, or an emphasis on individual choices that overlooks how larger systems shape those choices.

Critical realism proposes that the reality of life can be described using three distinct but interacting categories, that are called domains: the real, the actual, and the empirical. The *real* domain represents underlying forces that shape things that you cannot observe directly. For example, a national curriculum, and associated policies, are background structures that shape the practices of education in schools in a variety of ways. The *actual* domain represents things as they happen in life. This includes the ways in which teachers implement curriculum requirements through delivering their teaching in lessons. The category of the *empirical* domain is what people observe directly via their senses, and their interpretation of what they experience. For example, a researcher carrying out research about the national curriculum observes a lesson in a school and interprets what they observe.

These domains interact dynamically within educational settings. In education, underlying forces can include rigid assessment requirements enforced through inflexible policies (the real). Rigid assessment requirements can generate teaching practices focussed heavily on test preparation, limiting opportunities for children's choice (the actual). Consequently, children might experience education primarily as a process of achieving test scores rather than meaningful learning (the empirical).

Critical realism offers two concepts that help us understand how agency and structure interact over time: *structural reproduction* and *structural elaboration*. Structural reproduction happens when actions, even while expressing agency, ultimately reinforce existing structures – such as when children's efforts to succeed within a competitive assessment system end up validating and strengthening that very system. In contrast, structural elaboration occurs when agents' actions lead to meaningful changes in existing structures – for example, when children's feedback results in modifications to teaching methods or school policies. These processes help explain why some educational patterns and practices persist while others evolve through the initiatives of children and teachers.

This is particularly evident in institutional change. When schools implement systems to gather and respond to children's feedback, individual contributions can prompt broader transformations. A single child's suggestion might initiate discussions that, combined with other perspectives, lead to significant changes in teaching approaches or school policies. However, these individual contributions are themselves only enabled by the school's commitment to children's voice and the shared understanding that children's perspectives matter. This helps to explain why educational transformation requires more than isolated policy changes or new teaching methods. Meaningful change must address all three domains – the underlying structures (the real), their manifestation in practice (the actual), and how people experience them (the empirical).

Critical realism emphasises another important concept: *the causal power of absence*. What is not present in an educational setting can be as influential as what is. This becomes particularly clear when we consider opportunities for agency in schools. The absence of chances for children to make meaningful decisions does not just limit their current choices – it fundamentally shapes how they view themselves as learners and what they believe is possible for their future. This concept of absence helps explain why constraints in education have such profound effects on children's development. Consider, for example, when curricula fail to represent diverse cultural perspectives or when assessment systems recognise only certain types of achievement. These absences do more than create gaps in learning; they shape children's understanding of what counts as valid knowledge or legitimate success. A child who never sees their cultural background or personal interests reflected in their formal education might develop a limited view of their potential contributions and achievements.

The relationship between structure (the systems and rules that organise education) and agency (the capacity to act and make choices) becomes particularly important when we consider how these presences and absences affect learning. Some educators create a false division: either emphasising how physical settings, social contexts, and cultural norms determine educational outcomes, or focussing primarily on individual factors like motivation and personal learning strategies. Critical realism offers a more nuanced understanding by showing how personal and social outcomes emerge from the continuous interaction between structure and agency. Gao's (2010) longitudinal study of Chinese undergraduates provides compelling evidence of this interaction. The research examined how students' language learning strategies were influenced by contextual factors such as examination requirements and institutional structures. The study revealed that while students exercised individual choice in their learning strategies, these choices were significantly mediated by their social and institutional context. Gao's research demonstrated that students' learning behaviour emerges from the interaction between their individual capacities and the enabling or constraining features of their learning environments. More importantly, it shows how the same structural conditions can lead to different outcomes depending on how students interpret and act upon them, reiterating the importance of considering all three domains of reality – the real, the actual, and the empirical – in understanding educational experiences.

This critical realist framework provides a powerful theory for examining how children's agency operates within and potentially transforms educational structures. Building on this understanding of how structures and agency interact, we can identify specific dimensions through which agency manifests in educational settings. These dimensions help us understand the practical ways in which children's agency develops and operates within educational structures.

Dimensions of agency in educational settings

Our theory of agency resonates with Emirbayer and Mische's (1998) influential conceptualisation of agency as a temporally embedded process of social engagement informed by the past as well as oriented toward the future and toward the present. The temporal dimension manifests in how past experiences shape current actions and future possibilities: in educational settings, children's past learning experiences influence both their present engagement and future educational aspirations. Agency's fundamentally social character emerges through social engagement rather than existing as a purely individual attribute, as children's agency develops through their interactions with teachers, peers, and the broader educational environment. The dynamic nature of agency involves not just habitual actions but the capacity to imagine and pursue alternative possibilities while adapting to present circumstances.

Recent empirical research supports this multidimensional understanding of agency. Stoecklin and Fattore's (2018) study examining children's understandings of well-being, which involved 126 children aged 8–14 years in New South Wales, identified three key forms of agency that emerge through children's accounts. These were agency as competence in exercising abilities within social relations, agency as self-determination in making choices, and agency as practical action in everyday contexts. Their analysis revealed how children actively negotiate their agency through both symbolic resources (such as recognition from others, social relationships, and shared values) and concrete resources (like smartphones, physical spaces, and institutional opportunities). This demonstrated that agency is not just a simple matter of individual choice – rather, children's ability to act and make choices is shaped by both their individual capabilities and the social conditions around them.

Building on this understanding of agency, we can identify four key dimensions through which agency manifests and develops in educational settings:

1. The *contextual* dimension encompasses both the wider socio-cultural context and immediate educational settings. Societal attitudes towards education and success can influence children's aspirations and sense of agency. In contexts that highly value educational achievement, children may feel a strong sense of obligation and motivation to excel, whilst in contexts where education is under-valued, children might struggle to see the relevance of their academic efforts.
2. The *intrapersonal* dimension encompasses personal beliefs, motivations, attitudes, and actual capacities that shape agency. Children's internalised beliefs about their abilities fundamentally influence their sense of agency. When children believe in their capability to succeed and find personal satisfaction in their learning, they engage more actively and persistently in educational activities.
3. The *interpersonal* dimension recognises how relationships with teachers, peers, and parents profoundly impact children's sense of agency. Supportive teacher-pupil relationships can boost children's confidence and willingness to take risks in their learning. Collaborative learning and peer support shape children's agency by providing opportunities for shared experiences and collective problem-solving.
4. The *temporal* dimension reveals how past experiences ground present actions and shape future possibilities. A history of successful independent action and choice can bolster self-confidence, whilst repeated failures might lead to a diminished sense of agency. These beliefs about agency not only reflect past experiences but also inform future self-image and expectations.

These four dimensions – contextual, intrapersonal, interpersonal, and temporal – do not operate in isolation but interact dynamically to shape children's capacity for meaningful action in educational settings. For example, a child's interpersonal relationships with teachers might influence their intrapersonal beliefs about their capabilities, which in turn affects how they interpret and act upon contextual opportunities. Similarly, temporal aspects weave through all other dimensions, as past experiences in each domain influence future possibilities for agency.

Having established these four key dimensions, we can now examine how they manifest in children's lived experiences. This brings us to a crucial distinction in how agency operates in practice: the difference between children's sense of agency and their actual exercise of agency. This distinction helps us understand why similar structural conditions might lead to different outcomes for different children.

Sense and exercise of agency: a dual framework

Children's relationship with agency has two distinct aspects: their sense of agency and their exercise of agency. Sense of agency refers to children's belief in their capacity to act independently and create change. This belief develops through experience but also shapes future experiences by influencing how children approach new situations.

Exercise of agency involves putting this capacity into action through concrete decisions and behaviours – such as choosing learning strategies, pursuing personal interests, contributing to class discussions, or challenging established practices. The relationship between feeling agentic and exercising agency is complex: strong sense of agency often leads to more confident action, while successful actions reinforce that sense of agency. This distinction helps us understand several common educational situations: why children might feel agentic but not act on that sense of agency, why their experiences of agency might not match their actual opportunities for agentic action, and how school conditions can either support or undermine both aspects of agency.

These theoretical distinctions are supported by broader research into children's learning development. Studies of primary and secondary school children demonstrate that their belief in their ability to control their learning development significantly contributes to their propensity to exercise agency. Children who perceive control over their learning processes are more likely to take initiative, set goals, and persist in the face of challenges, even within potentially constraining structures. This empowerment fosters a proactive attitude towards learning, encouraging deeper and more effective engagement with educational activities (Mercer, 2011, 2012).

Reay and Wiliam's (1999) research provides compelling evidence of how educational structures affect children's sense of agency through their impact on self-perception and identity. Their study of children's experiences with national curriculum assessments revealed profound effects on children's self-understanding and perceived capabilities. The poignant statement from a Year 6 pupil – 'I'm frightened I'll do the SATs and I'll be a nothing' (Reay & Wiliam, 1999, p. 345) – captured how assessment structures can fundamentally shape children's sense of self-worth and agency. This child's fear reflected more than anxiety about a specific test; it revealed how institutional practices can become internalised as judgments about personal worth and potential. In *Miseducation* (2017), Reay builds on her earlier research to reveal the psychological impact of ability grouping on children's sense of agency and self-worth. Drawing on both new and previous empirical data, she documented how children placed in lower ability groups experienced pervasive feelings of guilt and anxiety. These emotions were not temporary but became deeply ingrained in their learner identities. This research demonstrated how ability grouping contributed to an 'emotional economy' in schools, where children's self-worth becomes closely tied to their assigned academic level.

More recent large-scale research has further strengthened these findings. Francis et al.'s (2017) mixed-methods study of Year 7 students found compelling evidence that ability grouping operates as a self-fulfilling prophecy. Their research revealed significant relationships between students' set placement and their self-confidence, not only in specific subjects like mathematics and English but also in their general learning capability. Particularly telling was their qualitative evidence showing how students internalised the implicit labelling that comes with being placed in different ability groups. As one student in their study observed, 'We can try to hide it, but it is blatantly saying, "You are less intelligent than this person"' (Francis et al., 2017, p. 102).

This internalisation of institutional judgments demonstrates how structural arrangements directly shape children's sense of agency and future possibilities, extending beyond specific subject areas to influence their broader learning aspirations and identities.

These empirical studies of ability grouping and assessment provide rich material for a critical realist analysis of how educational structures shape agency. From a critical realist perspective, they illustrate the complex interaction between the three domains of reality. In the domain of the real, institutional structures of assessment and grouping establish fundamental conditions that shape educational experiences. These structures generate practices of differentiation and labelling in the domain of the actual – the daily routines, interactions, and educational experiences that reflect and reinforce categories of ability. In the domain of the empirical, some children experience these structures and practices as diminished self-worth and restricted opportunities, developing what researchers describe as 'internal glass ceilings' that limit their educational aspirations and sense of possibility.

The power of these structural arrangements lies not only in what they provide but also in what they withhold. The critical realist concept of the causal power of absence becomes particularly relevant here. The lack of opportunities for agency and positive self-development in lower ability groups proves as influential as the presence of explicit limitations. Children placed in these groups often experience a dual disadvantage: the constraints of a restricted curriculum and reduced expectations, combined with the implicit message that they lack the capacity for autonomous learning and meaningful academic achievement. This combination of explicit and implicit messages creates a self-fulfilling prophecy. Children internalise the labels assigned to them, adapting their behaviour and aspirations to match institutional expectations. Their actions and choices, shaped by these internalised limitations, often reinforce the very structures that imposed these constraints. For example, children might avoid challenging tasks, participate less in class discussions, or resist taking academic risks – behaviours that appear to confirm initial judgements about their abilities and potential.

Consider also an educational setting with an inflexible curriculum. Children might understand their potential to influence their learning (sense of agency) but find themselves unable to act on this understanding due to the restrictive nature of the curriculum (exercise of agency). This misalignment between potential and action often leads to frustration, disengagement, and decreased motivation. Conversely, a flexible curriculum that values pupil input, encourages exploration, and provides opportunities for self-directed learning can significantly enhance both the sense of agency and its exercise.

These findings reveal how beliefs about contextual factors, from socio-cultural to familial to immediate classroom settings, affect children's willingness to exhibit agency. The extent to which contexts are imposed on children or created or chosen by them has considerable implications for their sense of agency. A child who feels supported and has opportunities for personal input is more likely to develop a robust sense of agency, providing the necessary room to experiment, make mistakes, and learn autonomously. In contrast, a child who feels restricted by their context may struggle to develop a sense of agency, leading to decreased motivation and engagement.

Children's agency can thus be conceived of as a 'latent potential', whose realisation depends on two factors: a child's sense of agency and the actual and perceived opportunities to exercise this agency in a given context. When opportunities are both available and recognised by children, they become *affordances* – actionable possibilities within an environment that individuals recognise and can act upon. The concept of affordances captures the mutual causality of structure and agency. According to a critical realist account, the enabling or constraining effects of structure manifest only in relation to agential intentions and actions. In practical terms, structural properties such as educational policies, school environment, classroom dynamics, and available resources remain neutral until agents – children and teachers – contemplate or attempt to engage with them. It is only when agents interact with these structures that their enabling or constraining effects manifest. Similarly, contextual opportunities become affordances only when children recognise the potential for action within them. This recognition transforms passive elements of the learning environment into active components of the educational experience.

These insights into the dual nature of agency – encompassing both sense and exercise – reveal how deeply intertwined individual capabilities are with institutional structures and social contexts. The argument we have presented demonstrates that supporting children's agency requires attention not just to their individual beliefs and capacities but to the complex web of structural conditions that enable or constrain their ability to act. This understanding helps bridge the theoretical framework of agency with its practical manifestation in educational settings, showing how children's capacity to act meaningfully depends on both their internal sense of agency and the external conditions that make agentic action feasible. This detailed examination of how sense and exercise of agency operate in educational settings demonstrates the value of maintaining this theoretical distinction while recognising their interdependence.

Agency as a socially situated capacity to act

This chapter has explored the complex relationship between children's agency and educational structures through the lens of critical realist theory. We began by defining agency as more than simply individual choice or action, showing how it operates within specific social contexts. Our analysis reveals how this socially situated capacity to act is fundamentally shaped by the interplay of structural conditions and individual capabilities, helping us avoid deterministic views that overemphasise structural constraints and individualistic perspectives that ignore them.

Our examination of the dual nature of agency – encompassing both the sense of agency and its exercise – reveals how children's capacity to act depends on both their internal beliefs and the external conditions that they experience. The argument and evidence presented in this chapter demonstrates how institutional practices, from ability grouping to assessment systems, can profoundly shape children's sense of agency and their propensity to exercise it. When children internalise institutional judgments about their abilities and potential, they may act in ways that seem to validate these judgments. This exemplifies how structural reproduction works in education – practices persist because students adapt their behaviour to match expectations.

To better understand these complex dynamics between institutional practices and children's agency, we turned to critical realism, which proved particularly valuable in understanding how educational reality operates across three domains – the real, actual, and empirical – and how these domains shape children's opportunities for meaningful action. This theoretical lens illuminated several key insights. First, agency develops through the dynamic interplay between individual capabilities and institutional structures, making it impossible to understand one without considering the other. Second, absences in educational settings – whether of opportunities, resources, or recognition – can be as influential as what is present in shaping children's agency. Third, supporting children's agency requires attention to multiple dimensions: contextual, intrapersonal, interpersonal, and temporal.

Building on these theoretical insights, supporting children's agency would require attention to multiple levels: creating enabling environments at the level of the real (such as flexible curriculum structures and inclusive assessment policies), nurturing supportive relationships in the domain of the actual (through teaching practices that encourage student choice), and fostering positive self-belief at the level of the empirical (through opportunities for children to experience themselves as intendent learners). This multi-layered approach would need to address both the explicit and implicit messages that educational structures convey to children about their capabilities and possibilities for action. It requires careful attention to how, for example, assessment practices, grouping arrangements, and pedagogical approaches might either enable or constrain children's sense and exercise of agency.

Drawing these threads together, the framework developed in this chapter challenges educators to move beyond simply providing choices or building task-specific confidence. Instead, it calls for creating educational environments that recognise and respond to the complex interplay between structural conditions and children's capacities to act. This means examining how institutional practices might be redesigned to support rather than constrain agency, how teacher-student relationships might foster rather than limit children's sense of agency, and how classroom environments might be structured to provide meaningful opportunities for the exercise of agency. Most importantly, this approach highlights how supporting children's agency requires sustained attention to both individual capabilities and institutional structures, recognising that meaningful change must address both simultaneously. This comprehensive approach to understanding and fostering agency offers a pathway toward more effective and equitable educational practices that truly support children's development as active agents in their own learning journeys. It recognises that while institutional structures can powerfully constrain children's agency, thoughtful educational practices can create spaces for meaningful change.

These theoretical insights raise important empirical questions about how agency manifests in different educational contexts and how various structural conditions enable or constrain children's capacity for meaningful action. While existing research has examined children's agency in specific contexts, such as literacy development, mathematics learning, or assessment practices, there remains a significant gap in our understanding of how agency operates across the broader educational experience, particularly in relation to national curricula.

Research undertaken prior to ours had focussed either on structural analyses of curriculum and policy (examining how these frameworks theoretically allow for agency) or on small-scale studies of individual classrooms or specific subject areas. What was missing was research that bridges levels of analysis – examining how school structures, particularly the national curriculum, manifest in everyday classroom practices and how children experience and exercise agency within these contexts. Additionally, while much has been written about the importance of children's voice and agency in education, there was very limited empirical evidence about how children themselves understand and experience agency in relation to school structures. Our research addressed these gaps by doing the following:

1. Examining the relationship between national curriculum structures and children's lived experiences of agency.
2. Investigating how children understand and exercise agency across different educational contexts.
3. Providing empirical evidence of how structural conditions enable or constrain children's capacity for independent action.
4. Offering insights into how schools might better support children's agency while working within national curriculum frameworks.

The next chapter outlines our methodological approach to investigating these questions. We describe how we designed and conducted research to capture both the observable manifestations of agency and the underlying mechanisms that shape its development and expression. This methodological framework allowed us to examine not just how children experience agency in schools, but how their experiences relate to broader structural conditions and how their sense of agency develops through their educational experiences. Our research design specifically addresses the complex interplay between structure and agency, examining how institutional practices shape children's opportunities for meaningful action while also exploring how children interpret and act upon these opportunities in various educational contexts.

References

Archer, M. S. (2007). *Being human: The problem of agency*. Cambridge University Press.

Biesta, G., & Tedder, M. (2007). Agency and learning in the life course: Towards an ecological perspective. *Studies in the Education of Adults, 39*(2), 132–149.

Bourdieu, P. (1984). *Distinction: A social critique of the judgement of taste*. Harvard University Press.

Emirbayer, M., & Mische, A. (1998). What is agency? *The American Journal of Sociology, 103*(4), 962–1023.

Francis, B., Connolly, P., Archer, L., Hodgen, J., Mazenod, A., Pepper, D., . . . & Travers, M. C. (2017). Attainment grouping as self-fulfilling prophesy? A mixed methods exploration of self-confidence and set level among year 7 students. *International Journal of Educational Research, 86*, 96–108.

Gao, X. A. (2010). *Strategic language learning: The roles of agency and context*. Multilingual Matters.

Giddens, A. (1984). *The constitution of society: Outline of a theory of structuration*. University of California Press.

Mercer, S. (2011). Understanding learner agency as a complex dynamic system. *System, 39*(4), 427–436.

Mercer, S. (2012). The complexity of learner agency. *Journal of Applied Language Studies, 6*(2), 41–59.

Priestley, M., Biesta, G., & Robinson, S. (2015). *Teacher agency: An ecological approach*. Bloomsbury Academic.

Reay, D. (2017). *Miseducation: Inequality, education and the working classes*. Policy Press.

Reay, D., & Wiliam, D. (1999). 'I'll be a nothing': Structure, agency and the construction of identity through assessment. *British Educational Research Journal, 25*(3), 343–354.

Stoecklin, D., & Fattore, T. (2018). Children's multidimensional agency: Insights into the structuration of choice. *Childhood, 25*(1), 47–62.

Yousafzai, M., & Lamb, C. (2013). *I am Malala: The girl who stood up for education and was shot by the Taliban*. Little, Brown and Company.

4

THE METHODS OF THE CHANT PROJECT

This chapter details our research design, explaining how we combined textual analysis with fieldwork to capture both the structural conditions shaping children's agency and children's lived experiences within these conditions.

The three domains of reality – the *real*, *actual*, and *empirical* – that we explained in the last chapter directly informed our mixed-methods research design. The research began with a critical discourse analysis (CDA) of England's national curriculum text which examined structures in the domain of the real. Longitudinal in-depth qualitative fieldwork investigated how these structures manifest in the actual domain and were experienced in the empirical domain by children and teachers in schools. Our research on children's agency and the national curriculum began in January 2021 and reached its conclusion in April 2024. The core of our inquiry revolved around three questions:

- How is children's agency represented in the text of England's national curriculum?
- How do children experience their agency, and in what ways do they exercise agency within the framework of schools adhering to the national curriculum?
- What role do structural elements, particularly the curriculum, play in shaping children's agency in primary schools?

To answer these questions, we used a mixed-methods qualitative research approach, combining the analytical power of critical discourse analysis with rich, nuanced insights from longitudinal qualitative fieldwork. Our research journey took us into three contrasting primary schools in England, where we observed the lives and experiences of the children and teachers over two years.

DOI: 10.4324/9781003227779-4

Research approach and design

Our research design aimed for a comprehensive understanding of the link between the national curriculum text and its meanings and children's agency from multiple perspectives. We began with a CDA of the national curriculum, examining the text to reveal how it positions and frames children's agency. This phase of the research provided a foundational understanding of the curriculum's official stance regarding children's agency.

Following this, we embarked on longitudinal qualitative research in three distinct primary schools in England. These schools were selected to represent diverse educational environments, including both the state and independent sectors. Over the course of the study, we conducted a series of observations, interviews, and participatory activities with children, teachers, and senior leadership teams. This immersive approach allowed us to capture the lived experiences of the children, providing a rich tapestry of data that reflected their perceptions, challenges, and successes in exercising agency.

The CDA illuminated how the national curriculum text treats children's agency. The fieldwork in the schools revealed the ways in which children navigated structural factors that shaped their opportunities to exercise agency within the school environment. Integration of these two sources of data provided a holistic view of curriculum and children's agency, highlighting the links between policy and practice, as well as the innovative strategies schools can employ to support children's agency within existing structural constraints.

Critical discourse analysis and critical realism

Underpinning the practical aspects of doing the CDA that we described earlier was an important set of theoretical ideas that underpinned the processes and analyses of the CDA. CDA does not offer standalone analyses of social phenomena. Instead, it draws on other theories to achieve an explanatory critique based on causal relations and a normative critique rooted in values and norms (Fairclough, 2018). Consistent with our study's approach to conceptualising agency, we adopted critical realism as our theoretical framework to inform and guide our analysis of children's agency in the curriculum. Critical realism is particularly apt for CDA as it aligns with some of the method's key philosophical assumptions. One such assumption is that texts have *causality*, meaning they can produce causal effects. Additionally, the causality of texts is contextual, contingent upon the environment in which a given text operates. These foundational principles provided a robust framework for understanding the impact of the curriculum text on children's agency.

Causality of texts

From a critical realist perspective, texts represent an aspect of social reality, and, like any other aspect of social reality, they have the potential to exert causal effects, that is, to bring about change. The most direct and straightforward effects of texts are seen in the knowledge they provide to people. However, texts can also produce changes in beliefs, values, and attitudes. These changes can be immediate or built over time, as seen when our consumer identities, gender roles, and political positions are shaped through continuous exposure to advertising and news. These changes can be intangible, as in the examples earlier, or material, such as when texts induce or inform modifications in our built environments, like new architectural designs (Fairclough, 2003).

The statement that texts have the potential for causal effects should be the basic starting point for any textual analysis. In education research specifically, it has long been appreciated that policy texts act as carriers of discourses imbued with intentionality that aim to steer the reading of the texts in a certain direction (see for example Lingard & Ozga, 2008; Lingard & Sellar, 2013; Ball, 2012), and the reading of political texts is contextually mediated, for example by teachers (Alexander, 2001).

The causality of texts is not something we simply assume – it is built into the critical realist ontology of reality, in which all aspects of structure are seen as having the potential to causally affect people, known as *agents*, who come into contact with the texts, even if this is secondhand via the various ways that curriculum policies are known about and discussed in schools. The presence of agents is a necessary condition for the realisation of the causal potential of texts. Texts cannot bring about change, individual or societal, merely by virtue of their existence. For any text to actualise its potential causal effects, it has to be actively engaged with – received, made sense of, and applied in a certain context. Thus, the causality of texts is not automatic but mediated by meaning-making. This means not only that the potential causal effects of texts may or may not manifest themselves but also that how and when they manifest themselves depends on who engages with them, in what ways, to what end, and in what circumstances. The causality of texts is therefore not regular but contingent on a variety of contextual factors – it is a product of the interplay between structure and agency.

Contextual causality

In addition to examining the text itself, we explored the broader contextual factors that influence how the curriculum is implemented and experienced. This included the following:

1. **Historical context**: Understanding the historical development of the National Curriculum provides insights into its underlying philosophies and assumptions about children's agency. Changes in educational policy over time reflect shifting societal values and priorities.
2. **Cultural context**: The cultural context within which the curriculum operates affects how it is interpreted and enacted. Cultural norms and values related to childhood, education, and authority play a significant role in shaping educational practices and children's experiences of agency.

3. **Institutional context**: Schools as institutions have their own cultures, policies, and practices that mediate the impact of the curriculum. Factors such as school leadership, teacher training, and available resources can either support or hinder the development of children's agency.

Examining causality in the curriculum

To delve deeper into the potential causality of the national curriculum, our CDA focussed on how it defines and promotes, or constrains, children's agency. We identified several key areas where the curriculum's language and structure could produce specific effects on children's agency:

1. **Educational objectives**: The stated goals and objectives of the curriculum play a crucial role in shaping educational practices. Objectives that prioritise knowledge retention or standardised test performance may limit opportunities for children to exercise their agency, whereas objectives that emphasise creativity, problem-solving, and self-directed learning could enhance it.
2. **Language and terminology**: The choice of words and phrases used to describe children's roles and capabilities can significantly influence perceptions of agency. Terms like 'obedient', 'compliant', or 'passive' can reinforce a sense of powerlessness, while terms like 'autonomous', 'critical thinker', or 'independent' can lead to empowerment of children.
3. **Pedagogical implications**: The teaching methods and strategies that teachers use as a result of the requirements of the national curriculum also affect children's agency. Teacher-centred approaches that focus on direct instruction and control can restrict agency, while student-centred approaches that encourage exploration and collaboration can promote it.

The process of critical discourse analysis

The CDA of the national curriculum text was conducted over a five-month period from May to September 2021.This phase of our research was foundational for subsequently testing, through fieldwork in schools, underlying narratives and assumptions about children's roles and agency within a powerful educational framework that had statutory and non-statutory elements.

The CDA involved an iterative and immersive reading process aimed at uncovering the nuanced ways in which children's agency is framed. Our approach was guided by a series of steps designed to extract meaningful insights from the curriculum text. These steps were as follows:

1. **Identifying the problem**: The central issue under scrutiny was the representation and treatment of children's agency in England's national curriculum.
2. **Defining the data**: The national curriculum text for Key Stages 1 and 2 (DfE, 2013) was selected as the policy text most likely to have influence on children's agency.

3. **Analysing content**: We closely examined the curriculum text, ultimately including the semantic details at sentence-level, to identify how children's agency was represented in the national curriculum.
4. **Generating findings**: The insights gathered from our analysis were interpreted to illuminate the curriculum's treatment of children's agency.

The analytical procedure involved close readings of the entire curriculum text, which enabled relevant insights to be uncovered, particularly about the curriculum's key assertions and assumptions. Each reading of the text facilitated the identification of prominent patterns and recurrent themes regarding the treatment of children's agency in the document. The findings from our critical discourse analysis provided a foundational understanding of how the curriculum appeared to shape children's experiences of agency. The intentions of any curriculum text have practical implications for educators, policy makers, and all stakeholders, including implications for how children's agency might manifest itself in their education in primary schools.

Limitations of critical discourse analysis

As mentioned earlier, Fairclough's approach to CDA rests on the fundamental principles of critical realist philosophy. Ontologically, it is grounded in the critical realist conception of social reality, in which equal weight is afforded to abstract social structures (e.g. education policies) as well as concrete social practices, phenomena, and events (e.g. the space of a classroom, the structure of a lesson, the content of the curriculum). Fairclough (2003) distinguishes between three distinct levels of reality that closely parallel the domains of critical realism discussed in Chapter 3:

1. **The actual, or the real**: The sum of all processes and phenomena that take place, regardless of our knowledge or even our ability to have knowledge of them (corresponding to critical realism's 'real' domain).
2. **The potential**: What is possible in principle under given circumstances (corresponding to critical realism's 'actual' domain).
3. **The empirical**: What we can directly experience and observe (corresponding to critical realism's 'empirical' domain).

Fairclough distinguishes between objective reality and our subjective interpretations of it, 'reality (the potential, the actual) cannot be reduced to our knowledge of reality, which is contingent, shifting, and partial' (2003, p. 14).

In the context of CDA, realism also has important epistemological implications. Namely, the reality of any text always exceeds our knowledge of it. Texts are knowable, but our knowledge of them is the following:

- **Always partial**: No textual analysis is ever definitive or complete.
- **Inevitably selective**: Any textual analysis is circumscribed by the specific questions we choose to ask at the expense of all other possible questions; the

particular theoretical frameworks we apply, deliberately neglecting other possible frameworks; our subjective motivations for selecting those specific questions and theories; and our personal beliefs underlying those motivations.

Similarly, our analysis of the national curriculum is circumscribed by the following:

- **Guiding questions**, such as how children's agency is treated in the curriculum.
- **Theoretical framework**, namely critical realism, with its distinct focus on the interplay between structure and agency.
- **Research motivations**: Understanding the potential impact of the national curriculum on children's agency.
- **Underlying beliefs**, particularly that children's agency is important and should be an essential consideration in curriculum design and delivery.

In recognising and acknowledging the inevitably partial nature of our analysis, we cannot avoid addressing the question of objectivity. Like Fairclough, we do not believe that a fully complete and objective textual analysis is possible. This, however, does not diminish the value of the effort. While our analysis may not capture all potential and actual effects of the NCE in relation to all stakeholders and contexts, it can nonetheless help to explore some effects, namely those pertaining to children's agency, in a specific context – namely that of primary schools – and on a particular group, namely primary-aged children. It is this purpose that our CDA of the national curriculum intended to achieve.

Longitudinal in-depth qualitative inquiry

The process of identifying and recruiting schools took place between February and April 2021. Our approach to sampling and sample sought three contrasting types of schools: an independent school, a community school, an academy school. This variety was intended to achieve variation in school types and contexts to ensure a breadth of examples of how children's agency is treated across different educational contexts.

The essential criteria for school selection included the following:

- **Adherence to the national curriculum**: Ensuring all selected schools followed the **national curriculum** was crucial for fulfilling the key aims of the research.
- **Co-educational intake**: Including both boys and girls to reflect a more generalisable student experience.
- **Commitment to the project's full duration**: Schools needed to commit to participating from the beginning to the end of the study.
- **Exclusion of schools with a weak Ofsted inspection rating**: This criterion ensured that the schools were operating at a recognised standard of quality.
- **Average level of fees per pupil (for the selection of an independent school)**: To ensure the selected private school was, to some degree, representative of typical private schooling in England.

Additionally, we identified some desirable features:

- **Presence of a student council or similar student-led body**: To facilitate the exploration of children's agency in practice.
- **Location of at least one of the schools in a high deprivation area**: This would allow us to reflect on how socio-economic factors might influence children's agency within the curriculum.

We leveraged our research centre's existing connections to secure the participation of a community school serving a deprived area in a city in the South of England and an academy school in the suburbs of a city in the north of England. To recruit an independent school, we utilised the Independent Association of Prep Schools' (IAPS) online directory, which helped us to identify a suitable school. Initial remote interviews with the senior leadership teams of the prospective independent schools were conducted to confirm their suitability. These discussions ensured that the schools met our criteria and were committed to the project's aims. All three schools subsequently signed a Memorandum of Agreement, outlining mutual responsibilities and confirming their participation. Formal ethical approval for the research was obtained in August 2021 via University College London ethical application procedures. All standard ethical procedures including informed consent, right to withdraw, pseudonymity, and secure handling of research data were adopted. To protect participants' privacy and confidentiality, all names of schools, teachers, and children used throughout this book are pseudonyms.

Fieldwork and data collection activities commenced in October 2021 and concluded in July 2023, adhering to the original timeline. This period allowed for comprehensive engagement with each school and enabled us to gather rich, longitudinal data. Throughout the data collection phase, a range of qualitative methods were employed, including the following:

- **Lesson observations**: To capture real-time instances of how children's agency was facilitated or constrained in different educational contexts.
- **Interviews with teachers and children**: To gain insights into their perceptions and experiences related to the curriculum and agency.
- **Focus group interviews with children**: To encourage a collaborative exploration of the themes under investigation.
- **Innovative participatory activities with children**: Designed to solicit children's experiences and interpretations of agency in and outside the classroom, such as 'My Agency Timeline' and 'My Learning Choice Diary'.
- **Document analysis**: Of school policies, lesson plans, and other relevant materials to contextualise our findings within each school's operational framework.

The careful selection and recruitment of schools, combined with rigorous ethical standards and a well-structured data collection timeline, laid a solid foundation for our investigation into children's agency within the national curriculum.

Data collection

In consultation with the schools, data collection activities commenced in October 2021. Before our first visit, each school received electronic copies of research information sheets and consent forms for teachers, parents, and children. These documents were designed to provide participants with comprehensive details about the aims and process of the research, ensuring informed consent. Each school assisted in selecting case study pupils, with two children from each of Year 3, Year 4, and Year 5 being chosen. The selection was based on the following considerations:

- **Children's attainment**: Ensuring a range of academic abilities.
- **Gender**: Achieving a balanced representation.
- **English language proficiency**: Including children with varying levels of proficiency.
- **Socio-economic background**: Ensuring diversity within the sample.
- **Ability to participate throughout the study**: Ensuring the children could remain engaged for the duration of the two-year data collection period.
- **Interest in contributing to the study**: Prioritising children likely to be engaged and willing to participate.

The schools provided tentative lists of potential case study pupils, which were confirmed during our first visits. The two-year duration ensured that we also engaged with the pupils when they had moved up to years four, five, and six, including the transitions to these new classes.

Data collection took place from October 2021 to July 2023, aligning with school terms but allowing for flexibility due to variations among the participating schools. Originally, the research design proposed two in-person visits per half-term to each school. However, unforeseen challenges such as Covid-19 outbreaks and staff shortages required occasional adjustments. When in-person visits were not feasible, we employed remote data collection methods, including online interviews and activities.

In total, the number of data collection points, fieldwork visits or online interviews, were as follows:

- **Independent school**: 18 (four online)
- **Northern Academy**: 21
- **State-funded school**: 19

The first visit to each school was undertaken jointly by Dom and Yana. The primary aim was to introduce the project and the team, and to become acquainted with the setting, teachers, and children. These visits involved the following:

- **Introductory interviews**: Conducted with Head Teachers and/or senior leadership team members (e.g. head of curriculum), as well as year lead teachers. These interviews were audio-recorded with explicit consent.

- **Meetings with case study pupils**: Informal conversations and ice-breaker activities were conducted to establish rapport. For example, children were asked to talk about their favourite places in the school. These interactions were not recorded to ensure maximum comfort for the children; instead, we took field notes shortly after the visit.

During the period of the research project we maintained continuous engagement with the schools to ensure the study's smooth progress. Regular communication, including updates and feedback sessions, helped to address any emerging issues promptly. This collaborative approach fostered strong relationships with the schools, enhancing the overall quality of data collection and ensuring that the participants remained informed and comfortable throughout the process.

The first visits provided preliminary insights into the functioning and day-to-day life of the schools. These insights were then used to inform the plan of activities for the next visits. These activities included the following:

- **Formal interviews**: Conducted with Head Teachers, senior leadership teams, and class teachers.
- **Observations**: Covering lessons, children's playtime, and other activities (e.g. *Golden Time*).
- **Observations of particular events**: Such as School Council meetings, School Assembly meetings, pupil meetings with the Head Teacher, and out-of-school trips.
- **Informal conversations**: Held with teachers and teaching assistants related to observations, and informal discussions (e.g. in the staffrooms).
- **Informal discussions during lessons**: Engaged both case study and non-case study pupils during lessons and activities.
- **Innovative activities with case study pupils**: Activities planned with an aim to explore the children's experiences of agency.

The innovative activities with case study pupils were meticulously designed to gain deeper insights into the children's lived experiences and their perceptions of agency within their school environment. These activities were instrumental in capturing rich, qualitative data that provided a nuanced understanding of how children perceive their ability to make choices and exercise independence in their educational settings.

The first activity, *The School Tour*, aimed to understand the children's emotional and cognitive connections with different spaces within their school. Each child guided us on a tour of their favourite places, explaining what they liked about these places and how they felt while visiting them. During these tours, we took detailed field notes and asked each child to write a short note capturing their feelings and thoughts in their own words. This activity revealed the emotional significance of certain spaces such as playgrounds, libraries, or art spaces. It also

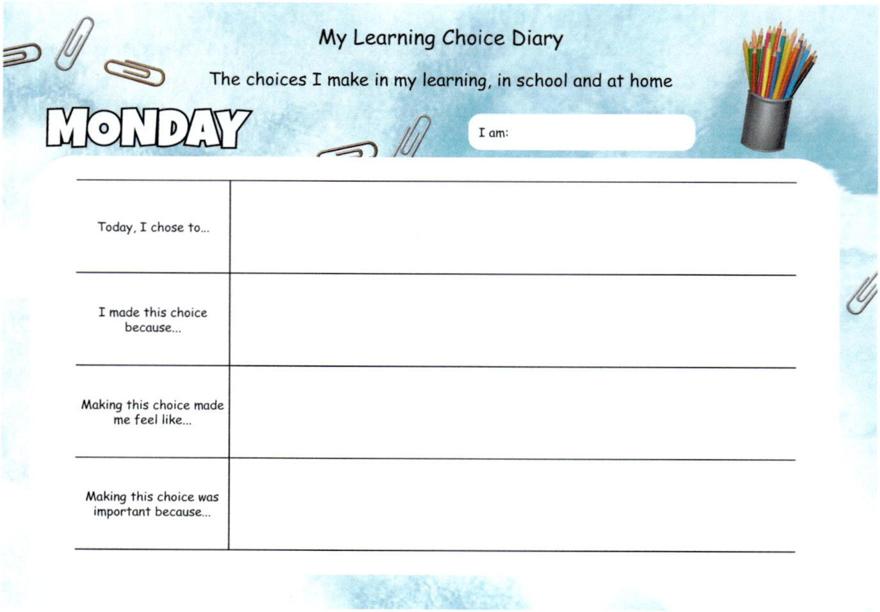

My Learning Choice Diary

The choices I make in my learning, in school and at home

MONDAY

I am:

Today, I chose to...	
I made this choice because...	
Making this choice made me feel like...	
Making this choice was important because...	

FIGURE 4.1 My Learning Choice Diary

provided insights into where children felt most engaged, which often correlated with areas where they felt a greater sense of agency and autonomy. Additionally, the tours highlighted how social interactions within these spaces influenced their sense of agency.

My Learning Choice Diary was another key activity designed to explore children's decision-making processes and the contexts in which they felt they could exercise choice. Children recorded the various choices they made over a week (Figure 4.1 shows a Monday page as an example), including decisions made both in and out of school. They were asked to reflect on why they chose to record those particular choices and how making those choices made them feel. We then reviewed the diaries with the children, discussing the recorded choices in detail. This activity revealed patterns in the types of choices children made and the frequency of these choices, providing insights into how different choices impacted their feelings of empowerment and autonomy. It also highlighted the contexts, such as home, classroom, or playground, where children felt more or less agency.

My Agency Timeline activity (Figure 4.2) aimed to identify specific moments during a school day when children experienced varying degrees of agency. Children created a timeline of their school day, noting times when they felt significant, little, or no agency. Terms such as 'choice' and 'independence' were introduced to help children understand and identify moments of agency. They were then asked to reflect on what contributed to their feelings of agency at different times. This activity helped identify temporal patterns, such as times during the day when children felt more empowered, and highlighted which activities, like group work or independent study, fostered a greater sense of agency. It also shed light on the barriers to agency, such as rigid schedules or teaching styles that limited their sense of empowerment.

This is my agency timeline

Date
My name

How much agency do you feel you are having today?

	😣 I feel powerless – no control!	🙁 I don't feel powerful enough – little control!	🙂 I feel more powerful now – good control!	😊 I feel quite powerful – a lot of control!	🤩 I feel very powerful – full control!
9am					
10am					
11am					
12pm					
1pm					
2pm					
3pm					
4pm					

FIGURE 4.2A   My Agency Timeline

Tell me more about each situation.

What made you feel this way?

😖

I feel powerless –
no control!

🙁

I don't feel powerful enough –
little control!

🙂

I feel more powerful now –
good control!

😊

I feel quite powerful –
a lot of control!

🤩

I feel very powerful –
full control!

Thank you 😊

FIGURE 4.2B My Agency Timeline

My Ideal School Day activity encouraged children to envision an ideal school day that maximised their sense of agency and enjoyment. Children designed a detailed timetable for their ideal school day, including preferred lessons and activities, and explained their choices in follow-up interviews. This reflection allowed them to articulate how these choices might enhance their sense of agency and overall school experience. The activity provided valuable insights into the activities that children found most engaging and empowering, as well as the characteristics of an ideal learning environment from their perspective. It also highlighted how much control children wished to have over their daily schedules.

Feelings at School activity (Figure 4.3) was designed to help understand children's emotional experiences throughout the school day. Children were asked to identify and record their feelings at different points during their daily school routine using a simplified emotions chart. The chart included four main emotional states:

5		Angry Out of Control
4		Upset Losing Control
3		Becoming upset Frustrated
2		Sad Worried
1		Happy Calm

FIGURE 4.3   Feelings at School

happy/calm, sad/worried, becoming upset/frustrated, and upset/losing control. By tracking these emotional states alongside various school activities, we could identify patterns between specific activities and children's emotional well-being. This activity was instrumental in understanding how social dynamics shaped children's experiences and agency within the school environment. Children's reported emotions served as valuable indicators of when they felt most empowered or constrained, with positive emotions often corresponding to moments of strong social connections. Conversely, negative emotions frequently aligned with situations where children felt their agency was limited. This emotional mapping revealed how social relationships and power dynamics within the school setting influenced children's sense of agency, demonstrating that their ability to exercise agency was deeply intertwined with their emotional experiences and social interactions throughout the school day.

The activities were designed to be non-intrusive and enjoyable, ensuring that the children felt comfortable and that their confidentiality was maintained. These activities not only enriched the data collection process but also empowered the children by giving them a voice in the research, allowing for a deeper and more comprehensive understanding of their experiences and perceptions of agency in their educational settings.

The fieldwork activities generated rich and diverse datasets. These datasets comprised several key components. Field notes were carefully edited after each visit, capturing detailed insights from interactions, observations, and reflections. These notes provided a comprehensive narrative of the day-to-day life within the schools and the children's experiences and perceptions.

Audio recordings were another critical element of the datasets. These recordings allowed for precise and thorough analysis of the discussions and provided valuable verbatim quotations and nuances that might otherwise have been lost.

Photographic data supplemented the written and audio-recorded materials. These photos included images of the case study pupils' learning materials and outputs, such as termly topic books, as well as photographs taken during out-of-school trips. These photos did not feature children, adhering to the ethical guidelines to protect privacy and confidentiality. Photos were also taken of school policy materials such as visual representations of curriculum planning.

Creative and written outputs produced by the case study pupils during the interviews added another layer of depth to the dataset. These outputs included the children's written reflections and notes from activities such as the My Learning Choice Diary, My Agency Timeline, My Ideal School Day, and Feelings at School. These materials offered direct insights into the children's thoughts and feelings, providing a personal and nuanced perspective on their experiences of agency within the school setting.

The dataset was further enriched by materials and information provided by the schools. This included school policies, procedures, and guidelines, which offered a broader context for understanding the institutional framework within which the children's experiences were situated. These documents helped to contextualise the children's experiences and provided a basis for understanding how institutional structures and policies might influence their sense of agency.

Recognising the importance of capturing children's authentic voices and respecting their preferences, not all interviews with children were audio-recorded. Some children preferred not to be recorded, and in these instances, handwritten notes were taken during and immediately after the interactions. These notes captured essential insights and occasional verbatim quotations, ensuring that the children's perspectives were documented even in the absence of audio recordings. These handwritten notes were subsequently integrated into the field notes, maintaining a cohesive and comprehensive record of each visit.

To foster transparency and collaboration, we conducted in-person visits to each school in June and July 2023 to share initial findings with the senior leadership teams. These sessions were an example of *participant validation* of the findings which were used to elicit reflections and feedback from the school leaders. The discussions during these visits were recorded, and these recordings became an integral part of the overall dataset. This collaborative approach ensured that the findings were not only accurate but also reflective of the schools' perspectives, enhancing the validity and reliability of the research outcomes.

Analyses

Our analyses were guided by the theoretical framework grounded in critical realism. By situating our findings within the critical realist philosophy, we were able to draw nuanced conclusions about the interplay between structural factors and children's agency in relation to the curriculum, pedagogy, and assessment. This approach allowed us to explore how broader institutional structures influenced individual experiences and actions, while also recognising the agency children exercised within these contexts.

The qualitative datasets produced during the ethnographic study were organised within a digital folder and file system. To manage and analyse these extensive datasets, we employed NVivo qualitative data analysis software. This tool facilitated the organisation and coding of various forms of data, including digital text, image files, and transcribed audio recordings.

The coding process was iterative and recursive. Initially, we developed a set of codes that emerged from preliminary readings of the data. These codes evolved as we engaged in a critical synthesis of the data, continually refining and expanding the codes to capture emerging themes and patterns. This iterative method allowed us to move back and forth between the data and the emerging codes, ensuring that our analysis was deeply grounded in the empirical evidence.

Through this process, we ultimately identified key themes. These themes were explored in depth through a comprehensive analysis across the various datasets. For example, we examined how children's agency was manifested in different contexts,

TABLE 4.1 Themes and codes

Theme	Theme definition	Code	Code definition	Subcode	Subcode definition
Choice	How children experience and exercise choice in school	Agency in learning	Children's ability to make decisions about their learning experiences	In lesson design	Children's input into how lessons are structured and delivered
				During lesson time	Choices available to children during actual lessons
		Agency in activities	Children's ability to choose activities outside formal learning	Free time choices	Decisions during breaks and unstructured time
				Extracurricular	Choices about clubs and additional activities
Subject hierarchies	How different subjects are valued and prioritised within schools	Core subjects	Treatment of mathematics, English, and science	Status	Perceived importance of subjects
				Flexibility	How much choice is given within subjects
		Non-core subjects	Treatment of other curriculum areas	Perceived value	How these subjects are viewed by teachers and children
Social dynamics	How different subjects are valued and prioritised within schools	Peer relationships	Interactions between children	Collaborative learning	Agency in group work situations
				Interaction outside the classroom	Agency in non-learning situations
		Teacher relationships	Interactions between children and teachers	Communication	How children express views to teachers

(Continued)

TABLE 4.1 (Continued)

Theme	Theme definition	Code	Code definition	Subcode	Subcode definition
School council	Formal structures for student voice	Representation	How children participate in decision-making		
		Impact	Actual influence on school practices	Changes in learning	Concrete results from council actions related to learning
				Changes in other areas	Concrete results from council actions related to other areas
Curriculum	How curriculum structures affect agency	Content control	Who determines what is taught	School control	School-directed aspects
				Children's input	Areas where children influence content
		Delivery methods	How curriculum is implemented	Flexibility	Room for adaptation to student interests
Assessment	How evaluation practices affect agency	Formal assessment	Impact of tests and examinations	Test preparation	How assessment shapes teaching
				Children's views of subjects	How assessments affect children's perception of different subjects
School and society	Broader contextual influences on agency	Family background	How home life affects school agency	Cultural factors	Impact of cultural expectations
				Economic factors	Impact of socio-economic status
		School culture	Institutional approach to agency	School values	How agency aligns with school ethos
				Local community	Community influence on school practices

such as classroom activities, school council meetings, and social interactions. We also looked at how institutional factors, such as curriculum and assessment, shaped these expressions of agency. An important final interrogation of the validity of the themes and codes was the processes of writing for publication. These processes necessitated revisiting and, as necessary, reanalysing the coding framework and the allocation of research events to codes. The final analysis themes and codes are shown in Table 4.1.

By employing a critical realist approach, we were able to achieve a nuanced understanding of the interplay between structural factors and children's agency. The use of NVivo for qualitative data analysis allowed us to handle large and diverse datasets effectively, ensuring that our findings were robust and well-substantiated. This approach enabled us to draw meaningful conclusions about the ways in which curriculum and other institutional structures influence, and are influenced by, the agency of primary-aged children within the school context.

Our methodology integrated CDA with longitudinal ethnographic research to examine both the structural conditions shaping children's agency and their lived experiences within these conditions. The combination of CDA and extensive field-work allowed us to trace how the national curriculum's treatment of agency mani-fested in school practices and children's experiences. This dual focus aligns with critical realism's emphasis on understanding both the causal power of texts and how that power is mediated through social contexts and human interpretation.

Chapter 5 presents detailed pictures of our selection of primary schools: South City Independent, South City State, and Northern City State, describing how each school's unique characteristics and approaches created different conditions for children's agency. These descriptions of the schools provide an essential context for understanding the findings that emerge from our research in each of the schools.

References

Alexander, R. J. (2001). *Culture and pedagogy: International comparisons in primary edu-cation*. Blackwell Publishing.

Ball, S. J. (2012). *How schools do policy: Policy enactments in secondary schools [eBook]*. Routledge.

Department for Education. (2013). *The national curriculum in England: Key stages 1 and 2 framework document*. https://www.gov.uk/government/publications/national-curriculum-in-england-primary-curriculum

Fairclough, N. (2003). *Analysing discourse: Textual analysis for social research*. Psychology Press.

Fairclough, N. (2018). CDA as dialectical reasoning. In J. Flowerdew & J. E. Richardson (Eds.), *The Routledge handbook of critical discourse studies* (pp. 13–25). Routledge.

Lingard, B., & Ozga, J. (Eds.). (2008). *The Routledge Falmer reader in education policy and politics*. Routledge.

Lingard, B., & Sellar, S. (2013). Globalization, edu-business and network governance: The policy sociology of Stephen J. Ball and rethinking education policy analysis. *London Review of Education*, *11*(3), 265–280.

5
THE SCHOOLS AND PARTICIPANTS

The three contrasting primary schools at the heart of our research each existed within a unique context, shaped by their geographical location, school type, and the socio-economic characteristics of their local communities. Through detailed profiles of the schools, this chapter provides essential context for understanding how different institutional environments approach and facilitate children's agency. Each profile examines the school's distinct characteristics, including its organisational framework, teaching staff, case study pupils, curriculum approaches, and specific initiatives that influenced children's agency. To protect participants' privacy and confidentiality, all names of schools, teachers, and children have been pseudonymised.

As explained in Chapter 4, our sampling approach followed children's progression through their school journey. We began working with Years 3, 4, and 5 teachers in the first year of fieldwork (2021–22), then followed these same children and their teachers as they moved into Years 4, 5, and 6 in the second year (2022–23). Children in these year groups are normally aged 7–8 years in Year 3, 8–9 years in Year 4, 9–10 years in Year 5, and 10–11 years in Year 6. This longitudinal approach allowed us to track how children's experiences of agency evolved as they progressed through the school.

This detailed examination of each school's unique features and practices sets the stage for understanding how different institutional contexts shape opportunities for children's agency in educational settings. We begin our examination with SCI, a school that demonstrates how traditional academic rigour can coexist with structured opportunities for children's agency.

South City Independent

South City Independent (SCI), established in 1958, was a selective co-educational primary school for children aged 3 to 11. With a maximum capacity of 175 pupils and average class sizes of 17, the school maintained an intimate learning

DOI: 10.4324/9781003227779-5

environment. Though non-denominational, the school welcomed children from diverse backgrounds. Data on free school meals eligibility was not available at this independent school, which served predominantly affluent families.

The school built on England's national curriculum, enriching it with additional subjects, particularly languages. An extensive extracurricular programme spanned sports, arts, and various clubs, with wraparound care available from 7:45 a.m. The well-resourced facilities supported both academic and extracurricular activities.

Each year group comprised one class, enabling teachers to provide targeted support and guidance. Attention to children's agency was part of the school's ethos, as articulated by the Head Teacher. However, this existed alongside intense parental expectations and a strong focus on preparing students for selective secondary school entrance exams. This focussed approach led to strong academic outcomes, with many children progressing to prestigious independent and grammar schools.

The teachers – 2021 to 2023

Dinesh – Year 3 (Year 5 in the second year of study)

Dinesh had a decade of diverse teaching experience from both independent and state sectors in the UK and abroad. His teaching career began in an independent school as a Year 3 Teacher of both English and mathematics, followed by a significant tenure at a British International School in Spain. During his two years in Spain, he served as both a Year 5 class teacher and Head of Physical Education. Following his return to the UK during the Covid-19 pandemic and a brief period in state education, Dinesh joined SCI as Head of Mathematics.

In his role as Year 3 Teacher, Dinesh extended beyond his mathematics leadership position, actively contributing to history teaching and engaging with children's wellbeing through PSHE. His teaching philosophy emphasised exceeding national curriculum expectations, exemplified by his introduction of diverse multiplication methods, such as Russian and Egyptian approaches. This variety aimed to add an enriching layer to children's mathematical understanding. Dinesh's experience teaching the English national curriculum to non-native English speakers in Spain significantly influenced his teaching approach at SCI. He successfully balanced maintaining national standards while accelerating the pace to prepare children for senior school entrance examinations.

Lauren – Year 4 in both years of study

Lauren's relationship with SCI spanned over two decades, beginning as a parent when her children enrolled in the school's Nursery. As her children progressed through the school, she took an active role in the Parent Committee, eventually becoming its head alongside another parent. While working as a teaching assistant in Reception, Lauren seized an opportunity for professional development. With support from the then Head Teacher, who allowed her to attend university two mornings per week, she pursued higher education, obtaining an English degree and later completing a PGCE at the University of Buckingham.

Her teaching career at SCI encompassed diverse roles across different year groups and subjects. She taught Years 4 and 5 as a lead teacher while actively engaging in teaching history, humanities, and English across various year levels. Her responsibilities expanded to include the position of Head of History and oversight of PE, particularly netball. Lauren's teaching approach emphasised fostering independent thinking and creativity. In history, she encouraged children to explore primary and secondary sources, moving beyond rote memorisation. Her English curriculum included aspects such as grammar-focussed days but also creative sessions designed to encourage free expression.

Recognising the diverse abilities within the Year 4 class, Lauren developed a practical approach to mathematics teaching. She introduced engaging activities such as quizzes and multiplication race games to make learning more dynamic. Through collaboration with the Deputy Head, she implemented differentiated instruction to provide targeted support for children with varying needs, demonstrating her commitment to creating an inclusive and stimulating learning environment.

Wayne – Year 5 (Year 6 in the second year of the study)

Wayne brought a unique blend of musical expertise and teaching experience to Year 5. His teaching journey began during his second year of university music studies, initially taking on part-time roles as a singing teacher before securing a full-time position at a state secondary school. Having completed the *School Direct* salaried route (a pathway designed for high-quality graduates with at least three years of transferable work experience) and gained experience at a special measures school, he joined SCI. At the study's commencement, Wayne was in his third year with the school, serving as both Year 5 Teacher and specialist music instructor for Years 3 to 6. Despite not initially considering primary education, he found SCI's supportive environment compelling during his interview, leading to his appointment.

Wayne's approach to music education demonstrated both creativity and adaptability. He preferred utilising the concise two-page national curriculum document as a foundation, enabling him to introduce composition to children from an early age. His teaching methods included using colour-coded notation for piano instruction, accommodating various learning styles. Wayne used the school's generous budget to provide children with diverse instrumental experiences, often catering to children's individual interests.

The case study pupils

Imran and Suraya – Year 3 to Year 4

Imran was a contemplative and thoughtful learner with a strong capacity for critical thinking and unique perspectives. While initially he was quite reserved in focus group discussions, he demonstrated particular strength in his ability to engage deeply with questions, offering considered views on his learning experiences. His approach to participation in research activities revealed a willingness to reflect on and share insights about his educational journey. Although somewhat shy at first, Imran gradually opened up during group discussions, contributing valuable perspectives that demonstrated careful consideration of the topics at hand. According to his teachers, Imran demonstrated consistent engagement in learning.

Suraya emerged as a notably self-directed learner who approached her studies with enthusiasm and determination. Her teachers described her as a smart and independent student who consistently sought out challenging tasks and learning opportunities. As a school council representative during the study period, Suraya demonstrated strong commitment to her leadership role, finding genuine satisfaction in contributing to school-wide initiatives and improvements. Her academic excellence and eagerness to embrace challenges reflected her proactive approach to learning.

Arun and Leyla – Year 4 to Year 5

Arun was described by his class teacher as academically average, yet he brought a distinct quiet determination to his studies. His proactive approach to learning was evident in the way he consistently engaged with learning materials. While Arun occasionally required support to maintain focus, he was genuinely curious and proactive in learning. He often approached teachers with questions about topics that captured his interest. Though reserved in his demeanour, Arun's diligence and initiative in seeking clarification demonstrated his commitment to understanding new ideas.

Leyla, while also characterised by teachers as performing at an average academic level, brought a vibrant energy to her learning experience. Like Aran, she demonstrated proactive learning behaviours, but she expressed it differently through her natural enthusiasm for sports and creative pursuits. What set Leyla apart was her deeply reflective approach to learning, particularly evident in her mathematics work. Her exercise books demonstrated her intellectual curiosity, filled with thoughtful observations and questions that explored the practical applications of mathematical concepts. Her interest in understanding how concepts like fractional complements applied to the real world highlighted her ability to think beyond the classroom and make meaningful connections with her learning. This combination of enthusiasm and reflection created a rich, engaged learning style that served her well across all subjects.

Raj and Sonia – Year 5 to Year 6

Raj was a musically talented student, particularly excelling in piano and demonstrating natural leadership in supporting his classmates with musical compositions. Raj embraced additional responsibilities within the school community, most notably in his role as *digital prefect*. In this position, he skilfully guided and supported his peers in their use of technology for learning, demonstrating both technical aptitude and leadership capabilities. His teachers noted that he was particularly susceptible to academic pressure, possibly influenced by parental expectations and the competitive academic environment.

Sonia was a gifted yet reserved pupil who consistently demonstrated keen interest in discussions about learning. Though naturally quiet, she displayed good insight during moments of reflection and contributed thoughtfully to discussions when invited to share her perspective. During research interviews, she offered particularly perceptive observations about the learning environment and educational experiences at the school. Her academic performance, while strong, placed her in the middle range of her high-achieving class, reflecting the high standards of the school.

The curriculum

The curriculum at SCI integrated national curriculum requirements with enhanced educational opportunities made possible by its independent status. The school pursued three main educational aims: academic excellence for selective secondary school entry, comprehensive subject knowledge across all curriculum areas, and integrated cross-curricular learning. Under the guidance of the Head of Curriculum, each Head of Subject developed plans that extended beyond statutory requirements. This approach was exemplified through cross-subject integration, particularly in humanities and STEM subjects, where topics and concepts were deliberately connected across different subject areas.

Parental expectations strongly influenced the curriculum design, particularly the emphasis on English and mathematics for senior school entrance examinations. However, the school maintained its commitment to delivering a broad and balanced education through various approaches to learning. The English curriculum exemplified this balanced approach to subject teaching. Each term was structured around a teacher-selected novel that formed the basis for all English activities. Creative writing, grammar instruction, and literary analysis connected to this central text, providing context for language learning. This approach ensured coherence across different aspects of English teaching while maintaining student engagement.

Building on this integrated approach, the school introduced the Vocabulary Ninja scheme in 2022 to further support language skills across all year groups. This initiative stemmed from the school's analysis of verbal reasoning and English assessment results from Reception to Year 6. The scheme incorporated daily five- to ten-minute vocabulary activities centred around a 'Word of the Day'. Following comprehensive INSET training for all staff members, the initiative extended beyond classroom practice through inclusion in the weekly newsletter, where the Head Teacher selected a 'Word of the Week' for both junior and senior children, often drawing from current events to encourage parent-child discussions about global issues.

While some subjects benefited from integration, others thrived as discrete disciplines. Arts education occupied a distinct place in the curriculum structure, with art, music, and drama taught as separate subjects to ensure focussed development in each artistic discipline. The music programme was particularly comprehensive, with all children learning an instrument in class. The success of this approach was reflected in the fact that approximately one-third of children from Year 3 onwards chose to pursue additional instrument lessons, indicating strong engagement with the music curriculum.

The school's responsive approach to curriculum development was particularly evident in its STEM provision. Following strong student performance in international competitions, where SCI secured first place internationally for two consecutive years and led the national quiz team rankings in July 2022, the school implemented dedicated weekly STEM lessons. These 35–40-minute sessions, introduced across all year groups from Year 1 upward, aimed to further nurture children's demonstrated enthusiasm for science and mathematics.

To complement classroom learning, the educational programme extended beyond traditional instruction through regular educational trips for all year groups and a residential trip in Year 6. These experiential learning opportunities were carefully integrated with classroom teaching to provide practical context for academic learning and support children's personal development.

The curriculum review process operated on a termly cycle, with Heads of Subjects conducting detailed evaluations of their areas through analysis of student progress, teaching effectiveness, and curriculum coherence. While teachers incorporated informal feedback from children shared during daily interactions, the school had no formal mechanism for children to contribute to curriculum development. The Head of Curriculum acknowledged that while they were aware of children's concerns about issues such as the packed timetable and time pressures, these insights came through informal channels rather than structured consultation.

Mental health assembly

The Mental Health Assembly represented a structured element of SCI's approach to student well-being. This dedicated programme went beyond traditional pastoral care, establishing formal channels for children to access support for their mental health, academic challenges, and personal concerns that might affect their studies. The school developed a distinctive approach to student support-seeking through the introduction of a formalised process that advanced beyond the practice of schools having classroom *worry boxes*. Children were encouraged to take an active role in managing their well-being by independently writing about their well-being issues on designated forms to request assistance. These forms, placed in a designated basket, served as a structured channel for children to indicate their need for support or discussion time. This process was intentionally designed not as a casual conversation request but as a formal acknowledgment of support needs, reflecting the school's commitment to treating mental health concerns with the same seriousness as academic matters.

To support this initiative, the school allocated dedicated staff resources, including a full-time mentor specifically focussed on children's well-being. This appointment was made in response to increased mental health concerns observed following the Covid-19 pandemic. While the school maintained a system where all staff members, including teachers and teaching assistants, remained available for brief conversations with children, the designated mentor provided regular, focussed support sessions. This dual approach ensured both immediate accessibility of support and the availability of more structured, ongoing assistance when needed. The programme incorporated both individual and group support mechanisms. The mentor also conducted various group sessions, including shared lunches with small groups of children. Students actively engaged with and helped shape the support available to them, taking ownership of their well-being needs. The success of these group sessions illustrated the programme's ability to respond to student preferences while maintaining its structured support framework.

School Council

The School Council operated as a formal platform for student representation and decision-making within SCI. The council's structure was based on democratic principles, with each class electing one male and one female representative through annual student votes held in September. The Council established clear communication channels to ensure comprehensive student representation. Non-council children could voice their opinions through two main avenues: their elected class representatives or classroom worry boxes. This dual approach to gathering student input ensured that all pupils had opportunities to contribute their views, whether directly through their representatives or more discreetly through the worry box system. Meeting schedules followed a regular pattern, with the Council convening every half-term and additional sessions arranged as needed for specific projects. These meetings followed formal protocols, ensuring systematic consideration of children's concerns and suggestions. The Council's work encompassed various aspects of school life, though notably focussed on matters outside academic learning, such as playground equipment and school lunches.

One significant initiative undertaken by the Council focussed on playground equipment refurbishment. This project demonstrated the Council's practical impact on school life, with children actively participating in each stage of the process. Council members engaged in detailed discussions about equipment preferences, contributed ideas for new additions, and collaborated on decisions regarding purchase and labelling of items. The project particularly emphasised creating inclusive recreational spaces that addressed the needs of both boys and girls. Another successful Council initiative centred on school meals. Representatives gathered opinions from their respective classes about meal preferences and new menu ideas. This systematic approach to gathering and implementing feedback demonstrated the Council's effectiveness in channelling children's voice into tangible improvements in school life.

However, at the time of the study the Council's scope notably excluded academic matters. Discussions where children might express views or advocate for changes related to learning, including curriculum content and delivery, were absent from Council meetings. This limitation meant that while children had established channels for input on social and organisational aspects of school life, their formal influence on academic experiences remained highly limited.

Lesson design

SCI adopted a primarily teacher-driven approach to lesson design, where teachers planned and structured learning experiences for their children. Lessons typically followed a traditional top-down model, with teachers providing clear frameworks and presenting carefully sequenced activities for children to complete. This structured approach aimed to ensure systematic delivery of content and objectives.

Within this framework, the school recognised the value of flexibility in teaching approaches. Individual teachers could incorporate varying degrees of adaptability into their lesson plans, introducing innovative practices that fostered elements of autonomy, choice, and independent decision-making. Teachers observed that such opportunities for choice enhanced children's motivation and enthusiasm for learning.

Through interviews with class teachers, it became evident that the extent of flexibility varied significantly across different subjects. The school maintained that certain disciplines, particularly core subjects, required a more structured approach, while others could accommodate greater flexibility. English and mathematics lessons typically followed more rigid teaching methods, driven by the specific goal of preparing children for standardised tests. This structured approach responded to parental expectations regarding academic performance and test outcomes. The mathematics and English lessons were designed to ensure systematic coverage of essential content and skills required for standardised assessments. Teachers in these core subjects employed instructional strategies that aligned closely with test formats, focussing on targeted content and assessment-specific skills. This systematic approach aimed to equip children with the necessary tools and knowledge for success in standardised testing environments.

A notable innovation within this structured framework was the introduction of red, yellow, and green folders in mathematics lessons. Initiated by the Head of Mathematics in 2023, this system represented a significant shift in how children's choice was integrated into core subject teaching. Unlike traditional ability grouping where children were directed to specific levels of work, this approach granted children the freedom to choose tasks across different ability levels, fostering independence and personal agency. The folder system operated through clearly defined processes. Each colour-coded folder, displayed prominently on the classroom wall, contained tasks of varying difficulty levels. The green folder offered more challenging work, yellow provided intermediate tasks, and red contained foundational activities. Children could select tasks from any folder based on their confidence and understanding of different topics. This flexibility enabled less confident children to challenge themselves with more advanced work when ready, while higher-achieving children could revisit foundational concepts when needed.

The system's dynamic nature was particularly evident in how children could move between different levels throughout their learning journey. They could adjust their choices based on their understanding of specific mathematical concepts, creating a responsive learning environment that accommodated individual learning patterns and preferences. As illustrated in Figure 5.1, this approach fostered both

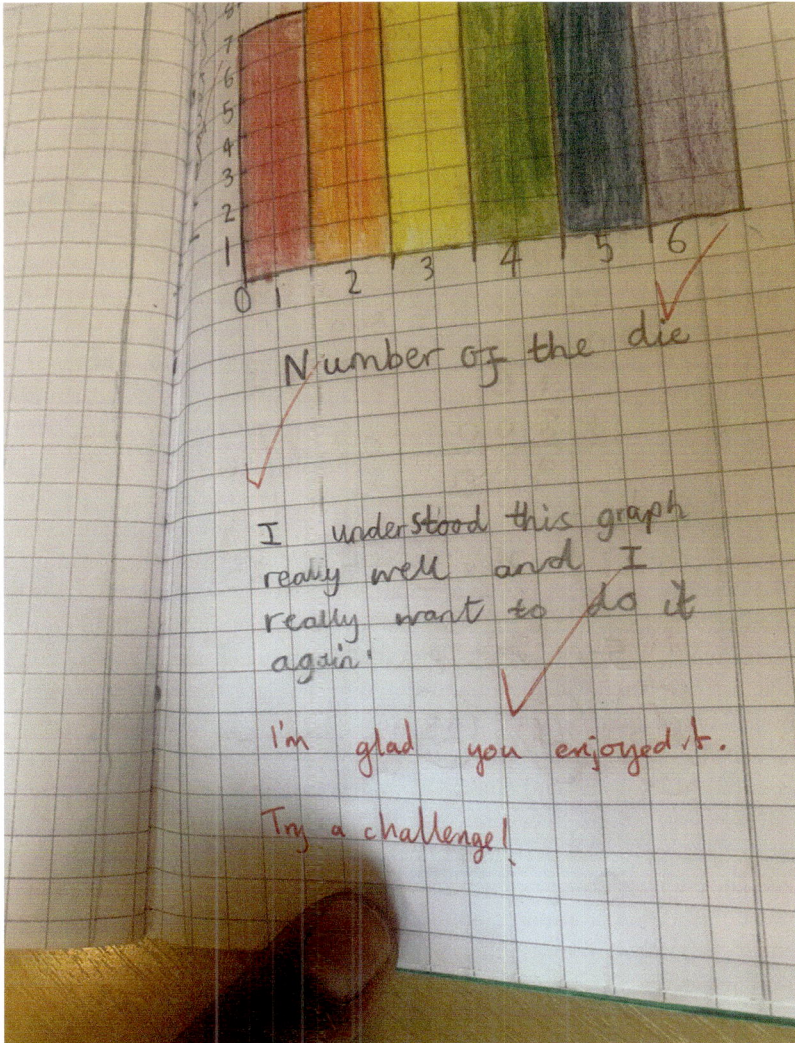

FIGURE 5.1 A Pupil's Mathematics Exercise Book

confidence and enjoyment in learning. In the observed instance, a child demonstrated enthusiasm while completing a dice-based activity. The teacher's encouragement to attempt a more challenging task showcased how the system supported children's growth while supporting their agency in the learning process.

This approach evolved from the school's existing concept of challenge folders, where children could select additional activities after completing their assigned work. The significance of the colour-coded folders lay in how they successfully integrated student choice into mathematics teaching, traditionally characterised by more rigid structures. This integration of flexibility into a highly structured subject demonstrated the school's efforts to balance academic rigour with children's agency.

Extracurricular activities

The extracurricular programme at SCI underwent significant expansion, growing from six clubs in 2018 to 28 different activities at the time of the study. This development followed the Covid-19 pandemic, when the school encouraged all staff members to contribute to the club programme. Activities operated within specific time slots: morning sessions from 8 a.m. to 8:45 a.m. and after-school sessions from 4 p.m. to 4:45 p.m., with certain exceptions such as ballet starting at 3 p.m. for younger children. The clubs operated with a flexible and inclusive structure. Children could join activities at any point during the academic year, without being restricted to term-based commitments. This open approach allowed children to explore their interests without the constraints of rigid timelines. The clubs welcomed various age groups, with activities tailored to meet different developmental needs and preferences.

Children's voices played an instrumental role in shaping the extracurricular programme. The chess club exemplified this child-led development, originating from pupils expressing preference for a structured chess club over informal lunchtime activities. The success of this initiative was evidenced by its growth to 46 participants, making it one of the school's largest clubs. Student interests also led to the introduction of a Rubik's Cube club, inspired by a Year 6 student's achievement in a national competition.

The Musical Theatre club, run by an external professional, focussed on developing both artistic skills and student confidence. The coordinator observed significant transformations over three terms, with initially shy children evolving into articulate, expressive performers through the use of scripted lines and guided actions. The club's instructional approach combined structured direction with creative freedom: although children followed specific performance guidelines, they were also encouraged to infuse their personalities into their roles. The coordinator selected content by blending their professional expertise with contemporary trends that captured children's interests, always ensuring age-appropriate material. Role assignment occurred through formal auditions, with talent as the primary criterion, although the coordinator made conscious efforts to distribute roles fairly. Despite varying levels of prominence in parts, children embraced their assigned roles, contributing to successful productions through collaborative effort.

The impact of extracurricular activities extended beyond their specific domains into daily school life. Skills and confidence developed through these activities, particularly in performing arts, and transferred to classroom activities and school events. Children demonstrated increased confidence during assemblies and class presentations, indicating the broader educational value of the extracurricular programme.

Overall, SCI's approach to education balanced traditional academic rigour with elements of children's agency and choice. The school maintained structured teaching methods, particularly in core subjects, while incorporating opportunities for children's voice and decision-making through various channels, most notably the extracurricular programme. While formal mechanisms for children's input in academic matters remained limited, the school demonstrated responsiveness to children's achievements and interests. This approach suggested a model of education where children's agency operated within clearly defined structures, balancing traditional academic expectations with opportunities for children's voice and choice.

Behaviour policy

The behaviour policy at SCI reflected a comprehensive and structured approach, with kindness serving as its core principle. The school developed a distinct system that balanced rewards and sanctions, effectively promoting positive behaviour while maintaining clear accountability for misconduct.

The House System formed the cornerstone of the school's behavioural framework, fostering both individual and collective responsibility. Organised into three houses, similar to Harry Potter's, children participated in an elaborate merit system that recognised both academic achievement through house points and good conduct through behaviour merits. The policy was notably proactive in its implementation, emphasising positive reinforcement through multiple recognition channels. These ranged from immediate acknowledgments in the form of house points to more significant celebrations like end-of-term prizes.

Children's voice and leadership played significant roles in the school's behavioural framework. Each class participated in creating their own 'Class Rules' and 'Class Charter', while the School Council actively contributed to discussions about rewards and sanctions. The school established multiple leadership positions, such as School Captains, House Captains, Prefects, Sports Captains, and Monitors, who were expected to lead by example and actively contribute to maintaining positive behavioural standards. Senior pupils were particularly empowered through practical responsibilities such as organising sports teams, encouraging wider participation, and modelling good sportsmanship. This comprehensive approach to pupil leadership, combined with participatory rule-setting, enhanced children's sense of ownership over their behaviour, contributing to children's agency in the school.

South City State

South City State (SCS) was a co-educational community primary school serving children aged 3 to 11. With a capacity for 800 children, it was a significantly larger-than-average primary school that included a nursery and admitted 90 pupils annually into Reception. The school's demographic reflected the diverse local community, with a notably higher proportion of pupils eligible for free school meals (almost 48% as of 2024) and those who spoke English as an additional language.

The school's approach centred on developing the whole child through a creative curriculum that balanced national requirements with innovative learning experiences. While firmly adhering to national curriculum content and standards as its foundation, the school enriched learning through extracurricular activities, with particular emphasis on outdoor learning and creative arts. Teachers followed clear progression maps and assessment requirements to ensure comprehensive coverage of curriculum objectives, specifically structured to support children from the school's disadvantaged area succeed academically. Through offering rich learning experiences that celebrated community diversity, the school worked to maintain high academic standards while developing well-rounded, independent individuals.

The school's commitment to community support was evident in practical initiatives, such as its food and essential items distribution system for vulnerable families. This reflected the school's broader mission to foster academic excellence while actively supporting the well-being of its local community.

The teachers – 2021 to 2022

Penny – Year 3

Penny's journey into teaching was sparked by a passion for geography and a desire to inspire young minds. Her undergraduate degree was in geography from University College London (UCL), and she completed her PGCE at the University of East Anglia. Penny's eight-year teaching career had led her through schools in rural Suffolk and Essex before finding her niche in an inner-city community.

Penny held a deep appreciation for the school's supportive culture and emphasis on staff and student well-being. Her approach to teaching reflected her belief in building a classroom community based on mutual respect and understanding. In her teaching, Penny thrived on engaging her children through dynamic and interactive learning experiences. Whether through quizzes, group activities, or hands-on projects, she strove to cater to diverse learning styles and interests, ensuring that every child felt valued and motivated to participate.

While Penny acknowledged the constraints of the national curriculum, she sought to introduce creativity and flexibility into her lessons, allowing room for children's agency within the prescribed framework. Recognising the importance of children taking ownership of their learning, she advocated for opportunities that empowered them to ask questions, explore ideas, and chart their own educational paths.

Mina – Year 4 in both years of study

As a Year 4 teacher, Mina was a dedicated and enthusiastic educator who brought a unique perspective to her role. Born into a Bangladeshi family, Mina's journey into teaching began with her undergraduate studies in Education at University College London (UCL). She continued her education by obtaining her Postgraduate Certificate of Education (PGCE) from the UCL Institute of Education (IOE).

Mina was drawn to the school's approach to education, particularly given its location in a deprived area. Despite initial reservations about the opportunities available in the area, Mina found the school to be a beacon of innovation and support, offering a wealth of resources and extracurricular activities uncommon in many schools.

Mina described her first year of teaching in the school as transformative, despite the challenges posed by the Covid-19 pandemic. Under the guidance of her mentor, Mina thrived in her role, finding the supportive atmosphere and opportunities for professional development invaluable. She credited the school's commitment to teacher training and mentorship as instrumental in her growth as an educator. With a class size of 29 children, she recognised the importance of catering to individual learning styles and abilities, dividing her class into different attainment groups based on formal assessments conducted each term.

Tanika – Year 5

Tanika's journey into teaching began with a three-year BA course at Middlesex University. While she had explored various schools, it was the tranquil and organised atmosphere of SCS that appealed to her. At the time of the study, four years into her tenure, Tanika found herself invigorated by the supportive community and the enthusiasm of both children and parents.

Tanika's teaching experience spanned different year groups, and she embraced the transition from Year 3 to her current Year 5 class at the time of our research. Although working without additional adult support in her classroom, she found her students remarkably self-directed, displaying a natural ability to engage independently with their learning. In her classroom, Tanika cultivated an environment of mutual respect and collaboration, empowering children to share their ideas freely and participate in collective learning experiences.

An advocate for a more inclusive curriculum, Tanika believed in addressing diverse cultural perspectives within the educational framework, especially in communities with significant multicultural populations like her own. While acknowledging the strengths of the national curriculum in core subjects like English and mathematics, she advocated for a more comprehensive approach that encompassed a broader spectrum of societal realities and experiences. While she had a passion for mathematics, she approached all subjects with equal dedication, integrating technology to facilitate learning through writing exercises and collaborative projects displayed on screen.

The teachers – 2022 to 2023

Sylvia – Year 5

Sylvia's journey into teaching started with an undergraduate degree in English Literature at Reading University. Initially unsure whether to teach at the secondary or primary level, she gained clarity during the Covid-19 pandemic while working in a nursery, realising her affinity for primary education. This realisation prompted her to pursue a PGCE at The University of Exeter, followed by a teaching position in a village school. Seeking a broader experience, she transitioned to a school in London before finding her place at SCS.

What drew Sylvia to the school was its supportive staff and focus on a holistic approach to education. She appreciated the emphasis on providing rich experiences for children, both within and outside the classroom, including integrating various aspects of children's lives, such as their food choices, into their learning experiences. She found her Year 5 children to be eager and curious, always willing to participate and engage with the material. The school encouraged a collaborative learning environment where children were given opportunities to share ideas and work together.

Sylvia's approach to teaching involved flexibility and responsiveness to her children's needs. She adjusted lesson plans based on their interests and responses, ensuring they remained engaged and motivated. She particularly valued student input in shaping lessons, especially in English where children had the freedom to choose their reading materials and contribute ideas to shared writing activities.

Fatima – Year 6

Fatima was an experienced teacher with over a decade of classroom experience and a deep-rooted commitment to fostering a love for learning in her children. After exploring supply teaching briefly, she found a permanent position at SCS. Having spent the prior part of her career in a different borough, her transition to SCS marked a new chapter in her professional journey.

Fatima's decision to move to the area was driven by a desire for a new challenge. Recognising the unique dynamics of the borough, she embraced the opportunity to make a difference in the lives of children facing diverse learning needs and behavioural challenges. Her familiarity with colleagues who had previously worked in the area facilitated a smooth transition to her new role. In her second year at the school, Fatima found immense satisfaction in teaching Year 6, describing her experience as 'epic' and attributing her enjoyment to the supportive environment fostered by the school's leadership.

One aspect of the school that Fatima found particularly intriguing was its curriculum design. She noted the breadth of subjects offered, which exceeded those of many other schools. The curriculum provided children with a rich and varied learning experience, incorporating subjects like Philosophy for Children (P4C),

Spanish, computing, and PSHE. Her approach to teaching emphasised flexibility and responsiveness to her children' needs, leveraging various teaching strategies, including peer teaching and experiential learning.

The case study pupils

Rita and Malik – Year 3 to Year 4

Rita was a bright student who exemplified academic excellence and a passion for learning. She shared a love for problem-solving and embraced challenges with enthusiasm. As one of the children working at 'greater depth' (a term used to describe a learner who demonstrates a deeper understanding of the subject material compared to the expected level for their age or grade), he demonstrated a drive for excellence in all aspects of her academic endeavours. Her methodical approach to her studies and her insistence on completing tasks with precision and order underscored her high standards for academic achievement. The teacher described Rita as someone who 'has to get things done' and does 'everything in order'. Beyond her individual pursuits, Rita also took on a teaching role with her peers, acting as 'a mini teacher' in the classroom. Her relentless pursuit of perfection and her ability to excel academically made her a well-rounded student.

Malik, described as 'quite chatty', was a lively and inquisitive student – one of the high attainers in the class, although not quite at the same 'greater depth' as Rita. He was characterised by his enthusiasm for problem-solving and art. Teachers observed that Malik put in significant effort and genuinely enjoyed figuring things out. According to his class teacher, Malik derived satisfaction from the learning process itself and the sense of accomplishment he felt when completing his work. Beyond his academic achievements, Malik's personality radiated with warmth and curiosity.

Ayla and Charlie – Year 4 to Year 5

Ayla was a quiet but academically capable student who consistently demonstrated high attainment across subjects. Her reserved personality coexisted with strong academic abilities – teachers characterised her as 'very able' while noting her tendency to remain quiet in class. She developed friendships with her peers while maintaining her focussed approach to learning. Her written work demonstrated exceptional attention to detail, and teachers noted her methodical approach to problem-solving. According to the teachers, Ayla had been successful in overcoming initial shyness and over time developed enough confidence to readily seek assistance when needed and engage in classroom discussions.

Charlie was a vibrant, lively student with a penchant for engaging conversations and shared a close bond with his younger brother, often fondly discussing their adventures together. In the classroom, while he found aspects of learning challenging, teachers noted that he 'puts lots of effort in' and demonstrated enthusiasm for hands-on activities. He liked spending time in the school library, which he referred to as his favourite place in the school. Teachers observed that he could become upset when receiving feedback on his work, requiring sensitive support to help him understand suggestions for improvement. Despite some socio-emotional challenges, Charlie's warm and friendly personality endeared him to his classmates and teachers. His dedication to learning manifested in his persistent efforts and his love of reading, particularly non-fiction books about history and science.

Paul and Miriam – Year 5 to Year 6

Paul was a vibrant and spirited student whose presence in the classroom added a dash of energy and enthusiasm to the learning environment. With an insatiable passion for all things culinary, he found immense joy and inspiration in the art of cooking. Paul's lively personality and quick wit made him a memorable character. His penchant for conversation often led to animated discussions on a wide array of topics, ranging from the latest cooking trends to humorous anecdotes from his daily life. With a mind as active as his body, Paul often found it challenging to adhere to the rigour of the classroom routine. Despite his chattiness and propensity for getting easily distracted, he demonstrated an innate ability to engage with complex ideas and concepts.

Miriam was a thoughtful and hardworking student who showed strong curiosity and dedication in her learning. She stood out for her inquisitive nature, with teachers noting her eagerness to ask questions and desire to explore topics in greater depth. Her excellent attention span and mature approach made her particularly strong at engaging with learning. She showed both academic ability and a genuine interest in understanding new ideas. Her consistent work ethic and ability to tackle challenging concepts made her a valued member of the class. Beyond her studies, Miriam showed a maturity beyond her years. Her thoughts and reflections provided important insights into how children experience agency and engagement within the school.

The curriculum

SCS's curriculum journey began with the adoption of the International Primary Curriculum (IPC), which was later found to be too restrictive for their children' needs. While retaining elements of the IPC, the school adapted its approach to better suit their context. The school adopted a thematic curriculum approach designed to align with the requirements of the national curriculum. Through thematic units, the school strove to create meaningful connections between different subject areas, fostering a holistic understanding of key concepts and topics. The themes served as a framework for integrating subjects like geography, history, and design technology (DT), allowing for meaningful cross-disciplinary learning experiences. For example, while exploring fashion, children looked into its history in history lessons and engaged in textiles and design in DT classes. A theme on ancient Egypt might include geography lessons on Egypt's physical features, history lessons on ancient

Egyptian civilisation, art activities inspired by Egyptian artefacts, and cooking lessons featuring ancient Egyptian cuisine. Themes were developed by the curriculum lead, with input from teachers, to create engaging and cohesive learning experiences.

The school's creative programme complemented the core curriculum by incorporating activities like gardening, cooking, art, and DT. This approach took its roots from the Open Futures programme (https://openfutures.com/), which was widely adopted by the school and had a lasting impact on its educational approach. Open Futures, an educational initiative that ran from 2005 to 2017, engaged over 80,000 pupils across 164 schools in England. By the time of its closure in 2017, the Open Futures approach had become a national model in primary schools and was also implemented in other settings, including nurseries, special schools, and further education. The programme consisted of four elements:

- AskIt: Developing critical thinking and communication skills.
- GrowIt: Engaging children in growing their own food.
- CookIt: Exploring connections between food and identity.
- FilmIt: Using filmmaking to support science learning and literacy.

Although Open Futures no longer delivered its full training programme, it continued to be integrated into schools where it had been adopted as a central tenet of learning and teaching. At SCS, activities in these four areas remained part of the curriculum, scheduled throughout the year with each half-term dedicated to one of these creative subjects. This staggered approach prevented overload and ensured integration with other curriculum content for maximum relevance and coherence. Philosophy for Children (P4C) lessons, which played a significant role in shaping curriculum design and teaching practices, were the inspiration for the AskIt element of Open Futures. The school used P4C to encourage children to ask questions, think critically, and engage in collaborative discussions, fostering transferable skills that supported learning across subjects. P4C lessons were designed to be fluid and responsive, with children exploring concepts and generating questions based on provided stimuli, such as videos, books, or artefacts.

According to the Assistant Head, the curriculum was dynamic, with ongoing adaptations based on feedback from teachers and children. The school recognised the importance of providing clear guidance to teachers while allowing flexibility to respond to student needs and interests. To achieve this, they developed progression of skills and knowledge documents for each subject, outlining specific learning objectives for each year group. This helped teachers understand expectations at each stage and provided a clear framework for planning and assessment.

A new addition to the curriculum at the time of the research was the use of *knowledge organisers* (Figure 5.2) and *dual coding maps*. These tools were designed to help children organise and retain key information by providing visual representations of concepts and vocabulary. Knowledge organisers contained key words and concepts for each half-term topic, enabling children to independently access and review

Knowledge Organiser: Are we responsible for our planet?
Y4 Spring 1

Things I know already:

- The equator is at 0 degrees latitude which separates the Northern and Southern Hemispheres.
- Longitude lines run perpendicular to the equator, latitude lines run parallel to the equator on a map.
- Egypt has a desert biome so its climate is dry and hot.

Things I will know:

- There are 5 major latitude lines: Tropic of Cancer, Tropic of Capricorn, Equator, Arctic Circle and Antarctic Circle.
- The Sahara Desert has a dry climate and is a desert biome. In the Sahara, the following physical features may be found, rocky areas and sand dunes.
- The Arctic and Antarctica have polar climates.
- Climate change is the process of our Earth heating up.

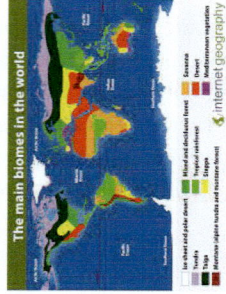

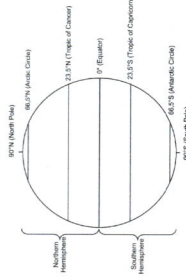

Words to help me:

Key Vocabulary	Definition
Equator	A line of latitude around the middle of the Earth.
Arctic circle	A line of latitude around the North of the Earth.
Antarctic circle	The most southerly latitude line.
Climate	Weather conditions in an area.
Biome	An area with a similar climate.
Tundra	A large barren region with no trees.
Desert	A place that has very little rain.
Global warming	The process of our Earth heating up.
Sustainability	Making small changes to look after the planet for the future.

The main biomes in the world

Tundra

The Arctic tundra

FIGURE 5.2 Year 4 Knowledge Organiser

important information. Additionally, dual coding maps provided pictorial representations of the same information to cater to different learning preferences and support visual learners. According to the school, the introduction of knowledge organisers and dual coding maps reflected their commitment to promoting independent learning and supporting children's agency. By providing children with tools to organise and review their learning, the school sought to empower them to take ownership of their education and develop essential study skills. Moreover, these tools supported differentiation and inclusion by accommodating diverse learning styles and abilities.

One of the main challenges faced by the school lay in the ever-expanding nature of the national curriculum, with additional content continuously being introduced without commensurate reductions. Consequently, time constraints often hindered the comprehensive delivery of curriculum content, leaving staff grappling with the dilemma of balancing breadth with depth.

Beyond the curriculum

The school recognised that authentic learning extended beyond the confines of the formal curriculum. Interviews with the SLT, particularly with the Assistant Head, revealed acknowledgment of the intrinsic value of addressing children's interests and curiosities. In an effort to promote creativity, critical thinking, and engagement with learning beyond the classroom, the school instituted a series of project competitions, held on a half-termly basis. These competitions provided children with the opportunity to showcase their talents and ingenuity through a variety of creative endeavours, ranging from posters and dioramas to multimedia presentations. Each project competition was aligned with the curriculum and current classroom topics, allowing children to explore topics in greater depth. Themes could vary widely, spanning topics such as African studies, historical epochs like the Vikings, or scientific phenomena such as inventions.

The competition format encouraged active involvement from children and their families, fostering a sense of collaboration and shared achievement. Children were tasked with conceptualising and executing their projects at home, with support and guidance from parents and guardians. This was meant to not only strengthen the home-school connection but also empower children to take ownership of their learning journey. Judging criteria for the competitions were carefully crafted to recognise creativity, relevance, effort, and originality. Winning projects were selected by a panel of judges, often comprising teachers, who assessed each entry based on its merits. Winners would be announced during celebratory assemblies and awards included gold, silver, and bronze distinctions. The projects themselves served as tangible manifestations of children's learning experiences and would be put on display in the school.

The school's commitment to holistic education was further evidenced by its emphasis on experiential learning and enrichment activities. For example, regular theatre trips were intended to help children develop into well-rounded individuals. These endeavours were informed by the school's recognition of the challenges posed by socio-economic disparities between the school's population of children and their more privileged peers. The demographic makeup of children played an important role in shaping the school's approach to teaching. There was a strong recognition among the school's staff that their children might lack access to enriching experiences like travel or exposure to a wide range of literature, which could hinder their creativity and imagination.

The school adapted its teaching practices to accommodate the diverse backgrounds and experiences of its student population. This involved providing additional support for literacy development, creating experiential learning opportunities within the school environment, and seeking alternative resources to supplement children' access to books and educational materials. For example, initiatives such as providing children with copies of key texts studied during projects aimed to bridge this gap, ensuring that every child had access to essential learning materials. Efforts were made to introduce children to local libraries and cultural institutions, such as the Ministry of Stories, a non-profit London organisation dedicated to helping children and young adults develop writing skills and to helping teachers inspire their children to write.

The language barrier faced by many parents represented another aspect of the community that necessitated extra efforts on the part of the school. The Assistant Head noted that parents who did not speak English could struggle to understand the level of text appropriate for their children, leading to situations where children attempted to read material far beyond their age level or were provided with books that were too simplistic.

Family backgrounds also influenced children's approach to learning and their attitude towards school in the classroom. The Assistant Head noted that parents who might not have had positive educational experiences themselves could struggle to support their children effectively in their learning journey. This might manifest in a lack of confidence in helping their child at home or a guarded attitude towards the school. The school recognised the importance of building parents' confidence and breaking down barriers to engagement with the school. To achieve this, the school implemented a Parent Engagement Lead role, which focussed on organising workshops and support sessions for parents. These initiatives aimed to empower parents with the skills and confidence to support their children's learning at home. According to the Assistant Head, these efforts were proving successful in fostering stronger relationships between the school and parents, particularly those who might be harder to reach or have had negative experiences with education in the past.

The School Council

At the time of the study, SCS was changing its student voice structure. The Head Teacher explained that the school had moved from a traditional School Council to a system of children's teams. These teams were organised around specific areas of school life, such as basic skills, inclusion, learning environment, and creativity. Each team consisted of a mix of children elected by their peers, along with adult facilitators who guided the discussions and activities. One of the key features of the children's teams was the inclusion of student leaders who took on roles of responsibility within their teams. These student leaders, selected through a democratic process, served as representatives of their peers and played a crucial role in facilitating discussions, coordinating activities, and communicating with school leadership.

The teams met regularly to address topics within their respective areas of focus, allowing children to contribute ideas, raise concerns, and propose solutions related to key aspects of school life. The child team leaders would then meet with the Head Teacher regularly to share ideas and provide feedback. The structure aimed to provide children with a voice and involve them in decision-making processes within the school. However, due to inconsistency in delivering the system, its effectiveness had been compromised. The implementation of children's teams had been hindered by adults' busy schedules, leading to missed opportunities for meaningful dialogue between children and school leadership. Meetings sometimes failed to occur regularly, resulting in a lack of follow-through on ideas generated by the children. At the time of the study, the Head Teacher was actively considering the implementation of Smart School Councils – a programme designed to engage children in school decision-making processes, promote student voice, and foster a more inclusive school environment.

Lesson design

The school's approach to lesson design primarily followed a model characterised by a top-down approach, where teachers pre-designed and led the lessons without soliciting input from children. This approach lacked student involvement in the lesson planning process. However, there was an element of choice embedded within this framework. Once children completed their mandatory assignments or tasks, they were offered the autonomy to select an additional challenge from a predefined set, varying in difficulty levels. This allowed children to tailor their learning experience based on their individual preferences and capabilities.

In contrast to this model, the school embraced a different approach in Philosophy for Children (P4C) lessons. These sessions were facilitated rather than led by teachers, fostering an environment where children had greater freedom to shape the direction of discussions. While teachers provided guidance and support, children played a more active role in steering the conversation. Typically, teachers prepared conversation prompts in advance to stimulate critical thinking and facilitate meaningful dialogue.

The school emphasised peer-to-peer collaboration as an integral part of the learning process. However, there was ongoing discourse regarding the best practices for facilitating such collaboration. Some teachers favoured structured approaches, advocating for differentiated grouping strategies to maximise learning outcomes. Others believed in providing children with more autonomy by allowing them to choose their partners and seating arrangements. This debate underscored the school's commitment to balancing structure and freedom within its educational framework. While structured approaches ensured efficient management of student behaviour and promoted equitable participation, allowing children to choose their partners encouraged autonomy and fostered a sense of agency in the learning process.

Behaviour policy

The school had a strong emphasis on behaviour management and fostering discipline alongside conducive learning behaviours. During her interview, the Assistant Head elaborated on what constituted good learning behaviour, emphasising children's understanding of effective learning strategies and tools. She highlighted that students exhibiting such behaviours demonstrated independence and adeptly navigated learning challenges. In contrast, those with poor learning behaviours often struggled with confidence and relied more on teacher guidance.

Acknowledging the disruptive impact of the Covid-19 pandemic and subsequent lockdowns on children's learning behaviour, the senior leadership team took proactive measures to mitigate the gap caused by these disruptions. They implemented interventions and provided additional support to children in need. This effort led to a significant transformation in behaviour management within the school, transitioning from disorder and low expectations to a structured environment with higher standards.

The change was facilitated by the implementation of clear and consistent behaviour policies, which struck a balance between structure and flexibility. Various initiatives were introduced to understand the root causes of behaviour and address children's basic needs. These initiatives included choice theory (an approach developed by William Glasser) and the Thrive program, which offered a trauma-informed approach to improving the mental health and well-being of children and young people. The demographic makeup of the community, particularly its large Muslim population with traditional values of discipline, influenced the school's approach.

Despite having strict rules and expectations, the leadership aimed to provide children with space within this framework. Interviews with the school's senior leadership team underscored the delicate balance between providing structure and allowing autonomy. There was a prevailing belief that while robust behaviour management policies might initially appear to limit children's agency, they ultimately fostered greater student ownership and engagement in their learning.

At the heart of the school's behaviour management strategy lay the Traffic Light System, an approach that provided clear guidelines for children regarding appropriate conduct. This system, which had been integrated into the school's culture over several years, employed a colour-coded framework to signify different levels of behaviour, each associated with corresponding consequences and rewards.

Central to the Traffic Light System were three distinct colours: green, amber, and red. Green signified commendable behaviour, reflecting adherence to school rules and positive conduct. Amber served as a warning sign, indicating minor infractions or disruptions, which could include talking out of turn or instances of unkindness. Red denoted more serious transgressions, signalling behaviours that were unacceptable and necessitated immediate intervention, such as physical aggression or the use of inappropriate language.

Flexibility was a key feature of the Traffic Light System, affording children the opportunity to move between colours based on their behaviour. Positive actions and improvements could move children from green to silver and gold statuses, which were celebrated weekly during School Assemblies. The system emphasised positive reinforcement, with praise and acknowledgment extended to children who consistently demonstrated exemplary behaviour.

Reading champions

To cultivate a love for reading among children, the school implemented a programme known as Reading Champions, specifically targeting Year 3 and Year 4 children. This initiative was designed to not only encourage children to engage with reading materials but also to nurture a genuine passion for literature. At the core of the Reading Champions programme lay the provision of a carefully curated reading box, stocked with a selection of books related to ongoing learning topics and projects. These reading boxes were prepared at the start of each half-term. The contents were chosen in collaboration with the English Lead, ensuring alignment with the topics being explored in the classroom. The selection was meant to cater to diverse reading preferences, including both fiction and non-fiction. Recent adjustments, such as the introduction of picture books and poetry, were intended to further enhance the programme's appeal.

Participation in the Reading Champions programme was incentivised through a system of rewards and recognition. Children were encouraged to log their reading progress, with the expectation of consistent engagement throughout the week. Those who demonstrated dedication and enthusiasm by consistently meeting their reading goals were rewarded. Rewards ranged from stickers and badges to personalised books signed by the Head Teacher.

Overall, the school's approach to education reflected its commitment to serving a diverse community while fostering children's development. The school's practices demonstrated adaptation to its community's needs, exemplified through initiatives like the food distribution system and targeted support for families where English was an additional language. This responsiveness to community context shaped both academic delivery and support structures. While traditional teaching methods predominated in most subjects, the school's creative curriculum, rooted in the Open Futures programme, provided opportunities for hands-on learning and student engagement through activities like gardening, cooking, and arts. This approach suggested an educational model where children's agency operated within a framework of strong support structures, designed to meet both academic needs and broader developmental requirements.

Having explored how both a selective independent school and a diverse inner-city state school approach children's agency, we now turn to our third school, which presents perhaps the most explicit commitment to child-led learning among our three cases. As an academy, this school used its greater institutional autonomy to develop innovative approaches to child participation, while still working within national curriculum requirements. This final case study provides an important contrast in how different institutional structures can enable or constrain opportunities for children's agency.

Northern City State

School overview

Part of a small educational trust, Northern City State (NCS) had been serving its local community since 2014. The school provided education from age 4 to 11, with an additional nursery provision, and served just over 600 children. Located in an oasis of relatively affluent families amid more deprived surroundings, the school had a low percentage of pupils eligible for free school meals at just 5.4% (as of 2024). As a non-denominational school, it welcomed boys and girls from all backgrounds, focussing on creating engaging learning experiences that could inspire every child.

NCS adopted an academic approach centred on a thematic curriculum that aligned with national curriculum requirements while being distinctively shaped by children's input. Each year's learning was organised into three termly topics, selected with active children's participation through an innovative consultation process. The school emphasised both skill development and subject knowledge, designing lessons to incorporate movement and choice. This approach balanced academic progress with children's agency, enabling children to advance at their own pace while meeting educational standards.

Cultural capital was a central element of the school's curriculum, woven throughout its approach to fostering community awareness and social responsibility. In the early years, children focussed on their immediate environment and local community, building a foundational sense of place and belonging. By later stages, children explored influential figures, locations, and historical events from the broader region, expanding their understanding of heritage and culture. To enrich this curriculum, the school incorporated field trips, social responsibility projects, and a range of extracurricular activities. The school also collaborated with various community partners to deepen the quality of its educational offerings. Altogether, this commitment to cultural capital was meant to equip children with the tools and insights they need to thrive in the workplace, in personal relationships, and as active contributors to society.

The teachers – 2021 to 2022

Rebecca – Year 3

Rebecca had been in her fifth year of teaching at the time of our first interview in 2021. Her journey into teaching began through the School Direct programme, a school-led route into initial teacher training (ITT) run by a partnership between a lead school, other schools, and an accredited teacher training provider. She trained at NCS, where she earned her Postgraduate Certificate in Education (PGCE), and remained there as a dedicated member of the team.

During the first year of the study, Rebecca's role had expanded to include curriculum design across the school, reflecting her commitment to fostering children's agency. When interviewed, she emphasised the school's child-centred approach, where decisions were led by the pupils. This approach, according to Rebecca, was intricately linked to student engagement, attainment, and a love for learning, with the curriculum serving as its cornerstone.

Rebecca's teaching philosophy revolved around empowering children as 'lead learners'. She had actively explored innovative approaches to children's agency, particularly focussing on incorporating cultural capital into the curriculum. She emphasised a calm yet enthusiastic manner in her teaching, championing the idea that pupils should be given opportunities to make decisions about their learning. Her proactive role in curriculum development and efforts to actively involve children in shaping their educational direction reflected her commitment to children's agency.

Coby – Year 4

At the time of the first interview, Coby had embarked on his second year as a teacher, having successfully completed his Newly Qualified Teacher (NQT) year at NCS in 2019. Opting to continue his career at the same institution, Coby was drawn to the school's innovative, child-centred approach. His decision to choose NCS for his second placement was rooted in the school's distinctive philosophy, allowing children the autonomy to participate in shaping the curriculum and lesson design.

Holding a degree in music from the Royal Northern College of Music, Coby's natural creativity permeated his teaching approach. His commitment to nurturing children's agency was evident in his teaching style, characterised by dedication to making lessons creative and dynamic. Coby's view was that unlike many schools, NCS provided him with the freedom to foster creativity in his classroom, be it through traditional teaching methods or unconventional approaches such as outdoor trips.

Recognising the positive impact of creative teaching on children's progress, Coby embraced the daily challenge of thinking outside the box. His planning involved detailed preparation for lessons, coupled with flexibility in subsequent sessions to cater to children's responses, fostering a dynamic learning environment. This commitment to creativity and flexibility aligned seamlessly with NCS's approach emphasising children's independence and agency.

Kris – Year 5

Embarking on his seventh year of teaching at the start of the project, Kris' journey into education marked a purposeful shift into a teaching career, driven by a genuine passion for working with children. He commenced his teaching journey with a two-term NQT stint at a local school. This initial experience proved challenging, marked by insufficient support and the relentless pressures associated with complying with Ofsted requirements. However, Kris' trajectory took a new turn when he joined NCS, describing the shift as 'a breath of fresh air'.

Kris had been at the school for four years. His roles included acting as a year lead teacher and a teacher development lead. His teaching philosophy was succinctly encapsulated in the mantra of 'engagement over compliance', a sentiment that resonated with NCS's core approach, placing children at the heart of their educational mission. One of the school's defining features that particularly appealed to Kris was its innovative approach to curriculum design, where children actively participated in shaping the educational landscape alongside their teachers.

In his interview, Kris portrayed himself as a facilitator, guiding and supporting children on their learning journeys. He emphasised fostering children's agency within the classroom and aligning lessons with children's interests and motivations. Navigating the balance between a learner-focussed approach and the national curriculum, Kris expressed appreciation for creative strategies to harmonise children's interests with educational requirements. He especially emphasised the significance of local and historical context in shaping children's agency, advocating for broadening experiences beyond the classroom.

The teachers – 2022 to 2023

Tracy – Year 4

At the time of the interview, Tracy had been on her teaching journey for roughly a year, bringing with her a unique background in archaeology and diverse experiences in community archaeology, alongside a brief stint as an estate agent. She entered the teaching profession in 2022, which marked the start of her first academic year as a class teacher at NCS. Tracy's passion for teaching was deeply rooted in her innate love for children and a strong belief in making learning enjoyable. Her academic background in archaeology provided her with a fresh and distinctive perspective on education. During the interview, Tracy conveyed her excitement about the child-led and child-centred approach employed at the school, a philosophy that strongly resonated with her beliefs.

Having undergone a School Direct course through a local university, Tracy highlighted the growing interest among fellow trainee teachers in the child-led approach. She expressed her conviction that traditional education often stifled children's innate curiosity, whereas a child-led approach empowered them to have a say in what, how, and when they learn. She perceived her role as a mediator, interpreting children's interests and facilitating their exploration of topics in greater depth. Actively engaged in curriculum mapping that year, Tracy appreciated the process while acknowledging its limitations. She advocated for first exposing children to various ideas before they expressed their preferences, aiming to broaden their awareness and enhance their ability to make informed choices.

Josie – Year 5

Josie embarked on her teaching journey by completing a PGCE in secondary English. Following her certification, she served as a qualified English teacher at the local secondary school for four years. Seeking a new challenge, Josie made a significant transition to primary education, joining NCS as a Year 5 teacher in the previous academic year.

The decision to shift to primary teaching was influenced by Josie's observations of the school's distinctive approach to learning. Witnessing the remarkable independence, enthusiasm for learning, and natural aptitude displayed by these children fuelled Josie's interest in exploring primary education. Her connection with NCS stemmed from her interactions with the current Head Teacher during a shared master's programme. This connection, coupled with Josie's curiosity about the school's unique educational approach, facilitated a seamless transition when a teaching opportunity within the Trust became available.

Now completing her second year in primary teaching, Josie candidly discussed the challenges and rewards of transitioning from secondary to primary education. She highlighted the dynamic nature of the primary classroom and emphasised the importance of aligning student interests with the national curriculum while also highlighting the crucial role of agency in promoting student engagement and effective learning behaviours.

Jane – Year 6

Jane Coleman was an experienced educator and the Year 6 teacher at NCS. Having embarked on her teaching journey 16 years ago as an NQT, she brought a wealth of experience to her role. Throughout her career, Jane had navigated various roles within the school, demonstrating versatility by working in early years, key stage one, and taking on additional responsibilities, such as a Teaching and Learning Responsibility (TLR). Her teaching journey had also led her to an enriching experience at another school within the Trust. Juggling part-time roles between the two schools, Jane had made significant contributions to shaping the educational experience for children in diverse settings.

In her interview, Jane offered valuable insights into the evolving nature of education at NCS, emphasising the unique challenge of balancing children's agency with the structured requirements of the national curriculum. She candidly addressed the challenges and rewards of maintaining a delicate balance between child-led learning and meeting external expectations, such as those set by Ofsted inspections. Jane's perspective shed light on the ongoing dialogue between structure and agency in education, emphasising the school's concerted efforts to meet both curriculum standards and the unique needs and interests of its children.

The case study pupils

Soraya and Molly – Year 3 to Year 4

Soraya joined the study in its second year, stepping in for a pupil who had relocated. Known for her quiet yet reflective nature, she displayed impressive academic abilities across all subjects. In class, she showed a strong ability to work independently on challenging tasks while also demonstrating strong collaborative skills during group work. Soraya was not only a high achiever but also expressed a genuine love of learning, often seeking out additional information about topics that interested her. She showed a deep appreciation for the school environment, often noting how it supported her academic endeavours. Soraya was consistently engaged during discussions about her learning experiences, often offering insightful reflections that demonstrated sophisticated metacognitive awareness.

Molly was acknowledged as one of the school's greater depth children, known for her confidence and remarkable articulation of views. In the classroom, she displayed natural leadership qualities and proactive attitude. According to her class teacher, she was an active and engaged learner known for her thoughtful contributions to class discussions. Particularly passionate about literature, Molly exhibited a talent for the written word and expressed an ambition to become a writer. She was actively working on a story at the time of the study. Teachers noted her ability to balance this creative pursuit with maintaining high standards across all academic areas.

Harley and Dahlia – Year 4 to Year 5

Harley was an active learner who was confident to speak out in class. His academic performance was described by his class teacher as consistently excellent, often working beyond the expected level for his age group. Beyond academics, he was an avid footballer involved in the Sports Academy. Excelling in both studies and sports, he was a standout pupil, contributing to the vibrant atmosphere of the Year 4 class. Harley's academic journey was supported by additional tutoring at home, an arrangement his parents had made to help prepare him for secondary school. When asked about this extra support, Harley explained that he often found himself ahead of the school's programme, and the tutoring allowed him to explore more advanced topics that would typically be covered later in his education. This reflected both his own capability and his parents' commitment to helping him realise his full potential. Harley's enthusiasm for learning extended beyond the classroom curriculum. He was particularly interested in mathematics and sciences at a level beyond his year group.

Dahlia joined the study in the second year, replacing Tracy, who had to withdraw due to family circumstances. A high-achieving pupil and a bright personality, Dahlia fit very well into the class. Her personality was characterised by intense curiosity and an active mind, and she consistently demonstrated a mature approach to her studies. She was an articulate person with well-formed views and a proactive attitude towards learning and school more generally. Like Harley, Dahlia also received additional tutoring support at home, which she viewed as an important step in preparing for SATs and securing a place at a prestigious secondary school. She spoke thoughtfully about her educational journey, emphasising the importance of maintaining high academic standards and making the most of every learning opportunity. Both Dahlia and Harley exemplified children with clear academic ambitions, supported by engaged parents who held high expectations for their children's educational achievement. Their approach to learning reflected not only their individual capabilities but also their families' commitment to maximising their educational opportunities.

Jaleel and Cecilia – Year 5 to Year 6

Jaleel was a curious, eager learner. While naturally quiet and shy in classroom settings, he demonstrated remarkable reflective capabilities and intellectual depth in conversations about learning. His mother, a teacher at the school, shared that Jaleel approached learning with impressive diligence; he rarely needed reminders to complete his homework and always ensured he was well-prepared for class. While he might not have been the most vocal participant in class discussions, his written work and individual contributions revealed a sophisticated level of thinking and understanding. Jaleel had a strong interest in football, and, while sometimes influenced by his peers in choosing activities, he also demonstrated a solid capacity for independent learning and self-monitoring.

Cecilia, a pupil with dyslexia, was known for her active engagement and her enthusiasm for reading, despite the challenges her dyslexia presented. Her determination to overcome reading difficulties exemplified her resilient approach to learning. Over time, she made notable progress academically, showing dedication and contributing meaningfully to the classroom's diverse environment. Though initially shy in group discussions, Cecilia gradually opened up during interviews over the course of the study, sharing some of her personal struggles, including feelings of insecurity related to her dyslexia. With supportive teachers who recognised her strong potential, Cecilia continued to grow in both confidence and ability. Her teachers noted that she often brought unique perspectives to class discussions, which we also observed during interviews and focus groups with Cecilia.

The curriculum

The school's approach to curriculum design was centred around active children's involvement and their individual interests. Aimed at being pupil-led, the curriculum was shaped by considering children's interests, prior knowledge, and cultural capital to make it personally relevant. The curriculum was developed through 'consultations between the teachers and the children'. In the initial step, children were encouraged to select an object representing a topic they would like to explore in the upcoming year. These objects could range from a plastic bottle to a gemstone or a picture of a famous person, reflecting the diversity of children's interests. The objects served as inspiration for conversations during 'transition days' which happened at the end of the final term of each academic year, when children met the teachers who they would work with in the following academic year. Based on these discussions, teachers identified three themes linking the objects, shaping the three topics for the year, each spanning one term. Each termly topic was then broken down into four quadrants, providing a comprehensive guide for children's learning throughout the weeks.

The school refined its curriculum consultation process after recognising that final teaching topics often drifted from children's original interests. One telling example involved a pupil who brought in an ammolite, inspired by Harry Potter's magical world. While this led to teaching about fossils and rocks, the lessons missed engaging with what had actually sparked the child's interest – the magical properties of crystals. This disconnect prompted the teaching team to reconsider how they could better cater to children's genuine interests and support their agency.

As a result, the school transformed its approach to curriculum design. Rather than limiting children's input to initial conversations about objects, they developed a more comprehensive, co-constructed approach to curriculum planning that operated across the whole school. The new curriculum consultations followed a clearer structure, focussing on the following:

• What children wanted to learn
• Identifying prior knowledge
• Recognising knowledge gaps
• Considering how cultural capital could enhance personal relevance

Teachers actively shaped sub-questions and broader inquiries, fostering powerful links between different concepts. Adult facilitation was crucial, particularly in questioning and modelling how objects were interconnected. For example, when a pupil brought in a polar bear, teachers prompted questions about its habitat and its resemblance to a cuddly toy. This led to the integration of topics such as habitats, adaptation, and evolution, illustrating the dynamic and interconnected nature of the school's curriculum. The

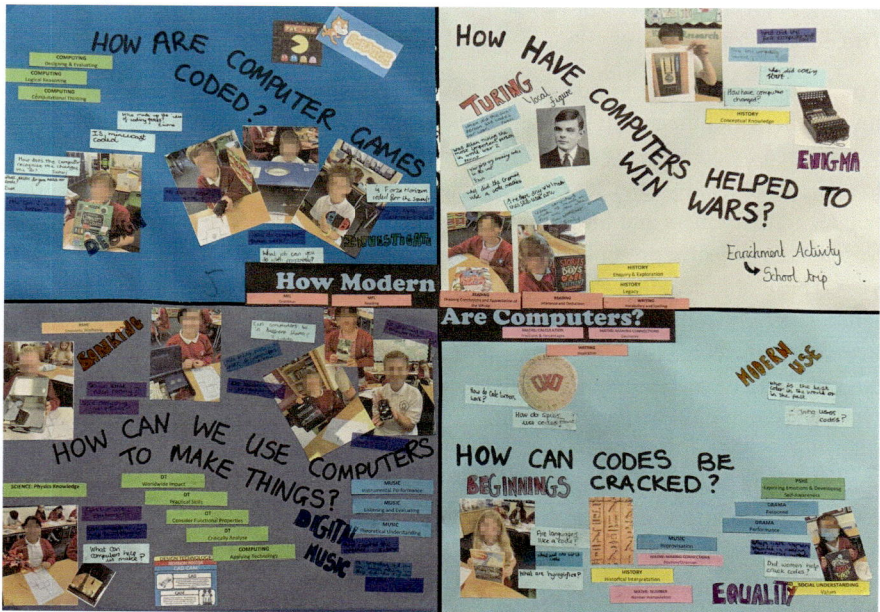

FIGURE 5.3 Termly Curriculum Map

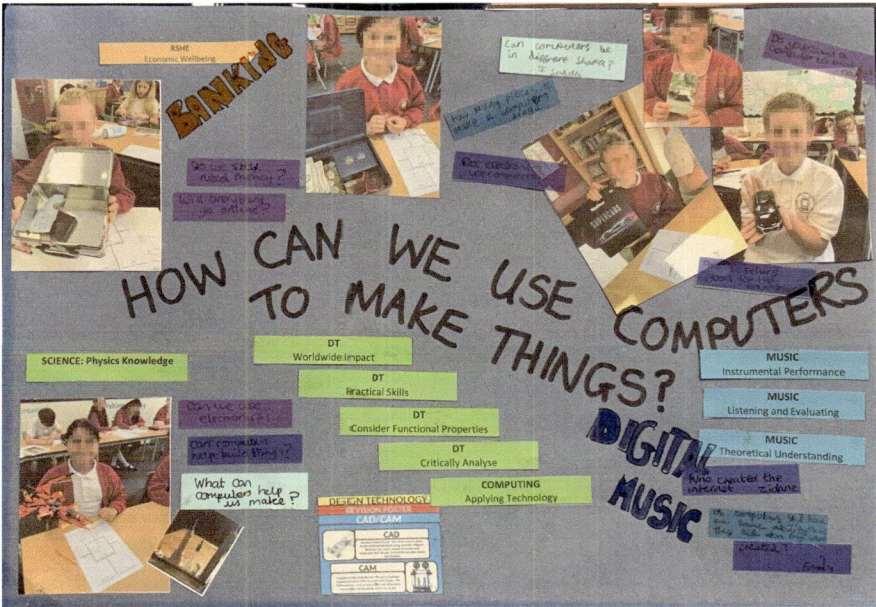

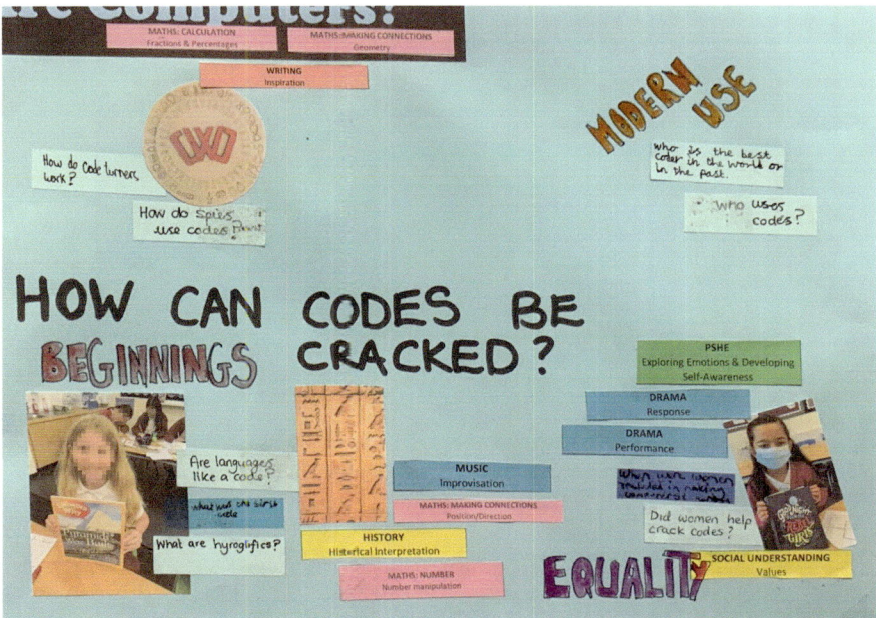

FIGURE 5.3 (Continued)

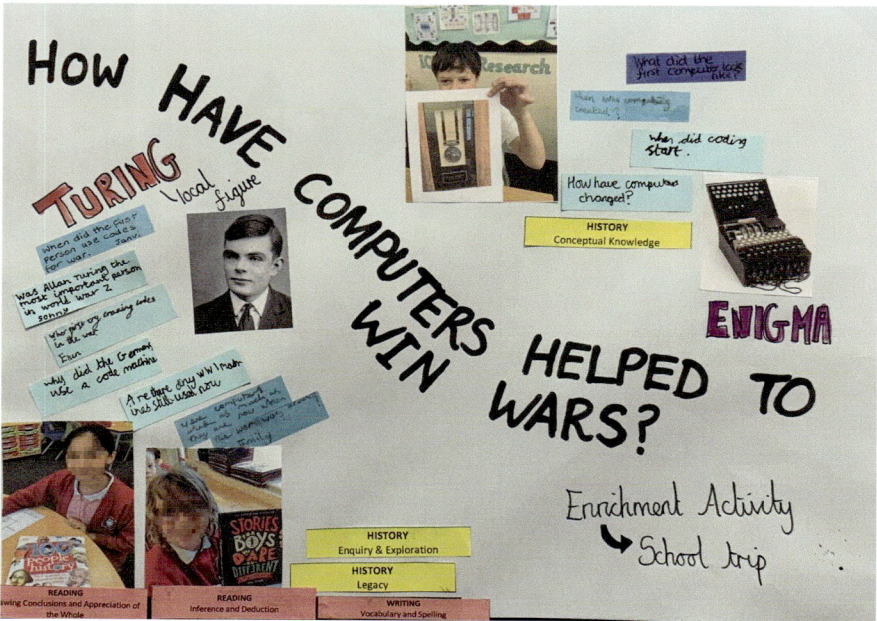

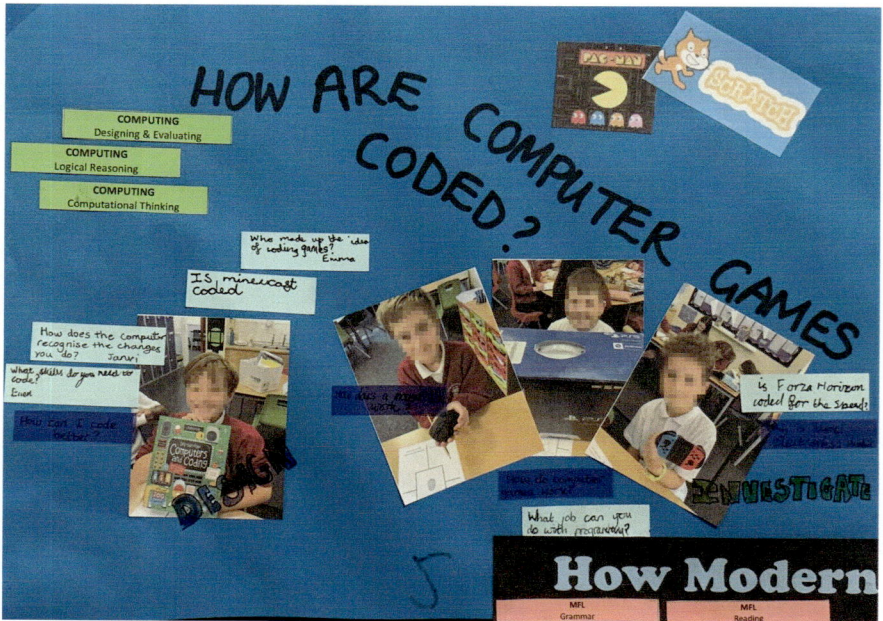

FIGURE 5.3 (Continued)

co-constructed curriculum maps, physically created by the children, served as tangible outcomes of this process, highlighting the collaborative nature of learning.

The revised process spanned two weeks, allowing more time for meaningful integration of children's objects into the curriculum. Consultations took place on two transition days – one before the summer break and another shortly afterwards. The first day involved bringing in objects and initiating discussions, while the second focussed on developing questions collaboratively with the children. This extended into the first week of the new academic year, enabling a seamless transition while enhancing the clarity and integration of children's interests.

While this object-inspired curriculum design emphasised children's voice, teachers skilfully mapped these child-initiated topics to national curriculum requirements. Each termly theme was carefully structured to ensure coverage of statutory content and skills. For example, when children brought objects related to space exploration, teachers integrated required physics concepts about forces and motion into the theme. Similarly, a child's interest in ancient artefacts would be expanded to cover mandatory history curriculum elements. This approach demanded significant planning and expertise from teachers, who needed to identify opportunities to weave mandatory content into child-chosen themes without diminishing children's sense of ownership. The success of this approach was evident in both children's engagement and academic outcomes, demonstrating that curriculum co-construction could support rather than hinder the achievement of national standards.

The School Council

The School Council played a pivotal role in facilitating child-led changes within the school and acted as a representative body for each class. Supported by two staff members, the council held periodic meetings, allowing time for children to engage in tasks between sessions. The agenda for each council meeting was structured around school development priorities. There were several councils within the school, each focussing on different aspects:

- The Eco-Council implemented environmentally friendly initiatives.
- The Play Council, where play leaders in Year Six and mini-leaders in Year Two worked to support their peers during break and lunchtimes, ensuring a positive and inclusive play environment.
- Well-being Ambassadors explored ways to develop and promote overall well-being.
- Forest Rangers worked towards maintaining the forest school area.
- The Creative Council was responsible for crafting items for the school, such as banners for events.
- The School Village Partnership involved children in activities within the local community, such as representing the school during the annual village festival.
- The Curriculum Council, a new addition, was initiated to oversee the delivery of the curriculum.

The Curriculum Council aligned with the introduction of the 'six C's' – curiosity, comprehension, compassion, creativity, collaboration, connectivity. This council conducted audits in classrooms, exploring how these elements were exemplified in teaching. The goal was to involve children in shaping changes in the delivery of the curriculum, seeking their input on improvements and adjustments.

A new initiative undertaken by the School Council in 2023 was the introduction of a student voice box. This platform allowed children from all levels of the school to share their thoughts, ideas, and suggestions by depositing them into the School Council voice box. The School Council, along with their facilitating adult, then collaboratively reviewed these submissions. They actively sought to address and implement changes based on the ideas and requests put forth by the children, fostering a sense of ownership and responsiveness within the school community.

The selection process for School Council membership varied across different groups. In the nomination process, each class selected a representative through child-friendly voting methods. The older year groups participated in democracy-style voting, where they wrote down the name of their preferred candidate. The younger children engaged in a blind vote, expressing their choice with closed eyes and raised hands. To provide diverse opportunities, council memberships changed from year to year, allowing different children to be actively involved in various roles. The chosen pupil from each class took on the responsibility of conveying the thoughts and opinions of their classmates during School Council meetings. They provided updates on meeting outcomes and discussions, ensuring that the voices of all children were heard. For instance, if a child overheard a discussion about assembly songs, they could bring up this topic in their School Council meeting. The matter was then deliberated among all School Council representatives, leading to an agreed-upon outcome.

Lesson design

The school implemented a unique approach to lesson design, providing children with the freedom to self-assess their learning progress and choose activities accordingly during lessons. Each lesson emphasised the development of six essential skills – Collaboration, ICT/Research, Communication and Problem Solving, Reflection, and Application. These skills were strategically integrated into the learning cycle, which comprised four stages: understanding, exploration, communication, and problem solving and reflection. Each stage corresponded to specific skill areas, providing a scaffolded progression for children as they deepened their understanding and application of knowledge:

- Stage 1: Collaboration
- Stage 2: ICT/Research
- Stage 3: Communication and Problem Solving
- Stage 4: Reflection and Application

At Stage 1, children worked collaboratively with a teacher and peers to solidify their prior knowledge, setting the foundation for further exploration. As they progressed through Stages 2 and 3, they engaged in independent tasks, utilising ICT tools for research, applying their knowledge in diverse contexts, and honing their communication skills. Stage 4 was intended to foster critical thinking. These differentiated learning experiences were offered at six skill-specific stations, and lessons were designed to facilitate movement and choice. Children had the autonomy to choose their preferred skill area, or areas, for each lesson.

Assessment was embedded in each stage and skill area. For instance, collaborative tasks at Stage 1 involved discussions with a teacher, Stage 3 might incorporate quiz questions, and Stage 4 involved reflection tasks encouraging children to engage in critical thinking. The flexibility of the lesson design reflected the school's commitment to children's agency. The goal was to enable teachers to adapt to individual student needs, providing opportunities for self-assessment and encouraging them to progress through the learning cycle at their own pace. This approach was intended to promote a dynamic and engaging learning atmosphere, a sense of community and shared learning.

The reward system

Golden time

Part of the school's reward system was 'golden time', which happened every Friday. During this time, children got to choose and do activities they liked in their classrooms. The activities were not decided beforehand; instead, children and teachers worked together to plan what they wanted to do. Activities could range from dancing and playing with toys to working on class projects. Golden time had been a tradition in the school for more than ten years. It was important to note that golden time was separate from the regular playtime during the school day. It went along with the school's rules on behaviour and acted as a reward for children who had behaved well throughout the week. Different classes might have had different golden time rules based on how well the children behaved as a group. If a child did not meet the behaviour expectations, they might lose some of their golden time. Instances of children losing their golden time were rare, suggesting that the reward system worked well to encourage good behaviour. When it did happen, the school saw it as a chance for children to learn about the consequences of their actions. Looking ahead, the school was thinking about ways to help children from different grades connect during golden time.

Dojo treats

Apart from the regular golden time, the school had an additional reward system called 'Dojo treats', given at the end of each half-term. These treats were a way to celebrate children who had embraced the school's values of social responsibility, life skills, choice, achievement, and independence. To be eligible, children needed to follow the behaviour policy and demonstrate positive learning behaviours. Exceptional pieces of work also contributed to eligibility for these treats. Those who met the targets by the end of the half-term were invited to the Dojo treat.

At the beginning of each school year, children in each class actively participated in deciding on Dojo treat ideas through a voting process overseen by the School Council. Children suggested various ideas, from bringing animals to the playground to festive activities like decorating gingerbread houses for Christmas. This inclusive approach ensured that Dojo treats reflected the interests and preferences of the children.

While some Dojo treat ideas came from children, teachers also contributed to the planning process. Some treats might be linked to significant events, such as the Queen's Platinum Jubilee. This collaborative approach ensured a balanced mix of student-generated and teacher-designed treats, creating a sense of ownership and excitement among the children.

The funding for these treats came from voluntary donations from parents and external fundraising initiatives. This flexible funding approach allowed for a variety of activities, from cost-effective options to more elaborate ventures. It ensured that Dojo treats remained inclusive, regardless of financial considerations, so all children could enjoy these rewarding experiences. The Dojo treat system went beyond individual achievements, serving as a collective celebration of positive behaviour, core values, and outstanding contributions to the school community.

Behaviour policy

At the time of the study, the school was actively implementing new learning principles, drawing extensively from ongoing research efforts. The school administrator actively participated in a National Professional Qualification (NPQ), part of which was focussed on learning behaviour and culture. Utilising resources such as the Education Endowment Foundation (EEF) and various research articles, the school sought insights into diverse approaches to behaviour management. Central to this developmental journey was the school's new behaviour policy, a critical document shaping the institution's approach to student conduct. This policy was a synthesis of diverse resources and research findings and was undergoing revision at the time of the study. The commitment to refining this document was evident in response to significant shifts in the educational landscape, particularly post-Covid. One of the developments was the introduction of the child-led CHAMP scheme, described in the following.

Anticipated changes in the behaviour policy marked a departure from outdated norms, recognising technological advancements such as the prevalence of mobile phones among children. The inclusion of new guidelines in response to these shifts underscored the school's commitment to staying relevant and responsive to the changing educational environment. While the new behaviour policy was still in the writing phase, it held the promise of a more contemporary and tailored approach to guiding student behaviour. Once finalised, the document would have to undergo a rigorous approval process involving governors and team leaders before being disseminated to the wider school community.

The CHAMP scheme (Calmly and quietly, Hands to yourself, Aware of others, Move slowly, and Pass on the left) was a key part of the school's 'behaviour for learning' initiative, designed to promote responsible and considerate movement throughout the school. After the disruptions caused by the Covid-19 pandemic, children faced challenges readjusting to movement within the school premises. The once-smooth transitions became lively and noisy. In response, children were actively involved in observing and reflecting on the state of the corridors. They highlighted noise and disruptions during transitions, promoting a collaboration between children and staff members leading to the creation of the CHAMP acronym.

The school spread the CHAMP message through strategically placed posters as visual reminders for children. Under the CHAMP initiative, when children were observed by adults displaying CHAMP behaviour throughout the school, their names were entered into a raffle box. Every Friday during the school's celebration assembly, six tickets were drawn from the box. The selected children received a special reward, allowing them to sit at the 'VIP' table in the dinner hall during lunchtime. They could bring a friend and were treated to a special prize consisting of a chocolate and juice, served in elegant champagne flutes. Implementing CHAMP was not an immediate change but marked a significant cultural transformation that needed the active involvement and acceptance of the children. Their ideas, observations, and collaborative efforts played a vital role in shaping CHAMP into an effective and widely embraced behavioural framework within the school community.

Overall, NCS exemplified an educational approach that placed children's agency at the heart of its vision and practice. The school's approach to teaching and learning reflected a belief that children should be active participants in their educational journey rather than passive recipients of knowledge. This philosophy manifested in various ways throughout the school, from curriculum development to classroom organisation, though always within a framework that maintained clear educational standards and expectations. Teachers across the school demonstrated commitment to this child-led approach, adapting their practices to facilitate children's voice while ensuring academic progress. The school's evolution of practices over time suggested an ongoing commitment to refining and strengthening children's agency, while acknowledging the need to balance this with educational requirements and standards. This emphasis on children's agency operated alongside, rather than in opposition to, academic achievement. The school demonstrated that prioritising children's voice and choice could coexist with maintaining high educational standards, suggesting a model where children's agency enhanced children's learning experiences and outcomes.

This chapter has presented detailed profiles of three distinctly different primary schools, each offering unique insights into how educational structures can relate to opportunities for children's agency. The schools' approaches reflected both their institutional contexts and their underlying philosophies about children's participation in education.

SCI exemplified a traditional academic focus coexisting with structured opportunities for children's agency. Through initiatives like differentiated mathematics folders and extensive extracurricular activities, SCI demonstrated how children's choice could be carefully integrated within a highly structured academic environment. Their approach to children's agency emphasised individual responsibility within clear boundaries, as evidenced by their Mental Health Assembly and formal School Council structure.

SCS demonstrated how schools can adapt to serve deprived communities with a strong focus on academic standards. Their prior implementation of the Open Futures programme represented a middle ground between teacher-led and child-led approaches, providing creative outlets for children's engagement through hands-on learning experiences. The school's Traffic Light System and team-based student representation reflected their efforts to balance structure with flexibility in a large, diverse setting. Their particular attention to community needs and family engagement showed how children's agency must be understood within broader social contexts.

NCS illustrated the most explicit and sustained commitment to children's agency, particularly through its innovative approach to curriculum co-construction and lesson design. Their development of multiple specialised councils and their object-based curriculum planning demonstrated how the institutional autonomy of being an academy school, including the option to not follow the national curriculum, school could be leveraged to maximise student participation. The CHAMP scheme exemplified their approach to co-constructing school systems with children, while their skills-based learning stations showed how children's choice could be embedded in daily classroom practice.

These three schools, while operating within the same national curriculum framework, developed distinctly different approaches to balancing structural requirements with opportunities for children's agency. Their varied contexts – from the selective independent setting to the culturally diverse state school to the innovation-focussed academy – provided rich ground for examining how children experienced and exercised agency in different educational environments. Each school's approach reflected different philosophies about children's agency: SCI emphasised balancing choice with high educational standards, SCS focused on broadening children's experiences and horizons, and NCS prioritised children's co-construction of learning.

The detailed examination of each school's structures, practices, and key personnel sets the stage for our next chapter, which presents the empirical findings from our research done directly with the case study children. Chapter 6 explores how children understood, experienced, and exercised agency across these different educational contexts, revealing both commonalities and contrasts in their perspectives on meaningful participation in their education. Through their voices, we gained crucial insights into how different school structures enable or constrain children's capacity for meaningful action as part of their educational journeys.

6
CHILDREN AND THEIR AGENCY

Having examined the distinct social and cultural contexts of our three case study schools, this chapter presents the findings from our research about how children experienced and exercised agency within these educational settings. Through analysis of interviews, focus groups, and innovative research activities with our case study pupils, we uncover patterns in how children's agency manifests across different school environments. While each school context yielded unique insights, common themes emerged around choice, subject hierarchies, social dynamics, and institutional structures like the School Council. These findings illuminate the complex ways in which children's agency takes shape within and beyond the classroom, influenced by both formal institutional frameworks and informal social interactions.

Our findings derive from focus group interviews with our sample of children, and innovative activities including *My Agency Timeline*, *My Learning Choice Diary*, and *Feelings at School*. These activities revealed common themes while highlighting distinctive patterns in how children engaged with different activities. My Agency Timeline activity generated particularly enthusiastic engagement at Northern City State (NCS), while Feelings at School activity resonated strongly with children at South City Independent (SCI). At South City State (SCS), My Learning Choice Diary prompted valuable reflections on individual choice. In presenting our findings, we focus on the activities that proved most illuminating within each school context, allowing us to capture both the unique dynamics of each school environment and the varied ways children experienced agency within their educational settings.

Talking about agency: our approach to introducing the term

In preparing to discuss agency with our case study pupils, we sought an approach that would make the concept accessible and relevant for children. We chose to use 'choice' as the primary entry point into the broader concept of agency,

DOI: 10.4324/9781003227779-6

complemented by terms like 'control' and 'power' within My Agency Timeline activity. This approach provided clear and tangible proxies that children could readily understand and explore.

The emphasis on 'choice' was particularly evident in My Learning Choice Diary activity, offering a practical way for children to discuss their experiences. This method proved especially effective SCI and SCS, where the concept of agency was relatively unfamiliar to both children and teachers. We tailored our approach to each school community's needs by using concrete examples of children's choices, from learning topics and activities to books and pencils. This strategy made the abstract concept of agency more accessible, establishing a foundation for ongoing discussions within the school community among both teachers and children.

In NCS, we encountered a distinctly different environment where school staff, including senior leadership and teachers, demonstrated sophisticated understanding of agency. During interviews, staff exhibited clear comprehension of the concept, eliminating the need for additional explanations. While we continued to use terms like 'choice', 'power', and 'control' in discussions with children, we could also incorporate the term 'agency' itself. The children consistently showed clear understanding of the reflections and examples we sought, suggesting that more abstract concepts could be introduced with greater confidence. The children's familiarity with agency appeared to stem from the school's strong commitment to child-centred pedagogical approaches and practices. Their consistent exposure to child-centred teaching methods, combined with active engagement in ongoing conversations about incorporating their views into school practices, seemingly contributed to their ease with the concept of agency. Let's now examine how children in each of the three schools navigated these discussions on agency, and what findings emerged from these conversations.

Children's agency and choice

South City Independent

The importance of having the freedom to make personal choices was prominent among the case study pupils in SCI. The freedom to make personal choices during learning activities appeared as a critical factor engendering positive feelings in children. The significance of social interactions in fostering children's sense of agency was particularly evident in Sonia's Learning Choice Diary (Figure 6.1). When documenting her choice to 'play with my friends at all break times', she explained that this decision was driven by her desire to 'have people who trust me and more friends to interact with'. Her reflection revealed how social choices enhanced her sense of agency and emotional well-being, noting that it made her feel 'full of joy and happiness' rather than lonely. Significantly, Sonia recognised that exercising agency in her social interactions helped her manage 'negative thoughts', demonstrating how the freedom to make social choices contributed to both her sense of agency and emotional well-being.

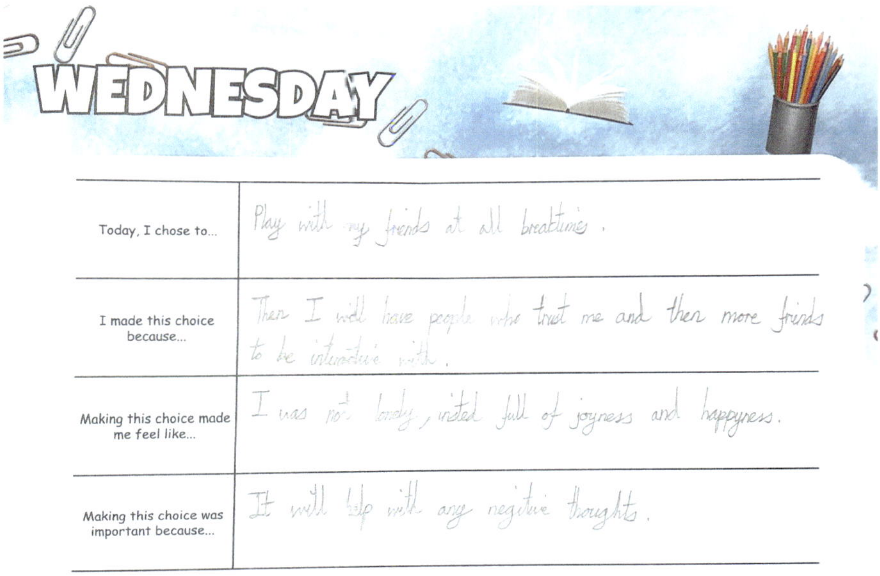

Today, I chose to...	Play with my friends at all breaktimes .
I made this choice because...	Then I will have people who trust me and then more friends to be introduced with .
Making this choice made me feel like...	I was not lonely, instead full of joyness and happyness .
Making this choice was important because...	It will help with any negative thoughts .

FIGURE 6.1 Sonia's Learning Choice Diary (Wednesday)

This sense of agency extended into learning activities as well. For example, Leyla linked her enjoyment of creative writing to a sense of ownership over her creative expression, 'I like creative writing the most because you always know that it will be your writing, and nobody can actually copy the exact same thing'. This emphasis on individuality indicates that the opportunity to exercise personal choice significantly contributed to the child's perception of agency within the learning process. The positive emotional connection between independent choice and motivation to learn was further demonstrated by the child's anticipation and excitement about creative writing. Leyla's expression 'And I just look forward to it' suggests that the freedom to make choices positively influences their attitude and engagement in the activity.

The children's reflections also revealed the negative emotional consequences of imposed learning experiences, highlighting their demotivating and disempowering impact. An example from Feelings at School activity illustrated this, where Imran narrated a story about an imaginary character who experienced a sudden change in the learning topic. The initial excitement about studying Greece turned into sadness and worry when the child was compelled to switch to studying Victorians. Imran described the character's feelings:

He was sad and worried, he was really good at this topic that they're doing in history, Greece, and then they changed it to Victorians. He is not good at Victorians, and then he doesn't want to do it. Then he gets all sad and worried that it's never going to pass.

This narrative reveals how forcing children to learn topics outside their interests can lead to feelings of discouragement and demotivation. The child's initial success with Greece demonstrates the positive impact of allowing children to explore subjects aligned with their preferences. The subsequent shift to Victorians, an area of lesser interest or proficiency, made the child feel 'all sad and worried'. These emotions were particularly linked to the fear of failing assessments in the less preferred topic. This highlights the potential for imposed learning to create anxiety and worry, especially when tied to formal evaluations.

The children's reflections on occasions when they felt a lack of agency highlighted another crucial aspect of their perspectives on learning in school – the perceived authority of teachers. Consider the following interaction during a focus group interview:

Yana: I'm really curious now to hear examples of when you don't feel agency.

Raj: Sometimes in our class we want to do Cahoots [game-based learning platform], but our teachers don't allow us to do Cahoots.

Yana: Why?

Imran: It's just the teachers, it's just a teacher's instinct. Instinct, it's natural, natural.

Yana: Why do you think it would be so?

Raj: Probably because they probably have something either already planned or . . .

Imran: Take away our fun.

Raj: On the school they have to be really strict . . .

This conversation highlights a prevailing acceptance of teachers' assumed authority, where their decisions are perceived as a natural state of affairs. The acknowledgment that lessons are pre-planned and teachers must be strict reinforces children's perceived lack of agency in questioning established school structures. Imran's interjection, suggesting teachers restrict activities to 'take away our fun', strengthens the connection between independent choice, enjoyment, and motivation. This implies that teacher-imposed subjects are seen as less enjoyable, contrasting with subjects that align with children's intrinsic motivation and interests. The emotional impact of compulsory engagement in unenjoyable activities emerged clearly in another example, where Sonia expressed boredom and powerlessness during math lessons:

Sometimes in maths I get very bored, and I feel like I have no power if we're doing a paper in maths. Like recently we did a paper and halfway through I literally just like, I did not want to do any more of it but I had to do it. So sometimes in maths, I feel that like I'm not powerful at all because I really don't like maths. . . . We just have to do so much, 11-plus papers.

Sonia's sentiment is particularly poignant when mentioning having to continue with work despite waning interest and motivation. The reference to '11-plus papers' emphasises the external pressures contributing to their sense of powerlessness. This example illustrates how the necessity to focus on specific subjects, particularly math for 11-plus exams, can transform learning from an enjoyable experience into a tedious task. The shift from voluntary engagement to forced obligation diminishes children's sense of agency in their learning journey. This conclusion was vividly illustrated through a striking analogy made by a child, who compared forced learning to forced eating, emphasising the explicit lack of agency in both scenarios. The following conversation provides insight into the profound psychological impact on the child's sense of agency:

Yana: Can you elaborate on the two examples of situations in which you felt powerless and out of control?

Imran: So, one of them was lunch, I can't remember the other one now . . .

Suraya: Maths.

Imran: No, it was English, it was English. English and lunch. Usually since nursery because I never ate and I really just don't like eating, all the teachers would usually ask me to eat, 'Why aren't you eating?' Or would usually force me to eat it and the dinner ladies would . . .

Yana: What do you mean by force?

Imran: In nursery they just put it on a spoon and then I'd have to eat it, then in Year 3, last year, the person that was usually on duty for lunch, she would usually make me eat it. She would force me to, she would just cut it up and then would make me eat it. Sometimes they'd watch me. Yes, she would watch me eat it . . . Now in Year 4 they don't do it much, but the dinner ladies always, once I think it was in Year 2, I said I wasn't hungry because the cookie was there, and it was like the only thing I was going to eat because they put the cookie out in something, and then because I said I wasn't hungry to the dinner lady, she took my cookie away. She just grabbed it and took it away, and then because she realised that was mean, she gave it back. And then for English we had to write about the silver . . . a book called *The Silver Swan*, and you had to write sentences, and I just felt . . . without power. I just felt I didn't have control because I didn't know how much to learn. I didn't want to do it.

Yana: Is it because you did not want to write?

Imran: No, and once the teacher that was teaching us, because I didn't say a sentence out loud, she made me do one, and that made me feel more out of power.

Suraya: She didn't make you.

Imran: Yes, she did, Suraya, she *made* me [emphasis in original].

The child's narrative highlights the profound impact of imposed choices and external pressures on children's sense of control and agency. Whether concerning meals or learning tasks, the experience underscores the psychological strain of compulsory engagement in unwanted activities. This illuminates the intricate dynamics of power and authority within the school environment, particularly between adults, notably teachers, and children.

When prompted to reflect on the relative influence of children and adults in their environments, some children expressed a strong belief in adults' greater power, contrasting it with their own perceived limitations. The stark comments shared by Imran, such as 'I'm a child and I can't do anything' and 'Adults can do whatever they want and children are stuck in prison somewhere', highlight a perceived imbalance in power dynamics and a clear lack of a sense of agency among these children.

The children expressed varying perspectives on the extent and importance of choice they get to make in their learning. Let's examine one particular interaction that took place during a focus group:

Yana: Okay, do you often get the chance to make choices?
Arun: Yes, we do get quite a lot of chances . . .
Leyla: We don't really get to choose what we do in the lessons, what we are choosing to do?
Yana: You mean the activities or the tasks or the problems that you solve? You don't get to choose those? Okay, would you like to?
Leyla: I'm not really so sure.
Yana: Why not?
Leyla: Because there might be a lot of things that we can do, and it can also be quite hard to choose, or hard options maybe or something really easy.
Suraya: But, Leyla, if you do something easy you won't learn anything.
Leyla: True, but it's just better if the teachers sometimes choose because then they know what we need to learn, and they just know what we need to do.
Arun: And they know all the aspects of the subjects.
Yana: Okay, and do you guys agree, [addressing the other two children]?
Suraya: Yes, like in English, was it maths or English? We did a subject. The teacher chose it because we had our exams, and so we revised with that because we weren't doing that work.
Raj: I think I agree with them, but sometimes in sport we do some stuff I don't like. I would like to do some other stuff, and some people would also agree.
Yana: Like what, for example?
Raj: Sometimes we do [unclear] or stuff to do with balancing yourself, but we all want to play either football or basketball most of the time.

This conversation reveals a complex interplay of preferences and perceived difficulties in decision-making among the children, and the role of teachers in guiding learning. Arun's statement that they have numerous opportunities for choice was challenged by Leyla, 'What we are choosing to do?' This indicates divergent perceptions regarding the extent of their choices. While some acknowledge opportunities for decision-making, others express uncertainty about wanting more control, citing potential challenges in making academic choices. The mention of preferences in sports activities emphasises their desire for more choice in areas of individual interest.

Collectively, the children conveyed a shared belief that teachers are better suited to make learning-related choices, indicating trust in teachers' expertise and guidance for comprehensive learning. This sentiment was reinforced by Leyla's expanded view:

> So, teachers choosing what we do is important because we might not know as much as they do, and they might know exactly what we have to learn, but then I think choosing our own things would be good because it is our own thing, and they might, sometimes in subjects they teach something easier that you already know, and sometimes I think it is to make your own choices to see where you have to keep working on or not just being stuck on something you have already done lots and lots before.

This perspective introduced nuance by highlighting benefits of both teacher-led choices and children's agency. Leyla recognised teachers' expertise in selecting learning materials while emphasising the value of children's choices for personalisation and self-directed learning. When prompted about important situations for making their own choices, children focussed on examples outside formal learning, such as after-school clubs and leisure activities. For example, Sonia emphasised the importance of influencing their school's physical environment:

> Sometimes choices are important if you can make certain places, like for example the school. If you wanted to make it better and the teachers won't let you, but they don't even let us try it out sometimes, and they may not know what is best for everyone.

These reflections illuminate children's understanding of autonomy and decision-making in school. They expressed a pronounced desire for agency in influencing the physical environment and choosing activities outside formal learning, underscoring the importance they ascribed to personal choices within and beyond school. However, they conveyed a sense of restriction in expressing and implementing their ideas. Sonia's candid statement that teachers may not always know what's best for everyone reflected a deeper desire for shared decision-making in matters directly impacting the school community.

This aspiration for collaborative decision-making in shaping the school's physical environment stood in stark contrast to children's passive acceptance of teacher authority in academics. This disparity became further apparent during a role-play activity where pairs of children interviewed each other about desired school changes. The open-ended activity revealed children's preferences across both academic and non-academic aspects. Their suggestions focussed primarily on non-academic matters: having a swimming pool, a bigger playground with more equipment, a buffet menu for lunch and no 'sloppy pastry', upgrading whiteboards, and increasing network speed. Learning-related changes centred on reducing disliked elements, such as shortening unfavoured subjects like English and having less homework. This emphasis on minimising rather than introducing new elements suggested limited agency in shaping learning experiences. We pursued this theme during a focus group, asking children about their learning preferences for the upcoming academic year:

Yana: What do you want to learn about the next academic year?
Imran: I don't know.
Yana: No pressure, Imran. You can take your time. So, you haven't thought about this before?
Imran: No.
Yana: This is a new question for you?
Imran: Yes, very new.

The lack of prior consideration suggested children weren't routinely prompted to reflect on preferred learning topics. This impression strengthened through another conversation:

Yana: Do the teachers ever ask you what you would like to learn about?

Children talking over each other: 'No', 'No, they never asked me', 'No, they don't ask'

Raj: They sometimes might ask. For us at least it was like, if you want to do this topic or this topic from next term, but they don't let us choose what topic we want.

Children's responses illustrated a common perception that teachers rarely sought their preferences, and even when they did, children felt minimal influence over topic choices. Despite occasional opportunities for input, children consistently viewed final decisions as teachers' domain. This recurring theme underscored the belief that learning choices were teachers' prerogative, given their perceived superior knowledge. Infrequent choice opportunities reinforced the sense that curriculum decisions were unilateral, fostering limited agency among children.

When asked about wanting more curriculum choice opportunities, children expressed desire for greater autonomy, particularly in topic selection. One child noted that choosing topics would allow exploration of new subjects rather than repetition. Another emphasised motivation, suggesting self-chosen topics would increase interest and engagement. Similarly, Raj believed teachers should consider children's suggestions to enhance learning motivation. His statement 'Then you like what you learn, and then it will have an impact' highlighted how personal interests drive intrinsic motivation. This aligned with findings across all three schools linking choice to increased agency, well-being, and motivation. However, conversations revealed a gap between children's desire for agency and how little influence they felt they actually had. The following dialogue was revealing:

Yana: How does it make you feel to be able to choose your curriculum?
Imran: Fine. . . . I don't care if I choose or not, really.
Yana: You don't care? That's very interesting. Why don't you care?
Imran: Because I just don't.
Yana: You're happy to learn what teachers tell you to learn?
Imran: I don't have to learn it at school, because if the school doesn't do it, then I'll just do it outside of school.

This exchange revealed how Imran had accepted his limited influence over curriculum choices. His indifference and comment about 'not caring' suggested that he felt his input would not change what he was learning. Tellingly, he preferred out-of-school learning where he had more freedom to choose. This highlighted the gap between children's desire for agency and their actual opportunities to shape their learning experiences in formal education.

South City State

In SCS, choice served as a central framework for discussing agency, providing children with a tangible way to understand the concept's relevance to their actions and decisions. Children's responses varied distinctly. Malik confidently asserted, 'I always have agency', while Charlie expressed the opposite view, 'don't have any agency'. However, Malik's initial claim of extensive agency was later moderated by his wish to 'choose my own subjects' if given the chance to introduce a new school rule. This suggested that even children who felt they had high levels of agency recognised areas where they wanted more control, particularly in shaping their learning experiences. Charlie's view of limited agency in school decision-making became particularly clear in discussions about his favourite place – the library. Although he usually spent his reward time there, when asked about visiting the library outside designated periods, his response 'I don't think I'm allowed to' highlighted both institutional boundaries and his uncertainty about what choices he could make.

Overall, children in SCS acknowledged having 'some agency', particularly during non-study times such as playtime, reward time, and extracurricular activities. These moments emerged as crucial for their sense of empowerment and choice. During less structured periods, children experienced greater agency, contrasting with the regimented learning environment. Ayla exemplified this by designating the playground as her favourite place, 'I can run around a lot, and I can play with my friends. Also, it's the time when I don't have to work. . . . I can do anything I want'.

This highlighted the clear connection between choice and empowerment, emphasising the distinction between prescribed 'work' and free-choice 'fun' activities.

Extracurricular activities, such as cooking and gardening, emerged as significant domains for exercising control and choice. Miriam's enthusiasm for cooking extended beyond the activity itself to accessing typically adult-restricted equipment, 'It's fun to do cooking yourself because, for example, at home only the adults get to cook. But in the kitchen, you've got the ovens, the stoves, and you get to cook whatever'. Another child's (not a case study pupil) comment about gardening captured a similar sense of ownership, 'when you grow your own plant, you can keep it'. These examples showed how children valued independent action, particularly in traditionally adult-led domains.

My Learning Choice Diary activity emphasised the social situatedness of children's agency. Case study pupils' reflections on day-to-day choices revealed how their opportunities to exercise agency could be enabled or constrained by their environments.

Miriam's Learning Choice Diary (Figure 6.2) highlighted how children exercised greater agency over their reading choices at home. She documented selecting Fiction Express (an interactive platform where students engage with professional authors in weekly chapter releases to co-create stories) instead of reading 'an actual

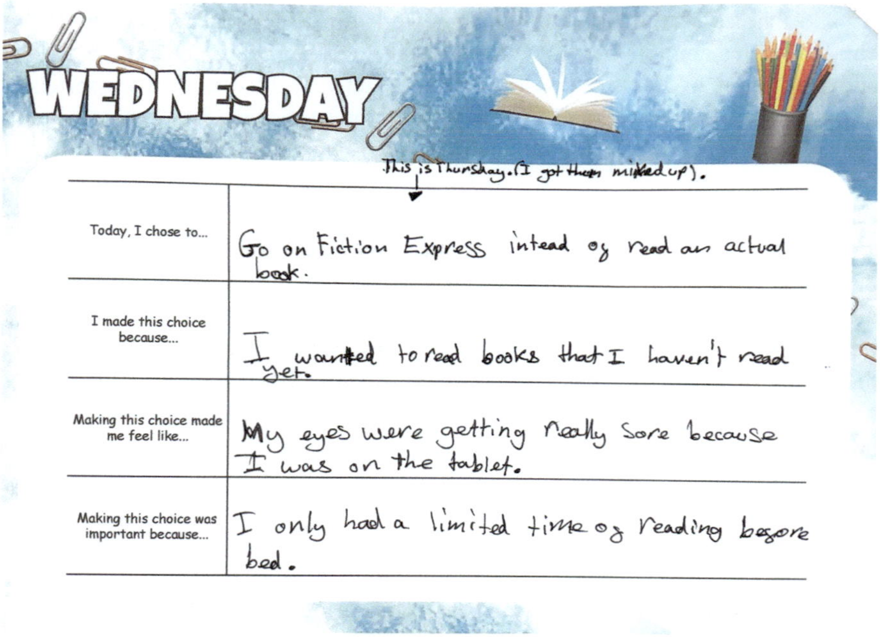

WEDNESDAY

This is Thursday. (I got them mixed up).

Today, I chose to...	Go on Fiction Express intead of read an actual book.
I made this choice because...	I wanted to read books that I haven't read yet.
Making this choice made me feel like...	My eyes were getting really sore because I was on the tablet.
Making this choice was important because...	I only had a limited time of reading before bed.

FIGURE 6.2 Miriam's Learning Choice Diary (Wednesday)

book' during her bedtime reading. 'I wanted to read books I haven't read yet', Miriam told us, highlighting how free choice in reading materials allowed her to explore new interests. While she noted that screen time made her 'eyes getting sore' and she had only 'a limited time to read before bed', the ability to choose both what to read and over what medium reflected the greater agency children experienced in home environments. This example illustrated how home settings often provided children with more opportunities to make independent choices about their learning and leisure activities compared to more structured school environments.

However, not all children experienced such freedom of choice at home. Paul faced challenges completing his Learning Choice Diary due to responsibilities helping his mum care for siblings. This situation limited his options for making choices that week, demonstrating how external responsibilities impacted children's opportunities and perceived agency. Similarly, Miriam expressed concern about limited choice opportunities during Eid, a significant Islamic religious festival, which involved highly structured family activities. This highlighted how external commitments influenced children's opportunities to make choices, affecting their perceived sense of agency.

The challenge of choice extended beyond practical limitations to questions of experience and expectation. Ayla confessed uncertainty about what to write in her choice diary, suggesting limited experience with deliberate decision-making. Her unfamiliarity led to feelings of being at a loss, highlighting the connection between lack of choice opportunities and diminished agency. This emerged further in her learning preferences. She lamented that 'they do not do science often', recalling how her request for more science was met with teachers claiming insufficient time. This led children to accept that science wasn't available for school learning and, importantly, that making requests of teachers was futile, 'We know they will just say no' – a statement heard repeatedly. This resignation to school authority created a narrative where children stopped expressing preferences, believing their input would not matter.

This sense of resignation emerged as a broader pattern, exemplified by Rita's feeling that individual choices lacked significance, 'You just choose things and then you just do them. You don't think much about it. . . . It doesn't really matter.' This sentiment reflected how choice-making seemed disconnected from meaningful impact on educational experiences. This became particularly clear in Rita's reflections on children's input about school improvements. She described how requests for a bigger playground went unaddressed due to practical constraints, responding with resignation, 'They wanted to see how they could improve. It doesn't mean they're going to do anything about it.' Rita's repeated assertion that 'We're not like other schools. . . . We don't decide, we just do what we're told to do' suggested limited agency within the school structure.

Nevertheless, Rita recognised the importance of children's voice, 'Our opinions are important. . . . My opinion is important because then I may not want to learn. How can I learn when I do not like the school?' This connected to her final observation about school enthusiasm, 'Nobody loves going to school. They want to spend time at home, play with their toys . . .'

This narrative revealed a tension between Rita's understanding of agency and her experience of its impact. While she recognised that expressing opinions affected her motivation to learn, her belief that making choices 'didn't really matter' suggested resignation. Her example of the playground request exemplified a pattern where children's input rarely led to visible change. Although Rita and her peers hoped their opinions influenced school decisions, the gap between expectation and reality bred disengagement. Her statement that 'nobody loves going to school' hinted at how this limited agency contributed to her broader dissatisfaction with education.

Building on these experiences of limited agency, the close link between choice, agency, and children's emotional responses emerged as a recurring theme in their reflections. One illustrative example was provided by Miriam as she described how her character felt out of control in a PE class:

Miriam:	In class she didn't know whether the teacher was being unfair to her.
Yana:	Okay, can you tell more how was the teacher being fair?
Miriam:	Telling her to do stuff she doesn't want to do.
Yana:	Okay, what lesson would that be can you imagine?
Miriam:	PE.
Yana:	Okay.
Miriam:	Then she starts losing her temper and going out of the room.
Yana:	Because of?
Miriam:	Her teacher telling her what to do and she loses control.

Miriam's narrative expressed a sense of injustice when describing how the teacher's directives controlled her character's actions against its will. The character's loss of control, culminating in leaving the room, illustrated how restrictive instructional methods affected children's perception of fairness and autonomy. This example demonstrated that opportunities for independent choice were vital for children's sense of agency in academic settings. The emotional response depicted in Miriam's story highlighted how limited autonomy in learning environments could impact both children's engagement and well-being, suggesting that incorporating choice in pedagogical approaches was essential for positive educational experiences.

Northern City State

In NCS, the My Agency Timeline activity inspired extensive reflections from the children, who demonstrated confidence in completing and reflecting on their timelines. These reflections revealed the dynamics of children's agency throughout a typical school day and the role of choice in shaping these dynamics. Children consistently expressed their highest sense of agency during break and lunchtimes, relishing these unstructured periods when their activities were not directed by teachers.

Let's explore Dahlia's Agency Timeline (Figure 6.3), focussing on key moments. The morning English lessons at 9 and 10 a.m. emerged as times of significant agency, where Dahlia felt 'quite powerful' with 'a lot of control' due to her strong grasp of the subject matter. However, this sense of agency diminished at 11 a.m. during the class reader session – where the whole class reads and analyses a book together, typically with little children's input into the book selection. During this time, Dahlia experienced 'little control' and didn't feel powerful. The middle of the day marked a return to higher agency, particularly at 12 p.m., when she felt 'very powerful' with 'full control' during playtime. This continued around lunchtime, where she enjoyed 'good control' while chatting with friends. The timeline concluded with another peak of agency at 4 p.m., when she returned home and could 'do what she wants', marking this as a time of complete autonomy.

Dahlia's description highlighted the fluctuating nature of children's agency throughout the school day, particularly how academic confidence, social

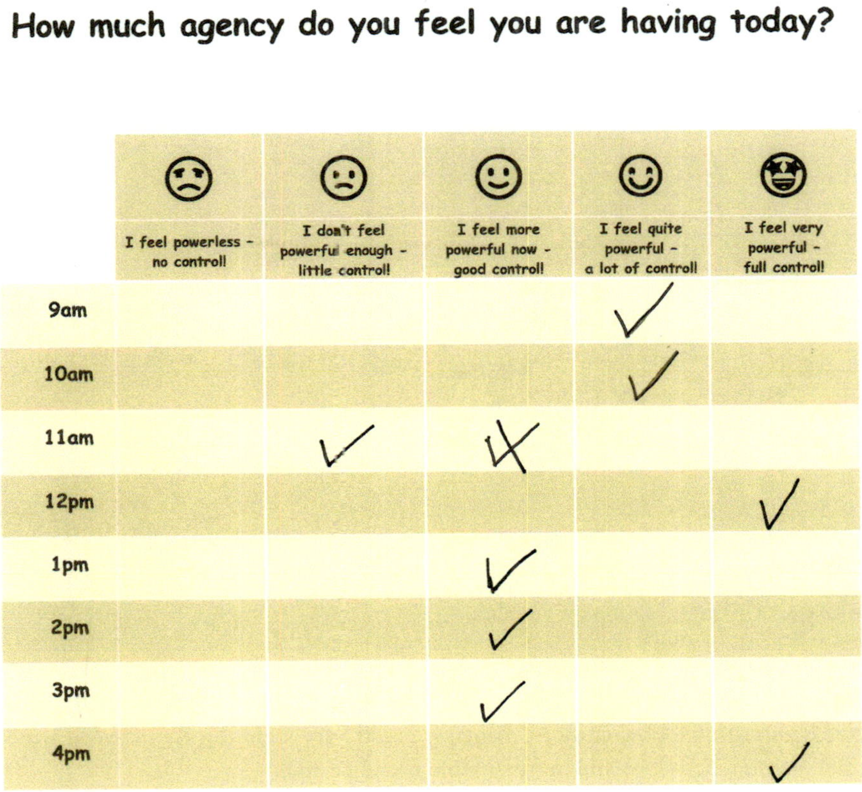

How much agency do you feel you are having today?

	I feel powerless – no control!	I don't feel powerful enough – little control!	I feel more powerful now – good control!	I feel quite powerful – a lot of control!	I feel very powerful – full control!
9am				✓	
10am				✓	
11am		✓	✗		
12pm					✓
1pm			✓		
2pm			✓		
3pm			✓		
4pm					✓

FIGURE 6.3A Dahlia's Agency Timeline

Tell me more about each situation.

What made you feel this way?

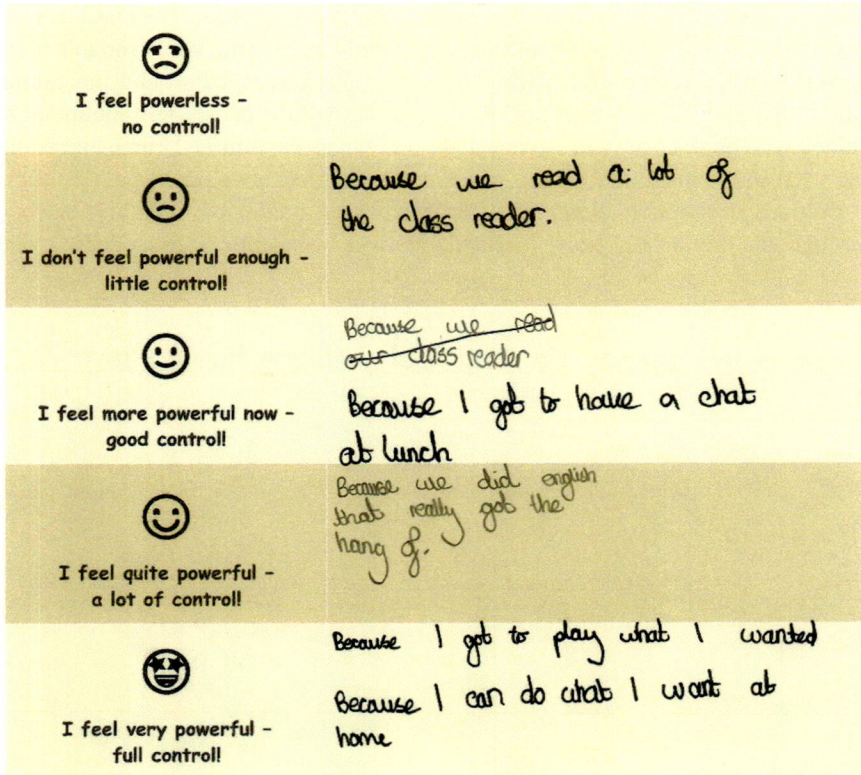

😫

I feel powerless –
no control!

🙁

I don't feel powerful enough –
little control!

Because we read a lot of the class reader.

🙂

I feel more powerful now –
good control!

Because we read our class reader

Because I got to have a chat at lunch

🙂

I feel quite powerful –
a lot of control!

Because we did english that really got the hang of.

🤩

I feel very powerful –
full control!

Because I got to play what I wanted

Because I can do what I want at home

Thank you 😊

FIGURE 6.3B   Dahlia's Agency Timeline

interactions, and free choice activities influenced her sense of control. Her experience demonstrated how children's agency could vary significantly between structured learning activities and more flexible social periods.

Her description resonated with the sentiments of her peers, who consistently emphasised these unprescribed times, characterised by free choices and shared moments with friends, as peaks of agency. Statements like 'I can do whatever I want with my friends outside' exemplified their descriptions of agency peaks.

Independent choice emerged as a crucial aspect of the children's sense of agency in the classroom. Jaleel expressed feeling empowered when given the opportunity to choose a learning station during lessons, stating, 'I feel quite powerful because I get to pick my independent activity'. This emphasises the importance of autonomy in structured learning environments, where the freedom to make choices significantly contributes to the child's sense of agency. However, situations where children felt less agentic were linked to instances without choice. A notable example highlighted a sense of powerlessness during a math lesson, where a focus task was assigned by the teacher, deviating from the school's usual practice of allowing children to choose activities based on their self-assessment. As Cecilia told us:

> I didn't feel powerful, little control . . . because when I was doing maths, I had to do the focus task because you get chosen at a certain point to do the focus task, whereas with all the other activities, you get to pick what you do.

Frustration could manifest even during break time if activities were imposed, as expressed by Dahlia, 'At break time, I might feel frustrated because, well, they [friends] might do something I don't want to do. And they kept telling me what to do, basically'. This highlights how imposed activities without choice diminishes children's sense of agency, leading to feelings of frustration and disempowerment.

While examples of situations where children felt powerless were rare, prominent instances related to the teacher-pupil dynamic in the classroom, highlighting the impact of different instructional approaches on children's sense of agency. A common sentiment was dissatisfaction with 'input mornings' – teacher-led activities focussed on delivering knowledge content. During these sessions, children expressed feelings of diminished control and powerlessness, emphasising the passive nature of listening without active participation. Harley succinctly captured this sentiment, 'I don't feel powerful enough, little control, because you just listen and you don't properly like to anything. You just listen'. In contrast, children highlighted instances when they felt more agentic, often associated with activities allowing for interaction and personal involvement. For instance, Jaleel mentioned feeling more in control when given the opportunity to chat and participate in activities aligned with personal interests, such as art, describing it as 'pretty fun' compared to the passive nature of morning input sessions.

These contrasting examples of active participation and passive listening emphasise how teacher-pupil dynamics shape children's agency within the classroom. Children's descriptions of feeling more in control during interactive activities highlighted the importance of an active role in learning. Their expressions of 'little control' and not feeling 'powerful enough' during input lessons underscore their frustration with passive listening. This suggests that opportunities for interaction and hands-on engagement significantly enhance children's sense of agency, while traditional teaching methods emphasising passive reception of information may diminish it.

In NCS, children consistently communicated a prevailing sense of control, both within learning and outside the classroom. Jaleel's statements that 'I don't actually ever think I've had no control whatsoever in my learning, or outside' and 'I really enjoy school and I really enjoy being able to pick what we do' reflected their appreciation for the extent of choice afforded to them. A strong positive correlation emerged between children's ability to make choices and their enjoyment of activities. The children consistently associated feelings of happiness and contentment with regular opportunities to make choices and engage in enjoyable activities throughout the day.

This positive correlation became evident in children's reflections. When asked about times of lacking control, Cecilia responded, 'It didn't happen because I really enjoy school and I really enjoy being able to pick what we do, and I feel like throughout the day, I have some level of power and control'. This statement underscored their belief that choice-making significantly contributed to their sense of power and contentment. Soraya echoed this sentiment when asked about instances of feeling out of control:

> I don't really know if there's a point in my day, or my character's day, that they get really out of control and really angry because usually the stuff is quite fun and we get to choose and be really happy most of the time, and I don't think there's a point in my day where I'd be angry and really out of control.

These quotes illustrated a common experience among the children in NCS. Their consistent expression of enjoyment and happiness in school activities emerged as a strong finding, with children attributing this positive engagement to their ability to make choices and exert control over their learning experiences. They emphasised the importance of picking activities and making decisions throughout the school day, contributing to their sense of power and control. This empowerment through choice emerged as fundamental to the school's approach, where children were active participants rather than passive recipients in shaping their learning experiences. Notably, the absence of instances where children felt completely out of control suggested the school's success in creating a highly agentic environment.

Children's agency and perceived subject hierarchies

A significant finding from our discussions with children concerned their perceptions of the importance of different curriculum subjects. Children consistently identified a clear hierarchy among subjects, with some regarded as more important, serious, or relevant to their educational and life goals than others. This perceived hierarchy held particular significance for children's sense of agency, their attitudes, motivation levels, and overall enjoyment of learning. Though subject hierarchies were evident across all three schools, their impact on children's learning attitudes manifested differently in each setting.

South City Independent

In SCI, children exhibited a clear awareness of subject hierarchies. During the Feelings at School activity, Imran described his character's sadness stemming from poor performance in their favourite subject. Consider our dialogue:

Yana: If it was his favourite, why was he getting 0%?
Imran: His parents weren't letting him do that subject. They thought core subjects were more important than doing that subject.
Yana: What core subjects?
Imran: Maths, English, and science.

This exchange illuminated the complex interplay between parental expectations, subject hierarchies, and children's agency. The character's sadness stemmed from parents prioritising 'core subjects' over personal interests, highlighting how external pressures could constrain children's educational choices. Imran's narrative revealed an internalised hierarchy where mathematics, English, and science held paramount importance, reflecting broader societal values about academic success. This prioritisation of core subjects over personal interests suggested a tension between external expectations and individual preferences, potentially affecting both the children's sense of agency and their emotional engagement with learning. An important implication of this hierarchy was that subjects deemed as 'work' were viewed as beyond the territory where children felt entitled to make choices. According to the children, these areas naturally fell under teacher domain. Leyla expressed this perspective:

> I feel I don't have the freedom to choose when we're doing English or maths or science because we have to work in there. We can choose how fast we work, but it's not much because our teachers normally choose what we do, and we can't really choose which pages we are doing and work topic.

This sense of constraint was reinforced by Raj, who emphasised that in 'main subjects', children didn't get to make choices. He acknowledged these limitations as intentional, 'That's because they [teachers] did it for a reason because they planned out because we need to learn that'. This remark suggested an understanding that certain topics were essential for their education, implying that some areas of learning were predetermined by educational goals.

The complex interplay of factors shaping children's attitudes towards different subjects emerged during discussions about their interests. When asked what he would choose to learn if given the chance, Raj initially expressed enthusiasm for learning new stitching techniques, particularly crosshatching. However, upon reflection, he changed his choice to an English booster – a specialised activity designed to help children prepare for the 11-plus exams:

Yana: Okay, what would you choose? Crosshatching or English booster?

Raj: I would choose English booster because it's going to help us into our senior school, and when I'm in my senior school, I could probably learn it then, how to crosshatch.

Children's acceptance of limited choice was often accompanied by a belief that this constraint served their benefit. As Raj explained in another context:

> I don't think that we can make our choices in stuff like science or geography and things like that because, especially in geography, we already have it planned, and we don't get a choice to do anything. We just have to do it as it is compulsory because it is good for our learning.

This perspective was further reinforced in group discussions:

Leyla: Well, you need English and maths. I think it's important to learn English and maths.

Children collectively: Oh, it is, yes.

Leyla: It's important to learn maths because when you get a job when you're older, my mum is a computer engineer, and so is my dad. And I also want to do that. So, I also have to calculate and do maths as well.

Suraya similarly emphasised the positive aspects of teacher-directed learning:

> So, I think that we don't get to learn what we want to do in the topic because they plan it before us, but it is also good because we learn new things. And also at home, we do clubs and classes – I do French and abacus class every Tuesday and Friday.

These examples illustrated the complex balance children navigated between personal interests and external pressures. Their experiences revealed an ongoing tension between agency and structure, as they attempted to reconcile their genuine interests with established academic expectations. While acknowledging the curriculum's purpose, children's responses revealed a complex relationship between structured learning and agency. Though they viewed teacher-directed learning in core subjects as necessary and beneficial, this came at the cost of their freedom to make learning choices. This highlighted the delicate balance between structured education and fostering children's autonomy in the learning process.

South City State

In SCS, children's perceptions revealed a clear subject hierarchy, where school-mandated activities were labelled as 'serious', while those chosen during free time were deemed 'fun'. This distinction highlighted how externally required subjects carried a sense of obligation, whereas self-chosen activities were associated with enjoyment. When discussing learning interests, children expressed belief that certain personal topics wouldn't be included in the formal curriculum because they were 'not normal' or 'not common'. Charlie articulated this by referring to mathematics and English as 'normal' and 'common' subjects, revealing how traditional subjects were prioritised within the curriculum. This theme was reinforced by Ayesha, who characterised core subjects as 'work' while describing activities like art and story writing as 'fun'. Her distinction illuminated the tension between formal curriculum requirements and children's diverse interests.

The school's project-based approach revealed interesting complexities in how children conceptualise knowledge. While the formal subject hierarchy remained clear in children's minds, their engagement with project-based learning showed a more nuanced understanding. For instance, when Ayla discussed receiving gold status for a project on digestive system, she and her classmate quickly identified this as science despite it being presented within a broader project framework. This suggested that while children recognised traditional subject boundaries, they could also engage with knowledge more holistically when it was presented in an integrated format.

Children's perceptions of subject importance appeared closely tied to assessment and curriculum structures. As the Deputy Head Teacher observed, children were acutely aware that subjects like English and mathematics were formally evaluated, which influenced how they viewed these subjects. This awareness created a clear divide where core subjects were perceived as 'work' while subjects like art and PE were categorised as 'fun'. Teachers' observations reinforced this pattern – Mina noted distinct differences in children's agency across subjects – while creative subjects like music offered choices such as instrument selection, core subjects like mathematics provided minimal room for children's input due to curriculum requirements. This structural difference was echoed by Sylvia, who noted that even in English, fundamental choices like book selection were teacher-controlled rather than child-led.

This hierarchical understanding of subjects was evident across multiple year groups. Paul's description of cooking as 'much more fun than staying in class and listening to boring speeches' exemplified how students categorised their school experiences into distinct spheres of 'work' versus enjoyable activities. The positioning of subjects like cooking and art as rewards rather than regular learning further reinforced this hierarchy – these subjects were seen as special privileges earned through academic achievement and good behaviour rather than integral parts of learning. This distinction was further reinforced by the school's timetabling and reward systems, as evidenced by Ayla's understanding that activities like drawing were restricted to reward times rather than being integrated into regular learning periods.

These distinctions in how knowledge was categorised and valued appeared deeply embedded in children's understanding of school life, reflecting both institutional structures and broader educational priorities. The consistent pattern across different year groups and teaching contexts suggested that children's perceptions of subject hierarchies were not merely personal preferences but rather reflected their understanding of how different types of knowledge were valued within the educational system. This understanding manifested in their clear demarcation between 'work' and 'fun' activities.

Northern City State

In NCS, children discussed their learning experiences without strictly adhering to traditional subject boundaries. This approach appeared to reflect the school's holistic curriculum, where content from various subjects was integrated into termly topics. While explicit subject separation was less emphasised and rarely mentioned by the children, subtle disciplinary distinctions emerged during our school interactions. A particularly revealing conversation occurred during a discussion about topic books – scrapbook-style documents where children captured their key learning takeaways from each term. These creative outputs served as tangible representations of each child's unique journey through the termly curriculum maps. In the following dialogue, we asked the child to discuss his topic book:

Yana: Okay, can you tell me a bit about the topic book generally? What is the purpose of the topic book?

Molly: Well, we write down about all the topics, for example, we've been doing ancient Egyptians and learning about Japan and cultures. And we just write stuff and do mind topics in our topic books as well. Like French and all the other kind of stuff.

Yana: Everything that you learn in school, basically?

Molly: Apart from maths and English.

Yana: Okay, why not those?

Molly: Because they're kind of just different. For the topic books, we choose what we want to learn about, but in maths and English, we just have to do it.

This dialogue illuminated children's perceptions of different subjects and their roles in learning. Molly explained the absence of mathematics and English from the topic book by characterising these subjects as 'different' and compulsory, unlike other areas where children had choice. Her acceptance of mathematics and English as subjects they 'just have to do' revealed an externally imposed learning priority. This distinction served as justification for excluding these subjects from topic books, which were meant to capture learning highlights, suggesting these compulsory subjects rarely aligned with children's most memorable or enjoyable learning experiences.

While this observation indicated Molly's recognition of subject differentiation, such remarks were infrequent, suggesting a relatively minimal influence of subject hierarchy on children's perceptions in NCS. The emphasis on children's agency in creating topic books reflected a pedagogical approach that encouraged broader appreciation for diverse subjects. This appeared to foster a more balanced view among children regarding subject importance, with the dynamics of subject hierarchy seemingly mitigated within the school environment.

Children's agency and social dynamics

In this section, we explore the relationship between social dynamics and children's sense of agency. Our analysis of children's experiences across the three schools reveals a nuanced interplay between social interactions, emotional well-being, and children's perceptions of control and empowerment.

South City Independent

In SCI, we found a recurring theme of feeling unheard or unseen. Children's narratives consistently revealed the emotional impact of not being heard. For instance, Arun described an imaginary character who 'was very upset and then he got a bit frustrated that people weren't listening to him.' This response highlighted both the immediate frustration and deeper emotional distress that came from not being heard, showing how being ignored affected children's sense of control over their environment. An exchange with Imran during a discussion on Feelings at School further illuminated this relationship:

Yana: Okay, he was upset and losing control because?
Imran: He has no friends. He was very lonely.

Here, Imran explicitly associated the character's diminished sense of control with a lack of friends and ensuing loneliness. The implication was that a dearth of social connection and the feeling of loneliness contributed to a reduction in children's sense of agency. The explicit connection between the character's lack of friends and the emotional state of loneliness suggested that social connections played a pivotal role in shaping Imran' perceived agency. The statement 'some days my friends aren't my friends' added another layer of complexity by implying a sense of unpredictability or variability in social relationships. On certain days, Imran perceived a shift in the dynamics of friendship, leading to a feeling of being out of control. This fluctuation in the child's social environment introduced an element of uncertainty, revealing a close interplay between social connections and agency.

Another illustrative example from Imran concerned an instance of bullying, 'some people started to bully him, so he got angry but he didn't know what to do.' This scenario showed how negative social interactions affected a child's sense of agency. The emotional response of anger highlighted the distress caused by the mistreatment, while Imran's admission that he 'didn't know what to do' revealed a deeper sense of helplessness. The lack of a clear course of action in the face of bullying emphasised how social challenges could undermine a child's sense of control.

These examples collectively showed how social dynamics shaped agency in SCI. Not being listened to, along with uncertain friendships, emerged as key sources of vulnerability for children, diminishing their sense of agency. The emotional responses highlighted the complex nature of agency, emphasising its interpersonal dimension.

South City State

In SCS, the intricate relationship between children's sense of control and their social experiences became particularly evident through the Feelings at School activity. This exercise revealed a profound connection between instances of feeling out of control and various social dynamics, offering a nuanced perspective on the interplay between agency and social integration. One compelling illustration came from Miriam's description of why her character felt out of control, 'She didn't know anyone there, and she was worried that she wouldn't meet anyone and be lonely.' This expression highlighted the emotional impact of social isolation and the fear of lacking social connections. Miriam's comment revealed a sense of vulnerability and apprehension linked to navigating unfamiliar social situations, emphasising the pivotal role of social acceptance and friendship in shaping children's perceived agency. The emotional toll described in the quote underscored how social dynamics profoundly influenced children's overall well-being within the school context. The fear of loneliness and uncertainty about forming new connections accentuated the challenges children faced when establishing social relationships in unfamiliar environments. These social experiences were intricately woven into their sense of agency, suggesting that a positive social environment was not only conducive to emotional well-being but also fundamental for fostering a strong sense of agency.

The children's stories about their imaginary characters revealed numerous instances where these characters felt out of control, primarily stemming from various social challenges. These narratives painted a vivid picture of how social dynamics – including bullying, social exclusion during lunch, or conflicts with friends – were intricately linked to feelings of frustration, anxiety, and reduced perceived agency. The connection between social challenges and diminished sense of agency was particularly evident in instances of bullying. The emotional toll of such behaviour translated into a palpable loss of agency, as characters grappled with feelings of powerlessness in the face of negative social interactions. Similarly, narratives depicting scenarios where characters had no one to sit with during lunch underscored how social isolation impacted children's sense of agency. The children's stories also highlighted how conflicts with friends were associated with diminished control. Falling out with friends introduced emotional distress and uncertainty, leading to reduced perceived control over their social environment.

The impact of these social experiences extended beyond the playground and into the classroom. The emotional fallout from social interactions during unstructured times contributed to shaping children's perceptions of themselves and their capacity for agency within the broader school environment. This holistic understanding emphasised that children's engagement and well-being in the classroom were intricately connected to their overall sense of agency, influenced by the complex tapestry of social experiences both within and outside formal learning spaces.

Northern City State

In NCS, children expressed a profound connection between their sense of agency and social interactions, both within and outside the classroom. This relationship was particularly evident during unstructured times, 'I feel very powerful when I have my lunch and break because I get to do things with my friends' (Jaleel) and 'I feel very powerful, full control because we're playing a game that I wanted to play, and all my friends were playing it with me' (Cecilia). These quotes highlighted how shared experiences with peers significantly enhanced children's sense of agency. The power dynamics extended beyond individual actions, amplified by the collaborative nature of these activities. Particularly noteworthy was how the ability to choose and lead games during playtime, with friends' active participation, enhanced children's perceived control and authority.

Conversely, children's accounts of powerlessness often centred on the absence of social connections, as noted by Soraya, 'Well, probably like in break times and lunchtimes when I'm with no one because no one is at break to play with me, or to sit with at lunch'. This poignant observation underscored how isolation diminished children's sense of control, highlighting the fundamental role of social interactions in sustaining agency. The significance of social validation extended into classroom experiences, particularly during collaborative learning tasks. As Harley expressed, 'I was really happy collaborating with the people on my table when we were answering the question. And I just felt really in control, that everybody would listen to my ideas and stuff'. This reflection revealed how peer recognition during group activities enhanced children's confidence and sense of control. These classroom interactions demonstrated that agency was not merely about making individual choices, but about having one's contributions valued within the social fabric of learning. Harley elaborated on this social dimension of agency, describing how group dynamics could both enhance and diminish their sense of control:

> I'm with a group of my friends and working together and then one of them might be messing around and it's really annoying. And then we all get split up, and it's not actually anybody else's fault, and I just don't feel very happy at that moment.

This account revealed how agency could be disrupted by peer behaviour – beginning with a sense of control when working collaboratively but diminishing when group dynamics broke down. The enforced splitting of the group and resulting dissatisfaction highlighted how social dynamics directly influenced children's sense of agency. These examples suggested that agency was not merely an individual experience but was deeply embedded in social contexts, with children's emotional states and sense of control closely tied to peer interactions.

The importance of social validation extended to teacher interactions, as demonstrated by Soraya, 'I feel quite powerful, a lot of control, is when I get answered, because when I get answered. . . . I feel this emotion because I don't feel ignored and I feel very powerful, full control'. This observation underscored how being acknowledged in the classroom environment significantly enhanced children's sense of agency. The simple act of being heard and responded to by teachers emerged as a crucial factor in children's perception of control and empowerment.

Collectively, these experiences highlighted the crucial role of social dynamics in shaping children's sense of agency. The power and control associated with positive social interactions demonstrated that agency was fundamentally tied to collaborative experiences. The need for acknowledgment and the emotional impact of being heard suggested that children's agency was inseparable from their social interactions. Within the educational context, this indicated that fostering positive peer relationships, encouraging collaborative learning, and ensuring each child felt valued could significantly enhance their sense of agency.

Children's agency and School Councils

A critical aspect in understanding children's sense of agency in school lies in examining formal structures designed to provide them with control within traditionally regulated environments. The School Council represents a prominent example of such institutional efforts to grant children agency. However, the effectiveness of these structures in fostering genuine agency and providing tangible opportunities for its exercise warrants careful exploration rather than assumption.

The School Council stands as a key institutional mechanism intended to empower children by involving them in decision-making processes. Its purpose is to recognise and incorporate student perspectives in shaping various aspects of school life. While such structures might reflect a commitment to promoting children's agency, questions persist regarding their actual impact and efficacy. The mere existence of a School Council does not inherently ensure true agency if the underlying processes and outcomes lack transparency, inclusivity, and genuine impact. This necessitates critical assessment of whether these structures genuinely empower children, allowing them meaningful opportunities to influence their educational experience.

Among the three schools, the School Council emerged as a prominent theme in NCS and SCI, both maintaining functioning councils despite irregular meetings. Children in these schools shared their views on the Council's purpose and its effectiveness in creating school change. SCS, however, presented a different picture. The School Council was not mentioned by children during interviews, and school leadership confirmed it was not active during the study period. Instead, the school was exploring 'Smart Councils' as a new structure to give children a more effective voice. Without an active Council, children in SCS lacked a formal avenue for expressing opinions, making it impossible to examine how such a structure might influence children's sense and exercise of agency in the school.

South City Independent

In SCI, the School Council was perceived as a crucial and effective structure for instigating positive changes within specific aspects of school life. This understanding emerged clearly in an insightful exchange with the children who were School Council representatives at the time of the study (they were not our case study pupils):

Yana: You think it's important to have a School Council?
Child A: Yes.
Child B: Yes.
Yana: Why?
Child A: Because then the school can improve and then people will . . .
Child B: Will be happier.

This dialogue highlighted children's belief that the School Council played a pivotal role in facilitating school improvements. Child A's emphasis on improvement, complemented by Child B's connection to happiness, underscored their perception that the Council served as a catalyst for enhancing the school environment and directly influencing children's well-being. This exchange illuminated the potential impact of children's involvement through formal structures like the School Council in fostering positive school experiences. While recognition of the Council's importance, in principle, did not automatically ensure children experienced it as personally effective, their responses to specific prompts about its impact proved revealing. The Council was regarded as a valuable platform, providing meaningful channels for expressing preferences. Imran stated, 'I always tell the School Council what I want,' reflecting a tangible connection between children's input and potential school changes.

Further insights emerged during a role-playing interview activity where children interviewed each other about desired school changes. A larger playground and swimming pool emerged as popular requests, and when asked about implementing these changes, children consistently mentioned approaching the School Council. This indicated they viewed the Council as an effective mechanism for influencing physical space improvements. To understand why children held this positive view of the School Council, we asked about instances of its tangible impact. Their responses revolved around practical and immediate aspects of the school environment, particularly changes to lunch meals and playground equipment. This indicated the Council's effectiveness in addressing children's day-to-day needs and preferences.

However, a significant shift emerged when discussing curriculum changes through the School Council. This idea appeared novel to the children, who expressed surprise and admitted they had not considered using the Council for this purpose. When asked why they had never tried suggesting a topic of interest, Raj responded, 'I never really thought about it.' This sentiment was echoed in a conversation with Imran:

Yana: Could it be something that you could discuss as part of the School
             Council meetings – the topics that you would like to learn about, have
             you ever thought about that?
Imran: No, I have not talked about that.
Yana: Why not?
Imran: I never thought of saying that.

The children's surprise and lack of prior consideration regarding the Council's potential role in curriculum matters was noteworthy. While they readily associated it with changes to physical environment, extending its influence to learning aspects seemed unprecedented to them. This limitation became clearer when Leyla expressed feeling 'sad' about not being able to choose learning topics. When asked about raising this concern with the School Council, she responded, 'I am not sure because they have to follow the curriculum, and if they don't, then they might get in trouble or something.'

This response highlighted the complex interplay between children's agency and structural constraints. Leyla's awareness of external requirements and potential consequences revealed perceived limitations on their ability to influence their education, contributing to a sense of powerlessness regarding curriculum matters. This sense of powerlessness was widespread, leading children to believe suggesting curriculum changes was futile. A revealing exchange illustrated this:

Imran: The teachers are probably always going to say no.
Yana: Why, do you have prior experience with the teachers like that?
Imran: No.
Dom: You just think they will say no?
Imran: It's a prediction.

Imran's further statement 'I just always thought that they are going to say no' reflected a form of learned helplessness, where children felt discouraged from expressing ideas due to anticipated rejection. His 'prediction' suggested how existing structures not only constrained current actions but also limited those merely contemplated.

This revealed a crucial distinction in the School Council's perceived effectiveness: while viewed as a powerful tool for influencing practical aspects of school life, it was not considered a platform for shaping learning experiences. The children's hesitation and assumption of teacher rejection regarding curriculum suggestions indicated an environment where they felt limited in their ability to contribute to decisions about their learning. This illustrated how structural constraints could influence both actual and potential expressions of agency – in other words, how it constrained not only the exercise of agency but children's sense of agency in relation to learning matters.

Northern City State

In NCS, the School Council operated with a nuanced structure featuring various sub-committees, such as the Arts Council and Curriculum Council, each focussing on distinct aspects of school life. This approach reflected an intention to engage children in decision-making across different domains. However, a focus group revealed a significant gap in children's understanding of the Council's intricacies. Children lacked comprehensive understanding of the Council's structure, and the roles assigned to different sub-committees. This became evident when Molly, who was chosen to represent the Art Council, was asked about her responsibilities, 'I am not quite sure because I have never been it yet'. This response reflected a notable gap in understanding roles within the School Council. Such lack of clarity suggested potential issues in communication and transparency regarding the functioning of the Council and its sub-committees. If children assigned specific roles were unsure of their responsibilities, it raised questions about the structure's effectiveness in conveying its purpose to children. The purpose of the Curriculum Council appeared particularly ambiguous, especially given the school's unique approach to curriculum development involving direct input from children. During a discussion, Cecilia suggested that the Curriculum Council's role was primarily outward-facing, engaging with visitors, 'So what they do is when guests come in, they talk about what we've learned in this academic year, and they talk about our curriculum to guests that come in to teach them'.

The ambiguity surrounding the Curriculum Council's role, particularly in relation to the school's distinctive approach to curriculum development, posed a potential challenge to children's sense of agency and the Council's effectiveness. Cecilia's perception of the Council's role as primarily visitor-focussed introduced uncertainty about their direct involvement in curriculum development. This lack of clarity regarding their role in shaping the curriculum could significantly impede children's agency. If children perceived their involvement as limited to discussions with visitors rather than active participation in curriculum development, it might diminish the Council's potential impact. Moreover, there appeared to be a disconnect between the Curriculum Council's perceived responsibilities and the school's unique curriculum development process. Given the school's emphasis on direct children's input in shaping the curriculum, the obscurity of this link for the children involved in the Curriculum Council might detract from the school's innovative approach.

The limited understanding among children regarding the School Council's inner workings raised questions about these bodies' effectiveness in facilitating children's agency. For children to truly exercise agency, they need a clear understanding of the structures in place and how their input contributed to decision-making processes. The importance of such understanding was recognised by the school, most evidently in their approach to curriculum design. During discussions on yearly curriculum mapping, both senior leadership team and teaching staff emphasised a crucial aspect: it was not enough to simply ask children what they wanted to learn about; equally important was making explicitly clear how their opinions actively contributed to shaping the curriculum. By emphasising transparency in the curriculum design process, NCS acknowledged the direct link between children's sense of agency and their understanding of how their input influenced educational decisions. This approach recognised that for children to feel genuinely empowered, they must comprehend the tangible impact of their contributions.

When prompted to reflect on tangible changes implemented through their Council involvement, children's examples predominantly centred around non-academic aspects of school life. One prominent example highlighted modifications to the school's reward system, specifically CHAMP, suggesting children perceived their impact on shaping behavioural incentives within the school community. Additionally, the introduction of designated zones for specific activities, such as football and dancing, alongside the regular playground, illustrated children's effective contribution to shaping the physical environment and creating spaces tailored to their interests. When asked about desired future changes through the School Council, children expressed practical aspirations, such as introducing more bins to reduce littering. These examples indicated not only a sense of responsibility but also active engagement in shaping their immediate surroundings, reflecting their sense of agency within the school community.

However, it was noteworthy that children's reflections did not delve into the academic domain. The absence of examples or suggestions directly related to learning could be attributed to the school's existing practices. The school provided consistent and tangible opportunities for children to actively shape their learning journeys through direct input into yearly curriculum maps and independent choices of learning activities during lessons. The School Council, therefore, appeared to play a more pronounced role in influencing aspects beyond the academic curriculum, emphasising the comprehensive nature of children's agency within the school context. This distinction between academic and non-academic influence revealed important insights about how different mechanisms supported children's agency. While the School Council facilitated agency in shaping the school environment and community aspects, direct curriculum input channels served as the primary means for influencing academic matters. This suggested that NCS had developed multiple, complementary pathways for children to exercise agency across different domains of school life.

Conclusion

This chapter's aim was to illuminate children's agency in their school settings. Agency operated as a complex interplay of institutional structures, social relationships, and individual experiences. Through identifying and examining four key themes – choice, subject hierarchies, social dynamics, and formal structures such as the School Council – we gained crucial insights into how children's capacity for meaningful action can be both enabled and constrained within school environments.

The findings reveal that children's agency cannot be understood in isolation but must be viewed as deeply embedded within school structures and relationships. Choice emerged not merely as an operational matter but as fundamental to children's sense of self and their engagement with learning. The stark contrasts between schools – from NCS' embedding of choice in curriculum development to the more constrained environments of SCI and SCSs – demonstrated how institutional approaches to choice profoundly shaped children's experience of agency. Importantly, where children experienced genuine opportunities for choice, this fostered not only immediate satisfaction but deeper engagement with learning itself.

Subject hierarchies emerged as powerful mediators of children's agency, revealing how traditional educational priorities can enhance or limit children's agency. NCS efforts to diminish these hierarchies through children's involvement stood in marked contrast to the approaches of the other schools, where a particular focus on core subjects or exam preparation often superseded children's interests and preferences. This highlighted how deeply embedded structural constraints, even when accepted as 'normal' by children, fundamentally shape their scope for agency.

The profound influence of social dynamics on children's agency revealed that agency is inherently relational rather than purely individual. Children's sense of power and control was intimately connected to their social experiences, from peer relationships to interactions with teachers. This showed that fostering agency required attention not just to formal structures but to the quality of relationships and social interactions within school communities.

The varying effectiveness of School Councils across the three settings demonstrated that formal mechanisms for student voice, while important, are not sufficient in themselves to ensure meaningful agency. Their success depended heavily on how they integrated with broader school cultures and practices, particularly in bridging the gap between practical and academic domains of school life. While prior research over many years has shown that some topics are 'off limits' for discussion at School Councils, the research that we report in this book offers a profound challenge even when School Councils are present and operating relatively well.

Our findings point to the need for a more nuanced understanding of children's agency in educational settings. Rather than viewing agency simply as individual choice or formal participation, we must recognise it as emerging from the complex interaction between institutional structures (such as curriculum and lesson design), social relationships (both peer and teacher interactions), and embedded school practices (such as how schools balance academic priorities with children's interests and integrate children's voice into daily decision-making). Chapter 7 builds on these insights by examining how broader educational structures shaped the possibilities for children's agency within the three schools.

7

EDUCATION STRUCTURES INFLUENCING CHILDREN'S AGENCY

There are many structural elements in education that influence whether and how children's agency is emphasised in schools. Building on the previous chapter's examination of children's experiences, this chapter analyses how educational structures – particularly curriculum frameworks, assessment systems, and institutional practices – shape opportunities for children's agency. The previous chapter's emphasis on the data from children contrasts with this chapter's emphasis on the data from Head Teachers and teachers. Consistent with our theoretical understanding, we identify structures as key dimensions in both our conceptual framework and in how agency manifests in schools and classrooms. While Chapter 6 highlighted the need to attend to children's agency from the perspective and experiences of the children themselves, this chapter presents our analysis of the structures: the social conditions and statutory frameworks that are integral to understanding children's agency in their daily school lives. It is only with the analysis of agency and structures that we will be able to turn our attention to the implications for practice and policy.

Curriculum, knowledge, and subject areas

One of the historically enduring topics about the curriculum in primary schools has been the amount of curriculum subject content required to be taught. This challenge manifested differently across our three schools, with each developing a distinct approach to managing curriculum content while attempting to support children's agency.

South City Independent

South City Independent (SCI) approached curriculum through their unique position as an independent school. Their commitment to children's agency manifested particularly strongly in extracurricular programming. Through student-led clubs

DOI: 10.4324/9781003227779-7

and activities, the school created opportunities for children to actively shape their experiences beyond the classroom. We observed this approach in action during one of our visits when several children, including one of our case study participants, presented the senior leadership team (SLT) with a proposal for a *Rubik's Cube* club. The Head Teacher and Deputy Head welcomed the children into the Head Teacher's office for a detailed discussion, where they articulated their vision and rationale for the club. Through thoughtful questioning, the leadership team guided the children to consider practical aspects such as finances, space requirements, timing, and expected participation. The children's proposal emphasised their intention to manage the club independently, with minimal staff oversight. In a follow-up interview, the Head Teacher highlighted this interaction as exemplifying the school's intentional approach to fostering children's agency.

While the Rubik's Cube club initiative demonstrated strong support for children's agency in extracurricular activities, our research primarily focussed on how agency manifested within the formal curriculum, especially in core subjects like English and mathematics. Here, the school's approach reflected a careful balance between academic rigour and curricular flexibility. As the Head Teacher explained:

> In English and maths, we tend to follow the [national] curriculum and then obviously there are some aspects of the Year 6 curriculum that perhaps have to go beyond the National Curriculum if they're going to be awarded academic scholarships to senior schools. . . . We aim to cover the whole curriculum by the end of Year 5, and it's the same in science, and that's why you then can focus on things like STEM and go beyond what is offered in the National Curriculum. We're really lucky as an independent school that we can do what we want when we want to.

This strategic approach to curriculum delivery centred on completing National Curriculum requirements by the end of Year 5 – a full year ahead of state school expectations. This accelerated timeline served dual purposes: demonstrating clear alignment with national standards while creating space in Year 6 for advanced study, particularly in areas like STEM. The decision to extend beyond the National Curriculum in the final year was strategically aligned with preparing children for academic scholarship examinations at prestigious senior schools. This emphasis reflected both the school's commitment to academic excellence and its responsiveness to parental expectations within their chosen competitive educational pathway.

The example of the whole of the children's final year at the school, Year 6, being used as extended curriculum was one significant example of the school's legal independence from the state-mandated national curriculum. There were other significant examples of approaches to the curriculum that highlighted the schools' independence. For example, an emphasis on oral language that included the introduction of initiatives like *Vocabulary Ninja*, and dedicated STEM lessons exemplified the school's approach to curriculum enhancement.

The introduction of Vocabulary Ninja, a commercially published scheme of activities focussed on developing vocabulary knowledge, was driven by the school's analysis of data related to verbal reasoning and English from Reception to Year 6. Verbal reasoning and vocabulary knowledge were important components of the entrance tests that pupils would have to take to get into elite secondary schools. Recognising the need to strengthen children's vocabulary skills, the SLT decided to adopt the scheme. All staff members underwent in-school training to familiarise themselves with the Vocabulary Ninja approach. The school's commitment to the approach was further reflected in the inclusion of a Vocabulary Ninja section in the weekly newsletter. The scheme consists of short daily tasks, lasting five to ten minutes, centred around a 'Word of the Day'. As part of the scheme, four children became so-called Vocabulary Ninja monitors, with one of them serving as a 'prefect' (a leadership role common in independent secondary schools). According to the Head Teacher, the children themselves expressed a desire to take on these responsibilities. They actively participated in creating resources for their respective year groups and expressed interest in developing independent resources for younger children.

Another initiative undertaken by the school to tailor the curriculum and enhance student learning was the introduction of dedicated weekly STEM lessons across all year groups, starting from Year 1. This development was motivated by the school's exceptional achievements in STEM fields. Over the three years prior to our first year of research in the school, children actively participated in and excelled at international STEM competition quizzes, securing top positions nationally and internationally. These accomplishments underscored what the school saw as the children's enthusiasm for science and mathematics. The implementation of dedicated STEM lessons aimed to capitalise on this existing passion, fostering further engagement and skill development in these critical fields. The school recognised the broader benefits of STEM education in cultivating well-rounded children with a competitive edge. By providing structured opportunities for STEM learning from an early age, the school aimed to equip children with the necessary skills and knowledge to excel academically and enhance their prospects of gaining admission to highly selective institutions. This initiative also reflected the school's commitment to adapting the curriculum to align with children's interests and achievements, and ultimately preparing them for future success in a competitive academic landscape.

The introduction of Vocabulary Ninja and dedicated STEM lessons underscored the school's strong emphasis on traditional academic disciplines. According to the Head Teacher, parental expectations significantly influenced the school's curriculum strategy. The Head Teacher shared his view, 'The pressure from the parents is – they would rather see more English than maths on the timetable than creative subjects'. This quote highlights the delicate balance the school had to navigate between their beliefs about education, meeting educational standards, and addressing parental aspirations. The emphasis on English and mathematics, driven by parental expectations, reflected the importance parents placed on certain subjects perceived to be critical for their children's educational success.

The teachers provided insightful examples of how the school endeavoured to accommodate children's learning preferences, particularly through curriculum development. One instance was shared by the Head of History, who was actively engaged in developing a new history curriculum at the time of the study. This updated curriculum sought to include topics such as colonialism, black history, and Indian history, aligning with the demographics of the student body. Lauren, the Year 4 Lead teacher, elaborated on her approach to tailoring lessons to meet children's interests. She explained how, when introducing a new topic like the Aztecs, she initiated discussions with her children, inviting them to share their existing knowledge and what aspects of the topic they were keen to explore further, such as diet or architectural materials used by the Aztecs. Lauren emphasised that this collaborative approach enabled her to gain insights into her children's specific interests and preferences. She adjusted the direction of lessons accordingly, ensuring that the content aligned with the children's curiosities to foster a more engaging and child-centred learning experience.

Another lead teacher, Dinesh, described his approach to accommodating children's preferences in the context of teaching mathematics. From his perspective, it was important to consider children's age and readiness for autonomy when accommodating their preferences in the learning process. Dinesh explained that with younger children, such as those in Year 3, the school's curriculum was primarily guided by the National Curriculum and the requirements for the 11-plus examinations. The 11-plus is an exam that has to be passed in order to be admitted to some selective secondary schools. Although it was not a feature in most local authorities in England, some authorities maintained the system, and SCI was in one of those authorities. He acknowledged the importance of providing more guidance to Year 3 children, as in his view their expressed preferences may not always align with effective learning. When asked to elaborate on what he meant by 'effective' learning, Dinesh shared an incident where children requested to watch *Maths Mansion*, an old TV show from the 1980s, during mathematics lessons. He reflected on the challenge of discerning whether the children's request was motivated by wanting to enjoy the programme just for entertainment rather than educational purposes. In contrast, with older children in Years 5 and 6, Dinesh adopted a more collaborative approach, offering them choices in their mathematics activities. For instance, he provided options that he thought would be fun for the children, such as working with geoboards or rubber bands for 2D shapes which some might see as more appropriate for mathematical work with younger children. He incorporated various stimulating activities into his teaching, such as logic puzzles and matchstick puzzles in response to the preferences expressed by his children:

I give them a lot of these challenge tasks because they say, 'I really enjoy the challenges. Can we do more challenges?' So I give them these logic puzzles and they want more of them. So we'll do that. Some days we'll do just logic puzzles. Then I gave them a matchstick puzzle. They said, 'can we have more matchstick puzzles?' So I gave them a whole bunch. So they do ask me a lot, and I try and give them. Now, I can't always.

This quote underscored Dinesh's commitment to accommodating children's preferences while also acknowledging the inherent constraints he faced, particularly regarding considerations of 'effective learning', as previously mentioned by Dinesh himself.

Wayne, another Year Lead teacher, shared examples of promoting children's agency in the context of teaching music. He provided specific examples from his teaching practice, highlighting how children frequently approached him with requests to learn specific instruments or explore particular musical genres. The teacher stated his openness to accommodating these requests, citing instances where they arranged for lessons in instruments not traditionally taught. Wayne emphasised the importance of tailoring the learning experience to the children's interests, noting that this approach enhanced their enjoyment and, consequently, their learning outcomes. At the same time Wayne expressed his view that certain subjects, such as mathematics, require a more rigid approach to ensure a solid understanding of foundational concepts. He emphasised the importance of having approval and support from senior leaders to experiment with different teaching approaches in subjects where the stakes are high (those in which children face extra pressure to perform well, such as English and mathematics).

The contributions from the Well-Being Lead shed further light on the school's approach to accommodating children's interests, particularly within the art curriculum. Aligning with other respondents, she emphasised the autonomy given to teachers in structuring lessons. She illustrated this point with an example of an art lesson focussed on sculpture construction. During this lesson, children were given wire and encouraged to create their own sculptures based on their interpretations and understanding informed by prior learning about Anthony Gormley's artwork. The Well-Being Lead underscored the significance of art lessons as a platform for children to integrate aspects of their culture into their work. She shared an example where a child offered insights about Islamic tiles and patterns during a lesson on Islamic art, highlighting how children actively contributed their cultural knowledge to enrich the learning experience.

South City State

At South City State (SCS), the Head Teacher noted significant pressure from curriculum content, including both national curriculum requirements and additional Department for Education (DfE) mandates. The school adopted a cross-curricular approach that attempted to integrate various elements while maintaining what they saw as essential knowledge. As the Head Teacher explained,

> [the school had a] cross curricula approach that brings in different elements of the national curriculum, but then also adds in elements of what we feel are the South City State curriculum, it enhances the rest of it. And I've got nothing that I can see in the near future that I would want to take out of the curriculum.

As our research was unfolding, the school decided to move away from the long-term planning that emphasised pupil activities towards emphasising the knowledge that they wanted children to acquire at each year of the primary school, hence the adoption of *knowledge organisers* (structured documents containing essential vocabulary and concepts for each topic) and *dual coding maps* (visual representations that pair text with images to enhance learning and retention). Regarding the involvement of children in curriculum design decisions, the Head Teacher readily acknowledged that the school had no formal process for soliciting their input. He noted, however, that the school's commitment to *Philosophy for Children* lessons helped to create a culture where children felt encouraged to voice their preferences and opinions. Also, teachers were encouraged to be responsive to children's interests and requests, modifying learning activities as needed to meet their needs while still aligning with pre-defined learning objectives. Overall, the Head Teacher emphasised that while there were structural constraints that limited the amount of choice and agency given to children, the school strove to create opportunities for meaningful engagement and collaboration between children and teachers.

The Assistant Head highlighted several key moments where children exercised agency. She mentioned 'teaching and learning reviews' as structured settings where children were encouraged to voice their opinions. According to her, these reviews provided a platform for children to reflect on their learning experiences and offer feedback on teaching methods and curriculum content. She described children as being highly discerning and critical in their feedback, indicating that they were capable of offering constructive criticism by identifying areas for improvement in teaching methods and suggesting alternative approaches based on their previous experiences. As she put it, 'they are so critical, they will be able to pull lessons apart and say, "well this should have been this way, we have done that before, it should be this way"'. Both the Head Teacher's and Assistant Head's accounts thus suggested that children in the school were at times actively engaged in expressing their views and empowered to contribute to discussions about their learning environment.

When prompted further, the Assistant Head elaborated on the ways in which children exercised agency and choice in learning. She explained, for example, that the school would leave summer term projects open-ended until the end of the year, allowing children to select topics based on their interests. She mentioned a project called 'journeys around the world', where children identified questions about a country or continent to guide their learning. This approach was intended to empower children to take ownership of their learning by driving the direction of their projects based on their interests.

One example of more frequent opportunities for pupils to make choices was the school providing different challenges for children to choose from. For example, after completing an initial whole class mathematics task, children were presented with two or three challenges from which they could select the one that aligned with their confidence level and abilities. The Assistant Head explained that this approach extended beyond mathematics to other subjects like geography, history, and religious education (RE). The example of RE was given where it was said that at the start of a unit of study the school would introduce a religion and invite children to generate questions based on their interests. According to the Assistant Head this child-generated inquiry drove the learning process throughout the week, giving children a sense of ownership over their learning.

One of the lessons that we observed during the research was an RE lesson. The children in the lesson were tasked with creating posters about the Five Pillars of Islam having done a 15-minute research session using iPads. The children had some autonomy in conducting research and designing their posters, but the overall structure of the lesson was teacher-led. The topic was set by the teacher, and children were assigned specific pillars to work on within predetermined teams, rather than being allowed to choose aspects based on their interests. The task permitted some self-direction within the pre-set structure of the lessons, but a greater degree of agency could have been achieved by allowing children to select their topics and form their own working groups.

The Assistant Head also commented on the integration of children's voices in the curriculum design. She discussed the balance between teacher-led and child-led learning, acknowledging the constraints posed by the national curriculum. While the school had to adhere to the requirements of the National Curriculum, they had introduced a more philosophical and conceptual approach to curriculum mapping. Each half-term was centred around a key question, such as 'Is there value in everything?' This approach enabled the school to link broader concepts, like the idea of value, with specific subjects. For example, in geography, children would explore the significance of fair-trade practices in Africa, making connections between the overarching question and the subject matter. By framing learning in this way, the school aimed to encourage children to think critically and philosophically, fostering curiosity and engagement in the learning process. The Assistant Head explained that while teachers designed the topics and questions, there was an element of openness in the key questions, allowing input from children. In this way, the school incorporated children's voices and interests into the curriculum design process.

The teachers who taught the case-study children offered their perspectives on giving children agency and choice during lessons. In the final interview the then former curriculum lead acknowledged the importance of offering choices to children in learning, mentioning her implementation of 'free writes' in English planning. She described how choices were provided within certain parameters, such as giving children a topic but allowing them to choose the form of their writing (e.g. letter, diary, poster). The Head of the Curriculum emphasised the benefits of giving children some freedom and choice in their learning, noting that it prevented them from feeling stuck in their learning, and allowed them to express themselves. She also highlighted the need for different levels of choice depending on individual children's needs and abilities.

Reflecting specifically on the link between particular subjects and children's agency, the Assistant Head acknowledged that some subjects may inherently offer more opportunities for children to make choices and be freer in their learning. She also described the efforts invested by subject leads into making core subjects more enjoyable and engaging. For example, the mathematics lead organised code-breaking competitions, while the English lead facilitated writing trips and workshops with external partners like the organisation called the *Ministry of Stories*.[1]

Mina reflected on her experience implementing choices in her classroom, particularly in response to discussions with colleagues, but also learning about choice theory[2] and its implications for classroom behaviour and learning. While lessons were pre-planned by the teacher, Mina ensured that her children had opportunities to exercise agency in various aspects of their learning journey. One way in which children exercised agency was through the choices they made regarding their effort and engagement in tasks. After completing the main tasks, children were given the choice to challenge themselves further. While acknowledging that some subjects may be more prescribed by the national curriculum than others, Mina strove to allow for children's input, such as allowing them to choose between different starter tasks, or levels of work in English or mathematics.

In terms of classroom organisation, Mina adopted a mixed-ability approach, considering both academic ability and behavioural dynamics. Although children did not choose their work partners themselves, Mina monitored their interactions closely and provided opportunities for adjustments in partnerships if needed. From her perspective this approach allowed for productive collaboration while promoting inclusivity and peer support within the classroom, for example, the teacher ensuring that children with a range of different abilities were encouraged to work together. Mina also talked about encouraging children to ask questions and raise topics of interest but acknowledged that she faced challenges in finding time to support their inquiries effectively. She acknowledged that while providing children with choices could be beneficial, it also required careful management and consideration of age-appropriateness.

Sylvia expressed a clear desire to empower her children with more agency. However, she highlighted several constraints that limited her ability to provide children with more opportunities for agency and choice in their learning. According to her, one of the main constraints was the need to ensure that children learned specific content and skills required by the national curriculum. For instance, in English lessons, teachers often selected books that contained the themes and vocabulary needed to support learning objectives. While this approach aimed to expose children to high-quality literature and relevant concepts, it restricted their freedom to choose reading materials based on personal interests or preferences. Similarly, she mentioned the pressure of addressing challenging topics and concepts during mathematics lessons, which did not always align with children's interests. While she wanted to incorporate fun and engaging activities, the curriculum often demanded a focus on more difficult or less appealing topics that she felt that children would not actively choose to explore. For her this emphasis on academic rigour tended to limit opportunities for children's agency in the learning process.

Despite these constraints Sylvia demonstrated a commitment to finding opportunities within the existing framework to accommodate children's interests. For example, she implemented a 'wonder box' session on Fridays, where children could ask questions about topics that they were curious about. This session allowed children to explore their interests and encouraged independent inquiry. Sylvia reflected on the positive outcomes she observed when children were given agency in their learning. She emphasised how this approach enhanced their school experience, leading to increased enjoyment and engagement. She suggested that granting children agency resulted in deeper learning experiences. Allowing children to choose topics of interest and make decisions about their learning made them active participants in the process, leading to a more profound understanding of the material. She also reflected on her struggles with using extrinsic rewards to motivate children, highlighting her preference for fostering intrinsic motivation. She believed that by giving children agency, schools could reduce the need for external incentives, encouraging a genuine desire to learn and explore.

Another teacher, Fatima, expressed concerns about the practical challenges of implementing choices within a structured curriculum and limited time frame. She worried about balancing the need to cover the core curriculum of national curriculum content with providing opportunities for choice and exploration. Fatima also raised the issue of ensuring that choices were meaningful and productive for children, noting that some children may struggle to take advantage of freedom if not given clear guidance and support. Additionally, she highlighted the importance of teachers' need to be supported by school leadership in implementing choice-based approaches without fear of repercussions.

Northern City State

In contrast to both SCS's state school approach and SCI's independent school model, Northern City State (NCS) developed a distinctive approach to curriculum. It was fundamentally shaped by their distinctive conceptualisation of knowledge, which the Head described as 'a unique interpretation of what knowledge is.' This development was partly in response to national-level discussions influenced by Ofsted, the national inspectorate. In 2017, Ofsted acknowledged that primary schools had become overly focussed on statutory tests at the expense of broader curriculum coverage (Spielman, 2018). Their revised inspection guidance aimed to expand curriculum focus, though this initiative became dominated by the 'deep dive' approach. Under this system, inspectors would examine a subject's policy and programme of study, culminating in classroom observations where they might sit next to a pupil and ask them specific factual questions – for example, questioning a pupil about Roman occupation dates in England. A student's inability to answer such questions would be considered evidence regarding teaching quality and school performance.

While England's national curriculum emphasised a knowledge-based approach, which Ofsted's inspections reflected, NCS developed a markedly different perspective. The Associate Head characterised their approach as 'how you shake the grounds, and really question the norms of what you do or don't understand.' This philosophy viewed knowledge as a social construction based on varying perspectives within each subject area, requiring critical examination for validity ('shake the grounds'). Such critical engagement demanded both sufficient subject understanding and awareness of how that subject is perceived, enabling meaningful questioning of received wisdom. This ambitious vision for children's knowledge acquisition became a central thread throughout their curriculum. The school aimed for children to engage with and challenge knowledge through 'mature themes that they [the children] wanted to learn about.' Thus, student agency was explicitly embedded in their curriculum rationale through consultation about learning content – a significant departure from both the national curriculum's knowledge conception and Ofsted's assessment approach.

Another significant influence on the school's conception of knowledge came through research. The Associate Head's master's degree research, which involved interviewing teachers about their knowledge conceptions, directly informed the school's curriculum development. Her research project had originated from concerns about schools' responses to the knowledge-based national curriculum and the Chief Inspector's emphasis on knowledge as knowing and remembering more. The Associate Head had encountered 'horror stories of schools generating fact files of knowledge and imposing them on children'.

NCS developed a sophisticated approach to curriculum design that balanced national curriculum requirements with their distinctive child-led development strategy. The school utilised various methods to ensure a holistic learning experience. Periodically, they suspended formal curriculum delivery for themed weeks that emphasised specific aspects of learning or personal development. During a themed week titled 'Me Time', children had extensive opportunities to deeply engage with personal interests such as cooking, creative arts, and gardening. The school also encouraged staff to think creatively beyond traditional classroom settings to make a positive impact in the community. During the 'Make Our Mark' week, teachers utilised external spaces as classrooms and explored ways to contribute positively to the community. This initiative fostered innovative collaborations with local organisations like car dealerships, conservation groups, and food banks, highlighting the school's commitment to broader societal engagement and meaningful learning experiences. This emphasis on community impact aligned with another key aspect of the school's teaching approach: leveraging and promoting children's cultural capital.

Despite the senior leadership's perception of the overall success of NCS' curriculum development strategy, teachers at the school were cognisant of its potential limitations. The teachers observed that relying on children's ideas and interests to shape learning topics often resulted in suggestions based on their existing knowledge and experiences. This approach could constrain the curriculum within the boundaries of what children were already aware of or exposed to, potentially overlooking lesser-known or unfamiliar topics that could be equally engaging and valuable for their learning. For example, children might not express interest in learning about the English Civil War simply because they lack awareness of it.

Teachers at NCS also noted the significant impact of children's family backgrounds on their agency and learning interests. Coby, a teacher at the school, highlighted that children with opportunities to explore diverse activities and ideas at home were more confident and articulate in expressing their interests and making informed choices about their learning. Conversely children with limited exposure to varied experiences might struggle to identify their interests and make decisions about their education. Coby emphasised the crucial role of family environments in fostering children's agency. In his opinion families that encouraged exploration, discussion, and exposure to different experiences empowered children to make positive choices and pursue their interests actively. In contrast, children without such opportunities might exhibit less developed agency and struggle to articulate their preferences and passions. Understanding and acknowledging the impact of family backgrounds on children's agency were important for teachers in supporting children to develop their interests, confidence, and sense of agency within the learning environment at NCS. A perception that children from certain backgrounds might struggle with exercising agency did not stop the school adopting their approach with all children.

Year 5 Teacher Kris and Year 6 Teacher Jane both reflected on the intricacies of developing a curriculum rooted in child-initiated topics. Kris emphasised the importance of critically evaluating children's suggestions, noting that not all proposed topics may offer substantial opportunities for deep learning. He viewed teachers as discussion partners, guiding children's inquiries towards more fruitful and curriculum-aligned areas of exploration. The goal, he noted, was not to 'indulge' all children's requests without consideration, but to scaffold their interests towards meaningful learning experiences by asking probing questions to deepen their understanding.

Echoing Kris' sentiments, Jane shared a similar perspective based on her experience co-constructing curriculum maps with children. She recounted instances where children brought in objects related to war, a topic they had already studied in Year 5. Rather than dismissing these ideas, Jane guided them towards exploring related topics like civilisations and engineering, encouraging deeper inquiry into their interests. Her approach aimed to challenge children to think critically about their learning goals and extend their inquiries into broader themes. Jane believed in directly connecting children's interests to the curriculum, seeing opportunities in topics like volcanoes or land formations to engage children more deeply in learning.

Similarly, Coby viewed the school's curriculum approach as a commitment to valuing and incorporating children's agency and interests while aligning with national curriculum requirements. He emphasised the importance of creatively integrating children's ideas into the learning process while ensuring alignment with educational standards. For instance, if children showed interest in historical figures, the school developed history units that met both children's interests and curriculum criteria.

Year 5 Teacher Josie viewed the national curriculum as a benefit rather than a restriction, finding that its requirements provided clarity and direction in curriculum planning, especially as a new teacher. She felt more confident and guided by these standards, ensuring essential topics in geography, history, and other subjects were covered comprehensively throughout the year. Josie embraced a co-constructed curriculum approach that considered children's interests while ensuring the academic subjects were covered thoroughly. Josie believed that the national curriculum was not only beneficial for herself but also for the children, helping them understand the importance and relevance of their learning. For example, if children expressed interest in oceans, she could connect this interest to specific academic subjects like geography, science, and history, demonstrating the interdisciplinary nature of learning. When asked about the importance of linking children's interests to specific academic subjects or the national curriculum, Josie emphasised the need to provide children with tools and foundational knowledge for their educational progress. Mapping interests to subjects gave purpose and direction to their learning journey, allowing children to build upon their knowledge year after year. Josie highlighted the importance of striking a balance between engaging topics that capture children's interest and ensuring they have a solid foundation of knowledge to carry forward into their future education.

Engagement was emphasised as a critical aspect by teachers at NCS who believed that giving children agency was essential for ensuring a successful learning process, especially in promoting effective behaviour for learning. The distinction between engagement and compliance was highlighted, particularly by Kris in the context of student learning and classroom dynamics. Kris explained that compliance referred to children following instructions or directives without being personally invested or interested in the learning content. In contrast, engagement signified a deeper level of involvement, enthusiasm, and ownership over the learning process. He pointed out that while compliance may lead to children adhering to rules or instructions, it does not necessarily translate into genuine interest or active participation in learning activities. The challenge arises when children lack engagement due to a lack of intrinsic motivation or interest in the subject matter, which can impede learning outcomes and make teaching more challenging. Kris emphasised that the school's approach focussed on fostering engagement over mere compliance. The distinctly child-centred approach allowed children to shape their educational experiences, creating a learning environment where children felt excited, curious, and motivated to explore topics that genuinely interested them.

Year 4 teacher Tracy highlighted the challenge posed by fixed curriculum timelines on children's agency. Tracy recalled an incident where a child expressed interest in learning about the Suffragettes mid-year but was unable to influence the curriculum because it had already been planned. Incorporating ongoing opportunities for children to influence learning topics based on emerging interests and experiences throughout the year, from the teachers' perspective, would offer a more comprehensive role for children's agency in curriculum development. This approach would allow children to have a more active and participatory role in shaping their learning experiences based on their evolving interests and curiosities.

Year 5 teacher Kris and Year 4 teacher Coby, in separate interviews, discussed the varying perceptions children had regarding the importance and enjoyment of different subjects within the curriculum, and both emphasised efforts to reshape these perceptions through engaging activities and real-world connections. Kris acknowledged that children may perceive certain subjects as more important or serious based on the amount of instructional time devoted to them. For instance, if a school places greater emphasis on teaching mathematics and English compared to subjects like Spanish or music, children might infer that mathematics and English are more significant or essential. To address this perception Kris emphasised the importance of framing all subjects as valuable and meaningful, advocating for connecting each subject to real-world applications and demonstrating how skills acquired in different areas can lead to various career paths or personal achievements. For example, excelling in design and technology (D&T) could pave the way for a career in architecture, while proficiency in music could lead to becoming a renowned composer or performer. Kris also stressed the role of educators in fostering enthusiasm and engagement across all subjects by delivering lessons in creative and interactive ways, such as incorporating role-playing, outdoor activities, or technology into mathematics and English lessons. By making learning experiences enjoyable and dynamic, teachers can help dispel the notion that certain subjects are merely 'work' while others are 'fun', while also advocating for consistency in enthusiasm and creativity across all subjects to ensure children receive a well-rounded education that stimulates their curiosity and encourages them to excel in diverse areas.

Similarly, Coby addressed the perceptions children have regarding subject importance and enjoyment. Coby noted that while subjects like English and mathematics are often perceived as serious or essential, others such as physical education (PE), D&T, music, and art are sometimes viewed as less academic or purely recreational, leading children to undervalue the learning experiences offered by these subjects. To combat this, Coby implemented activities demonstrating the educational value of subjects like PE. For instance, during cross-country activities, children learned about sports analysis as a career, watching videos of professionals in action and reflecting on their own performances. By integrating learning experiences with real-world applications and career pathways, Coby aims to help children recognise the significance of all subjects in their educational journey. Additionally, Coby highlighted the importance of teachers articulating the relevance of subjects to children's future lives and careers beyond their practical uses, showcasing how subject-specific skills are employed in various professions. Coby also sought to make subjects like English and mathematics more enjoyable by framing activities in engaging ways, such as using practical activities like relay races for times tables or integrating interesting texts that resonate with children's interests.

Both Kris and Coby's approaches focussed on bridging the gap between perceived importance and enjoyment of subjects by incorporating real-world connections, career exploration, and engaging activities to showcase the educational value inherent in all areas of the curriculum. This approach aimed to foster a more holistic and positive view of learning among children, ensuring they recognise the significance and enjoyment of each subject encountered in their educational journey.

Overall, the teachers at NCS did not perceive the national curriculum as an insurmountable barrier to children's agency. Unlike in some schools, where teachers might feel their hands were tied by national curriculum requirements, the teachers at NCS successfully aligned the requirements of the national curriculum with their philosophy and practices of engaging children's choices and interests. They leveraged children's agency to creatively achieve learning objectives across subjects, ensuring that children's interests were not merely accommodated but skilfully integrated to meet curriculum standards. They believed that this approach fostered deeper engagement and relevance in learning. The teachers' reflections underscore the nuanced approach needed to effectively integrate children's agency into curriculum design. It entailed balancing children's interests with curriculum goals, guiding meaningful inquiries, and aligning child-driven topics with educational objectives. This reflective and dialogic process was aimed at promoting deeper children's engagement while upholding arguably more important aspects of learning and education.

Assessment, accountability, and children's learning

Assessment practices and their influence on children's agency manifested distinctly across the three schools, revealing complex tensions between accountability requirements and opportunities for children's agency.

South City Independent

At SCI, assessment revealed distinct tensions between independence and standardisation. Although not required to participate in the national statutory tests (SATs) mandatory for state schools in England, SCI had traditionally administered them alongside a range of additional assessments including Cognitive Ability Tests, Verbal Reasoning Tests, and National Foundation for Educational Research (NFER) progress tests. Teachers also conducted regular classroom-based assessments as part of their weekly instruction.

This multi-layered assessment approach prompted senior leadership to reevaluate their testing strategy. They identified two key drivers for change: first, the desire to more fully embrace their status as an independent school, viewing assessment autonomy as fundamental to the meaning of 'independence'; and second, the need to align assessments more closely with teachers' instructional needs and student support. Through consultations with school governors, leadership made the case that children were experiencing assessment overload, leading to their decision to discontinue participation in state school statutory testing.

The school's Well-Being Lead provided crucial perspective on this decision, noting how the existing emphasis on academic achievement and preparation for selective examinations like the 11-plus stemmed largely from parental expectations. Drawing from direct experience with student mental health, the Well-Being Lead identified exam performance as a primary source of anxiety among students, observing particularly elevated stress levels as children progressed through Year 5 and beyond.

The 11-plus examination emerged as a critical external influence on SCI's curriculum, driven by parental aspirations for their children's admission to prestigious secondary schools. The school identified the 11-plus as more academically rigorous than national SATs tests, particularly in its emphasis on independent thinking. This recognition led them to view SATs preparation as potentially counterproductive, requiring children to 'relearn' different testing approaches when preparing for the more challenging 11-plus examinations.

The Covid period's suspension of statutory testing requirements provided SCI, like other schools, temporary relief from SATs administration. However, unlike state schools, SCI could choose to permanently discontinue these tests, a decision that aligned with their broader educational philosophy. The Deputy Head articulated this shift toward 'whole education'.

> So not only did we scrap SATs. We also scrapped something called EPIPS. Well, actually, we're getting that information from the NFERs [tests] and from the CATs, and actually, that's a bit more accurate and kind of on par with where we feel as teachers the children are at. So luckily because we are independent, we were allowed to [say], 'we don't want to do that'. We're putting too much pressure on these children. They should be getting the whole education. So again, that teaching to test – we don't do that.

While our classroom observations generally showed minimal focus on test preparation, one visit revealed nuanced insights into the school's assessment practices. During a 'non-verbal reasoning' lesson, we observed children working with stapled photocopied booklets and red Manila folders as the teacher reviewed answers from their textbook. The exercises involved describing shape transformations, such as 'rotation', which the teacher later confirmed was part of general 11-plus preparation. On the same day, we observed a different class conducting a spelling test, representing a distinct assessment tradition in English primary education. Unlike statutory tests or 11-plus preparations, spelling tests have been fundamental to primary education since its beginnings in England. Yet these tests, like all assessments, inevitably shape curricular content and delivery. In this observed lesson the teacher made sure the children were ready, then began the test using the following kinds of prompts:

Teacher: Test 6 . . . right, number one, 'stardom'
Teacher: 'Motherhood', number 2 . . . Number 3 'citizenship'.
Teacher: Who knows what 'chiefdom' means.
Pupil: An area owned by a chief.
Teacher: What do we call that word?
Pupil: Context.
Teacher: Excellent, someone's awake this afternoon.
Teacher: Has everyone got their spellings for this week?
Teacher: Casserole.
Pupil: Is it a kind of food?
Pupil: It's a dish made with noodles.
Teacher: Is it indeed – that's not the casserole that I have!
Teacher: How many of you reviewed your 11-plus practice paper last night?

Despite SCI's decision to discontinue voluntary participation in national statutory assessments, testing continued to shape their curriculum significantly, though through different channels. The 11-plus examination, in particular, exerted substantial influence over educational practices, largely driven by parental expectations. This emphasis on selective examination preparation notably constrained children's agency in their learning experiences.

While the school recognised the dominance of core subjects in their curriculum, they actively sought to enhance the status of subjects like music and art. However, their approach to elevating these subjects' importance paradoxically relied on introducing new assessments. This strategy, though well-intentioned, inadvertently reinforced the notion that a subject's educational value was fundamentally tied to its assessment structure, perpetuating rather than challenging the test-driven culture they had hoped to move away from.

South City State

At SCS, significant time pressures emerged from attempting to cover all necessary national curriculum elements for assessment. The Curriculum Lead highlighted the significant pressures of time that the school faced in attempting to cover all necessary national curriculum elements. A key issue was the lack of opportunity to delve sufficiently deeply into subject matter due to the need for relatively superficial coverage caused by an overly content-heavy curriculum. Statutory tests, known as 'SATs', were noted as a major contributor to this pressure, as they often result in a narrower focus in the curriculum to ensure children are prepared for the tests.

This emphasis on formal assessments, particularly in core subjects like mathematics and English, was also noted by the Assistant Head, who discussed the impact of these assessments on children's perceptions of different subjects. She observed that children often see subjects like art and PE as enjoyable, while subjects like mathematics and English are viewed more as 'work', largely because of the pressure associated with formal assessments. To counter this, the school actively worked to elevate the status of subjects like art, music, geography, and history. Initiatives such as half-term project competitions and the introduction of online assessments for geography and history were designed to engage children and highlight the importance of these subjects beyond the so-called core curriculum.

The Head Teacher noted the impact of the Covid-19 pandemic, including the first ever cancellation of national statutory tests in England since their inception from 1988 onwards. School inspections that were carried out by the inspectorate Ofsted were also postponed. The impact of the pandemic on all schools was profound. Families of children at SCS experienced a significant number of bereavements during the peaks of the pandemic. The school had to organise to deliver food to a significant number of families who were in particular difficulties. Teaching for most children had to be done online. The school was also designated as one that could remain open for children whose parents were deemed to be essential workers, for example staff in England's National Health Service. The normal school population of about 720 children was reduced to 100 children whose parents/carers were designated as essential workers, including some children from other schools that were closed. The Head Teacher reflected on this period, noting that with the pressures of Ofsted, SATs, and league tables removed, the school had been able to adopt a more creative and flexible approach to education. During that time the small number of children attending school had greater input into the activities they participated in, with more time for dialogue and opportunities for choice. This period, described by the Head Teacher as 'off curriculum', allowed for more experiential learning opportunities, such as working in the school vegetable garden and planning and cooking recipes in the school's fully equipped classroom kitchen that included at least 15 cookers: one cooker per two children in a class of 30.

This shift during the pandemic underscored the significant impact that formal assessments have on shaping the curriculum and limiting children's agency. When these pressures were temporarily lifted, and when pupil numbers were significantly reduced, the school was able to provide a more holistic and child-centred educational experience.

There were fewer examples where assessment was identified as a key issue in our time spent working with the school. We reflected on whether this could have been related to the school's ethos of striving to support children and their families in a very deprived area: a focus on helping children to jump the assessment hurdles that government required. The Head Teacher and teachers naturally strove to ensure that children performed as well as possible in statutory assessments. It was felt by the school that the background of the children necessitated the ways of working that we describe in this chapter. Assessment issues featured more prominently in our experiences with the other schools, so we remain uncertain as to why assessment seemed less of an issue in relation to SCS.

Northern City State

NCS took a distinct approach to assessment. The school recognised that the national statutory tests could have an undesirable narrowing effect on the curriculum. However, their strong educational rationale enabled them to mitigate this narrowing while acknowledging certain compromises, such as teaching formal grammar more frequently than before the 2014 national curriculum which they approached through brief, regular sessions. They maintained confidence that their pupils would pass the Year 6 statutory tests 'with flying colours'. They attributed their pupils' success to the school's curriculum design, particularly the connections made between subjects and the breadth of study children experienced. They also differentiated between the quality of various statutory tests, expressing particular concern about the grammar test which they described, with diplomatic understatement, as

> a little bit more frustrating because it is quite a binary check, and I don't think it does justice to the rich grammatical understanding that children leave primary school with. But I think that [grammatical understanding] comes across in the [children's] writing which is where it should do.

Their use of 'binary check' referred to the grammar test's simplistic assessment of factual knowledge, such as noun identification in sentences. Instead, they emphasised the importance of assessing grammar through purposeful writing, which they believed the statutory teacher assessments of writing achieved more validly.

Assessment practices at NCS manifested notably in their approach to class grouping. Ability grouping, where children are organised based on academic abilities to target specific learning needs, was implemented particularly in Years 5 and 6 for subjects like English. The groups were structured as follows:

High Achievers: Children performing beyond national expectations received more challenging and specialised materials, including 'stretch and challenge' questions to enhance their learning.

National Expectation Level: Children working towards meeting national expectations focused on materials aligned with standard benchmarks.

Lower Attainment Group: This smaller group received additional support through a curriculum broken down into more manageable steps, with adjusted learning pace to ensure comprehension and progress.

The Pupil Research Lead at NCS explained that this ability grouping approach aimed to support children's performance in standardised assessments like SATs. The perceived success of this practice in improving examination experience and performance led to its extension to Year 2.

This practice of ability grouping, while aimed at optimising educational outcomes, can have implications on children's agency and choice in learning. One of the potential effects is limited diversity of learning experiences: when children are grouped solely based on their academic abilities, there is a risk of limiting their exposure to a wider range of learning experiences. In addition, children miss out on interacting with peers who have different learning styles and perspectives, which could enrich their overall educational experience. Ability grouping often dictates the pace and content of instruction for children within each group. This can result in reduced autonomy for children in selecting topics or deciding on the depth and breadth of topics they want to explore. Children will have less opportunity to pursue areas of personal interest or passion outside of the predetermined curriculum for their ability group. Another significant implication of ability grouping is its impact on children's self-perception and confidence. As discussed in Chapter 2, ability grouping can significantly damage children's self-esteem and their identity both as learners and more broadly. Children in lower attainment groups might develop feelings of inadequacy or lower self-esteem, while high achievers may experience pressure to continually perform at a high level. Ability grouping can unintentionally reinforce stereotypes about children's academic capabilities based on perceived ability levels. This can perpetuate fixed mindsets and limit opportunities for children to challenge themselves or break out of assigned categories. Finally, children's motivation and engagement can be influenced by their placement in ability groups. Those in higher groups may be more motivated by challenging tasks, while children in lower groups may feel demotivated or disengaged if they perceive their assignments as too easy or repetitive. The negative impacts of ability grouping seemed to be mitigated at NCS through comprehensive practices promoting children's agency. Peer collaboration opportunities, diverse learning experiences, and a child-led curriculum approach were implemented across all year groups, suggesting a nuanced approach to maintaining children's agency despite structural constraints.

The school and society

The relationship between schools and their broader social contexts significantly shaped how children's agency was understood and supported across our three settings. Each school's approach reflected distinct responses to their communities' needs and expectations.

South City Independent

At SCI, the relationship between school and society manifested primarily through the school's perceptions of parental expectations and the pressures of preparing students for elite secondary schools. While the school demonstrated efforts to incorporate children's interests and cultural perspectives into curriculum design, deeper examination revealed limitations in children's involvement in curriculum development itself. In our interviews with the Head Teacher and teachers, we probed into whether children not only express their views on existing curriculum offerings and learning approaches but also actively participate in shaping their design. We sought to assess the degree to which children were afforded opportunities to exercise agency in relation to their learning experiences. By understanding the extent of children's involvement in curriculum development, we aimed to uncover the depth of collaborative decision-making processes within the school and assess the extent to which children played an active role in shaping their educational journey.

The Head Teacher described two key practices promoting children's agency in the school. First, Year 6 children actively participated in curriculum development, contributing age-appropriate ideas for different year groups. While we were unable to verify these contributions without access to the relevant documents, the Head Teacher emphasised their commitment to incorporating children's opinions and preferences in curriculum decisions. Second, the school empowered Year 6 children through summer term projects, where they could pursue research topics of personal interest, fostering engagement through independent learning choices.

Interviews with staff revealed an awareness of the benefits that came with the school's increased autonomy in shaping the curriculum. This flexibility allowed teachers to make curriculum decisions that aligned with their pedagogical strengths, the requirements of the national curriculum, and the assessed needs of their children. Teachers were committed to selecting topics they believed would effectively engage and resonate with their children. However, children's voices were absent from these decision-making processes. When asked about the possibility of giving children more freedom, voice, and choice in their learning journey, teachers highlighted the challenges associated with implementing such practices. They pointed to constraints arising from familial and societal expectations, particularly those related to academic standards and assessments.

Practical considerations were also emphasised. Certain subjects, especially those considered foundational for progression to prestigious institutions, required a more structured approach to ensure essential content was covered and children were adequately prepared for critical assessments like the 11-plus exams. Dinesh specifically highlighted concerns related to student age, maturity, and the academic culture of the school, noting the pressures of exam preparation. Lauren expressed concerns about the logistical difficulties of accommodating diverse interests and the potential challenges in reaching a consensus among children with varied preferences. She also acknowledged her own lack of confidence and empowerment in involving children in the curriculum development process, suggesting that such initiatives would likely need to originate from the management level rather than individual teachers. As she put it, 'It would probably come from management down. Do we want to meet with children and ask them what they want to do?'

The discussions with staff at the school illuminate the complexities of balancing curricular flexibility with the pressures of academic standards and societal expectations. While teachers appreciated the autonomy to tailor the curriculum to better suit their children, the absence of children's own voices in these decisions reveals a gap in promoting agency in the learning process. The challenges of implementing children's choice and voice are compounded by practical and cultural factors within the school, suggesting that a shift towards greater children's involvement in curriculum development would require both institutional support and a reconsideration of the existing educational priorities.

South City State

At SCS, located in an area of high deprivation, the Head Teacher reflected on broader structural factors affecting the role of children in shaping their educational experiences. While he felt that the concept of 'child-led learning' had gained traction in education at various times, the Head Teacher emphasised the need for balance, especially, as he saw it, in school communities that included families with limited financial resources, and by implication experiences, such as the community that the school served. He noted the significant impact of demographic factors, such as child poverty and what he saw as parents' limitations in providing educational support, on the school's approach to education and curriculum. In an area marked by high levels of deprivation, the school took a proactive approach to provide enriching experiences and opportunities that it was felt were not readily available to children outside of the school environment. Hence a large part of the curriculum was pre-planned and therefore less open to children's own input.

At SCS, the approach to children's agency was multifaceted, influenced by both theories of education held by the head and staff, and factors external to the school. The Head Teacher acknowledged the impact of government policies and local initiatives on teacher and children's agency within the school community. An example was provided where a group of Head Teachers in the borough were presented with the mayor's education pledge, which included goals that the Head Teachers disagreed with.

> And there's just been a new elected mayor come into power in [name of Borough], and we got presented with the mayor's education pledge, and a lot of it that we as Heads disagreed with, so there was that whole thing of, 'hang on a minute, we've got absolutely no agency here'. We're being presented with a set of goals that we don't agree with. Some of the things that we as a body of Heads would want aren't on there, and that's without even getting to the children's level of saying, 'actually, where's their voice?'

This quote highlights a lack of agency felt by the Head Teachers, and the frustration felt when they were presented with a mandate that they felt did not align with their values or goals. Despite being key stakeholders in the education system, their voices were seen to have been marginalised or ignored in decision-making processes. This firsthand experience informed the Head Teacher's empathetic perspective on children's agency in the school. He emphasised the importance of local decision-making and agency at all levels, including among children, even though in practice affording agency to staff or children was mediated by the range of beliefs, for example about children's home lives, and other factors we have described so far in this chapter.

The SCS approach demonstrated a profound commitment to serving their children and families. While the school valued children's agency, they recognised an inherent tension between promoting agency and addressing what they perceived as the specific needs of children from their economically disadvantaged area. Teachers provided examples of how children's agency was incorporated into certain lessons, while also acknowledging the limitations on expanding such opportunities. Although children's agency featured prominently in the school's educational philosophy, it had not been formally integrated into the institutional structure of education delivery.

Northern City State

NCS developed distinctive approaches to connecting school and society, particularly through their behaviour management systems. NCS utilised *ClassDojo*, a widely used behaviour management system in schools, to promote children's agency within a structured framework. This system operates on a points-based reward model where children earn 'dojos' for various achievements and behaviours. Children who met their target by the half-term had the opportunity to qualify for a special 'dojo treat'.

During the pandemic, NCS responded to children's desires, following Covid-19 lockdowns, by implementing dojo treats based on their feedback. These treats were designed to provide memorable experiences aligned with children's preferences, extending beyond academic rewards. Children actively participated in selecting treats through class discussions, voting, and input via the School Council. Treats included creative activities like a beach experience recreated at the school, a farm visit with rabbits and sheep, Easter egg hunts, and decorating gingerbread houses.

We observed a ClassDojo treat which celebrated the Queen's Platinum Jubilee. This particular treat was not chosen by the children. However, the Pupil Research Lead emphasised the importance of children's choice in shaping the experience. For instance, children had the opportunity to decorate their own crowns and select items for the festive menu. By involving children in these decisions, NCS aimed to cultivate ownership and engagement, enhancing the impact of rewards on children's motivation and enjoyment, although children's level of involvement in this was less profound than some of the other curriculum strategies that the school had developed to support children's agency.

Similar to Dojo treats, the school leveraged Golden Time to promote children's agency and engagement in school life. At the time of the study, the traditional concept of Golden Time, where children have unstructured free time as a reward, was being reconsidered. The school's leadership expressed discomfort with this approach, feeling it teaches children to endure the school week for the sake of a brief period of unstructured play. Instead, the school was redefining golden time as an opportunity for meaningful relationship building. One initiative was 'Flashback Friday', which allowed children to spend time with peers from other classes, sharing their knowledge and learning experiences. The aim was to transform golden time from a scheduled break into a valued part of the week centred around building connections and boosting self-esteem through sharing knowledge and experiences.

By the end of our research project the school had continued to develop their thinking, not least because they had started working with a primary school that had newly joined their Trust. This new school had many more children with backgrounds in lower socio-economic status. The NCS experience of helping the school to improve meant that their philosophies about curriculum came into 'tensions with external verification': the need to improve statutory test results and the Ofsted grade the next time the school new to the Trust was to be inspected. The Executive Head began working with the new school by empowering the school staff because it was felt that in the past they had not been involved in the processes of curriculum development. As part of a small group interview, the Associate Head described the journey that she felt she had been on with the new school in order to help them improve their curriculum:

So that is what our work, our conversations have been sort of focusing on, around what are our parameters, what are our beliefs? What do we hold strong to? What do we let go? What do we adopt? Where we work collaboratively let's not reinvent the wheel, let's learn from each other. So there's been a lot of giving and taking, hasn't there, I suppose around the way we view that. And the conversations have kept going back to curriculum intent and purpose and the why. And that is I suppose where the demographic [SES] kind of conversations come in, because for our sponsor school, yes, the demographic is very different, but it's not an excuse for the curriculum. It's a purpose for how the curriculum is designed, and therefore it's an ambitious curriculum that meets the needs of those children. And our two intents [of the two schools] look very, very different, and that is right that they look different. However principally . . . [the staff in the other school] follow the same purpose and pathway. So creativity, curiosity, comprehension, connectivity, all those elements of curriculum design are there. The way they manifest themselves looks different in the different schools.

NCS' curriculum approach offers a potential model for other schools to adapt. The key to their success lay in maintaining core beliefs, purposes, and pathways, while allowing flexibility in implementation details which were 'very different'. The effectiveness of this approach was evidenced by dramatic improvements in statutory test results, with the percentage of Year 6 children achieving the national average in reading, writing, and mathematics, rising from 33% or 36% to 80% in the school that had relatively recently joined the trust. Through careful collaborative management, their curriculum development successfully balanced the demands of external verification with their commitment to an agentic curriculum.

Our study of these three schools revealed distinctly different approaches to children's agency, each shaped by unique institutional contexts and constraints. SCI, despite having the greatest statutory independence, found its approach to agency limited by parental expectations and examination pressures. NCS developed a comprehensive philosophy of children's agency that permeated all aspects of school life, while SCS balanced agency against their perceived responsibilities to their disadvantaged community. Each school's distinctive response to the structural constraints provides valuable insights into supporting children's agency within different institutional contexts.

The findings of our research prompt crucial questions about how educational structures might better support children's agency while meeting educational standards and requirements. This complex interplay between institutional structures and children's agency lies at the heart of contemporary primary education in England but also shares many characteristics with other countries and regions. In our final chapter, we explore the broader implications of these insights for educational policy and practice, examining how schools might foster environments that enable meaningful agency while maintaining academic rigour and addressing societal expectations. By bringing together our analysis of both children's experiences and institutional frameworks, we can better understand how to create educational environments that truly support children's agency within the realities of modern schooling.

Notes

1 See *How Writing Works: From the invention of the alphabet to the rise of social media* by Dominic Wyse for a chapter reporting the evaluation of a three-year study of The Ministry of Stories.
2 The teacher did not specify the source of the theory, but we assume they were referring to William Glasser's Choice Theory, which is often applied in schools for classroom management.

Reference

Spielman, A. (2018). *The annual report of Her Majesty's chief inspector of education, children's services and skills 2017/18* (HC 1707). Her Majesty's Stationery Office.

8

CHILDREN'S AGENCY AND PRIMARY EDUCATION

Throughout this book, we have explored the fundamental issues of children's agency and the curriculum in relation to social structures. Against the backdrop of growing international recognition of children's rights and evolving approaches to curriculum design, this final chapter brings these elements together to examine how they interact and shape children's experiences in school. Our research across Northern City State (NCS), South City Independent (SCI), and South City State (SCS) demonstrates how children's agency is shaped by the structures within and outside the school walls. The final part of this chapter puts forward recommendations for education policy and practice based on our new concept of 'structured freedom'.

Children's choice and agency in primary schools

Our research revealed a profound connection between opportunities for choice, children's agency, and their motivation and engagement in primary school settings. This finding aligns with broader international evidence about the value of learner-centred approaches and the importance of children's participation in their education. The interaction between choice and agency manifested differently across our study schools, each offering unique insights into how these constructs play out in practice. NCS provided particularly rich evidence of how school structures can enable agency. The school's institutional commitment to children's agency was manifested through child-led curriculum design and ongoing participatory decision-making. These structural foundations enabled meaningful, comprehensive and sustained agency in practice, where children actively participated in shaping their curriculum, their learning activities, and the physical and cultural environment of their school. The child-led curriculum proved especially significant, allowing children to explore personal interests with the teachers meeting national curriculum

DOI: 10.4324/9781003227779-8

requirements, effectively embedding opportunities for individual choice in one of schooling's most essential aspects. Children's own descriptions of their engagement with learning, both in and outside formal learning hours, revealed how this approach consistently nurtured their sense of agency.

The initial structural conditioning through child-centred policies and participatory mechanisms enabled social interaction through children's active engagement in shaping their learning environment. This interaction led to reinforcing and expanding agency-supporting structures. At NCS, this emerged as a distinctive school culture where agency became embedded in daily practice. The transformation of structural opportunities into lived experiences of agency demonstrates how affordances develop through interaction. Opportunities at the structural level become actualised through children's recognition and engagement in practice, leading to an enhanced sense of agency in their daily experiences. This process shows how structures can be transformed through human agency over time.

While NCS exemplified a high degree of integration between structure and agency, SCS and SCI offered insights into how agency operates within more constrained contexts. These variations mirror broader patterns of schooling regionally, nationally, and internationally, where different educational contexts have developed varying approaches to balancing structure and agency, as discussed in the first two chapters. In these schools, structures were characterised by a more top-down approach, particularly in curriculum and lesson design. Yet even within these more structured environments, opportunities for agency emerged in specific spaces, from extracurricular activities and after-school clubs to the shaping of physical environments and summer projects, reflecting the multidimensional nature of agency.

Our examination of School Councils across the three schools provided particularly revealing insights into how institutional mechanisms operate. At NCS, the Council existed as a formal structure for student participation, representing a concrete manifestation of the school's commitment to children's agency. In practice, this manifested through children's involvement in decision-making across various aspects of school life, from curriculum choices to environmental improvements. Despite some gaps in children's understanding of the Council's formal structure, they nevertheless experienced a genuine sense of agency through seeing their input create real change. This generated a self-reinforcing cycle in which successful experiences strengthened children's sense of agency, empowering them to take further agentic action.

SCI presented a different and more nuanced pattern. The School Council wielded significant influence in non-academic areas of school life, yet its absence from academic matters proved significant. The lack of structures for agency in academic domains created a divided experience of agency for children. This division highlighted how institutional structures can simultaneously enable and constrain agency in different spheres of school life. At SCS, the absence of a Council structure demonstrated even how the lack of formal mechanisms can limit opportunities for children's agency.

This comparative analysis suggests that fostering children's agency requires a comprehensive approach. The global movement toward recognising children's rights, combined with evolving understanding of curriculum development and implementation, highlights how supporting children's agency demands attention not just to formal mechanisms but to how these mechanisms translate into actual practices and meaningful experiences for children.

The impact of assessments and the implementation gap

While formal mechanisms like School Councils represent one way of supporting agency, our research revealed that systemic factors, particularly assessment systems, played an equally powerful role in shaping children's experiences. National assessment requirements, performance metrics, and institutional accountability frameworks including school inspections create fundamental conditions that shape educational experiences. These structures profoundly influence teaching practices, curriculum delivery, and assessment preparations, which children experience through their perceptions of subject hierarchies and their sense of agency in learning.

Reflecting broader international patterns in educational assessment, these influences manifested distinctively across our study schools. At SCI and SCS, high-stakes assessment structures were a strong influence on school life, leading to practices that prioritised English and mathematics over other subjects. Children experienced this prioritisation as a clear subject hierarchy that constrained their ability to explore broader interests. Even at NCS, where structures promoting agency were strong, the power of assessment requirements, and other accountability pressures such as Ofsted inspections, at times overrode these, for example during periods of statutory national tests and other assessments. This pattern shows how assessment pressures can reinforce particular teaching approaches despite a school's broader commitment to children's agency. The emphasis on high-stakes assessments, particularly evident in SCI's focus on the 11-plus exam, created what Bernstein (1975) termed 'strong classification' – rigid boundaries between subject areas that reinforced existing power structures. Such classification creates practices of compartmentalised learning that children experience as constraints on their agency, reflecting wider tensions between standardised assessment and child-centred education observed globally.

Our research uncovered examples where a significant disconnect existed between teachers' intentions to foster agency and children's actual experiences of agency in their learning. While teachers consistently expressed strong beliefs in the importance of children's agency, aligning with contemporary understanding of children's rights and capabilities, the day-to-day realities of school life often communicated different messages to children about their ability to influence their learning. This misalignment became particularly evident in the approach to gathering children's input. Rather than establishing consistent procedures for involving children in curriculum design, schools often relied on ad-hoc feedback mechanisms.

This approach risked creating what Hart (1992) describes as 'tokenism' in his Ladder of Participation model related to children's rights – situations where children appear to have a voice but lack genuine influence over their learning experiences.

The consequences of this misalignment extend far beyond immediate learning situations. Our research revealed its impact not only on children's current opportunities to exercise agency but also on their developing sense of agency and future propensity to act independently in their learning.

When children repeatedly encounter environments where their attempts to influence their learning seem ineffective, they often develop a diminished sense of agency. This operates as a self-reinforcing cycle, particularly evident in the absence of consistent mechanisms for children's involvement in curriculum design. Such absence proved as significant as any existing structure in shaping both practices and experiences.

The pattern unfolds in several stages: first, limited opportunities for genuine agency lead to reduced engagement in decision-making. This results in a diminished sense of agency, which in turn reduces children's likelihood of recognising and acting upon future opportunities. Rather than transforming established patterns, this cycle tends to reproduce itself through distinct phases: initial conditions create limited opportunities for meaningful participation; this leads to reduced attempts to exercise agency; and finally, these limiting structures become reinforced rather than transformed.

Addressing this challenge requires fundamental restructuring of educational systems. The recommendations of the Independent Commission on Assessment in Primary Education (ICAPE) (Wyse, Bradbury & Trollope, 2022) represented a significant recent attempt to break this cycle by recommending systemic change. In critical realism's *real* domain, ICAPE recommended moving away from high-stakes assessments, where all children in England are tested at the same time, to an approach to national assessment based on sampling. ICAPE also recommended fundamentally rethinking accountability measures for schools. These changes could create *structural elaboration* – the transformation of existing structures to enable new possibilities for agency.

By broadening curriculum structures and reconceptualising assessment frameworks, the ICAPE recommendations sought to create enabling conditions for agency to flourish. The proposed changes would generate new patterns through the implementation of formative assessment practices and innovative teaching approaches. On the basis of our research reported in this book, we think that these changes would be likely to transform children's lived experiences of education, potentially enhancing their agency in learning, broadening recognition of diverse capabilities, and fundamentally transforming educational experiences.

The role of social dynamics in fostering agency

The research reported in this book revealed how social dynamics emerged from the interplay between individual and collective agency in schools. This interaction reflects both the wider emphasis on children's collective participation rights and the growing recognition in curriculum frameworks internationally of the need to balance individual learning with collaborative experiences.

School Councils, previously discussed as formal mechanisms for student voice, revealed important insights about collective agency and social dynamics. In schools where Councils operated, the interaction between representatives and their peers demonstrated how individual agency could transform into collective action. Representatives learned to navigate complex social dynamics when gathering feedback about playground equipment, building consensus around proposals for new after-school clubs, or mediating different opinions about school lunch options. These everyday examples showed how representatives developed sophisticated skills in balancing diverse interests – learning when to push for change and when to compromise. For instance, when proposing new after-school clubs, representatives had to consider not just their immediate friends' preferences but the broader interests of different year groups.

At NCS, collective decision-making systems showed how the principles of child-led curriculum design can be realised in practice. The school's commitment to children's agency enabled practices that children experienced as genuine opportunities for participation, aligning with contemporary understanding of how curriculum frameworks can support both individual and collective agency. Similarly, at SCI, the establishment of pupils-run clubs demonstrated how institutional support for student-led activities enabled children's collective organisation, which in turn led to the development of new opportunities and leadership roles.

However, our research also revealed how social dynamics can constrain children's agency, reflecting the challenges of implementing participatory approaches. Social influences, particularly peer pressure, sometimes limited individual expression and choice across all three schools, mirroring wider societal tensions between individual rights and group dynamics. We observed instances where children's decisions were influenced more by their peers' opinions than their own interests, highlighting complex dynamics that curriculum frameworks rarely address explicitly. This tension requires teachers to actively manage classroom social dynamics to ensure they support rather than hinder individual agency, demonstrating why professional development in participatory approaches remains crucial internationally.

Managing these social dynamics effectively requires careful attention to how structures and agency interact in practice, a challenge faced by education systems worldwide as they attempt to implement more participatory approaches to learning. Schools benefit from establishing structures that promote collective agency while implementing practices that balance individual and group needs. Ireland's curriculum framework, launched in March 2023, demonstrates this balance, where children's agency is positioned alongside other educational goals (National Council for Curriculum and Assessment, 2023). Similarly, Scotland's Curriculum for Excellence 2024 (Education Scotland, 2024) shows how children's choice can be embedded systematically within formal curriculum structures. This involves creating opportunities for authentic collaboration while protecting individual agency, as also seen in Wales' rights-based curriculum approach where schools are required to draw on children's voices in developing their educational programs.

Teachers can facilitate open discussions about peer influence and decision-making, helping children become more aware of external pressures on their choices – skills increasingly recognised as essential for participation in contemporary society. The implementation of anonymous voting systems for group decisions can help to mitigate peer pressure effects and allow for more honest expression of individual preferences, reflecting practices advocated by international children's rights organisations. Regular rotation of leadership roles in group activities helps prevent the formation of rigid social hierarchies and ensures all children have opportunities to develop leadership skills, addressing equity concerns central to modern educational reform.

While collective agency was not initially our research's main focus, it emerged as an important element in shaping children's experiences of agency in schools. Our findings suggest several important avenues for future research in this area, building on global developments in understanding children's collective rights and educational engagement.

Understanding how collective agency emerges from individual agency in school settings could help educators better facilitate the development of both, contributing to ongoing international discussions about effective pedagogical approaches. Investigation of the long-term impacts of collective agency experiences on children's civic engagement and leadership skills might reveal broader societal benefits of fostering agency in schools, connecting to wider concerns about preparing children for active citizenship in an increasingly complex world. Examining how collective agency can be fostered in diverse and inclusive educational environments could ensure equal opportunities for all children to exercise their agency, addressing persistent concerns about educational equity and access. These considerations of collective agency lead us to examine more closely the fundamental relationship between institutional structures and children's capacity for action, both individually and collectively.

Interplay between structure and agency

Our analysis of structure-agency dynamics across schools reveals the complex relationship between institutional structures and children's capacity for action. Effective agency requires not just opportunities for choice but meaningful engagement with those choices within supportive frameworks. For children to develop a true sense of agency, they need to understand the implications of their decisions, and crucially they need to actively witness their impact.

NCS' approach to curriculum design exemplified this complex interplay. The school created structures that enabled children's meaningful participation in curriculum development while ensuring alignment with national requirements, demonstrating how agency can operate effectively within necessary constraints when appropriate enabling structures exist. The experiences at SCI and SCS revealed how broader societal pressures influence educational practices. At SCI, the drive to prepare children for elite institutions, heavily influenced by parental expectations, constrained children's opportunities for choices. Similarly, at SCS, the emphasis on discipline and enrichment, shaped by perceptions of the needs of the local community in relation to socio-economic status, created tensions between the schools' desire and commitment to implement holistic learning but also the need for children to master what were seen as basic skills.

These tensions between structure and agency in educational settings connect to other foundational works in educational theory. Freire's (1970) critical pedagogy offers valuable insights into how power structures shape educational experiences and possibilities for agency. His critique of the 'banking model' of education, where students are viewed as passive recipients of knowledge, resonates with contemporary understanding of children's rights and capabilities, and with our metaphor of children as ghosts in the education machine. His concept of 'conscientisation' – developing critical consciousness of social, political, and economic contradictions – helps us understand how children might recognise and respond to constraints through small but meaningful acts of resistance within their immediate sphere of influence. These might include choosing alternative ways of responding to assigned tasks, helping peers despite instructions for independent work, or finding creative ways to incorporate their interests into prescribed activities.

The international context enriches our understanding of how these dynamics manifest in the diverse settings of our research. Bordonaro and Payne's (2012) research with street children in Cape Verde introduced the concept of 'ambiguous agency' to capture how children exercise agency within constraining circumstances. Their work revealed how children's actions often defy simple categorisation as either resistance or compliance, showing instead how agency can manifest in ways that simultaneously challenge and reinforce existing power structures.

Although Bordonaro and Payne's concept of ambiguous agency attempts to capture the complexity of children's actions within constraining circumstances, we argue that this framework inadvertently reinforces adult-centric judgments about what constitutes legitimate forms of agency. The very notion of ambiguity in children's agency implies that there are 'clear' or 'desirable' forms of agency against which children's actions can be judged. This raises fundamental questions: who determines what constitutes 'good' or 'bad' agency? Such judgments inevitably rest on assumptions about desired educational outcomes, which themselves are subject to debate and critique.

The current emphasis on academic outcomes in educational systems represents just one way of framing the purpose of education. Alternative perspectives might prioritise children's well-being, social development, or preparation for democratic citizenship. Given this multiplicity of potential educational aims, we argue for approaching children's agency as fundamentally valid and morally neutral, acknowledging children's fundamental right to act on their own behalf.

We need to recognise that children navigate school structures in sophisticated ways that defy simple categorisation or moral judgment. Children encounter structural constraints such as assessment systems and curriculum requirements, alongside institutional mechanisms that might enable agency. Their responses to these constraints demonstrate a range of strategic approaches, from working within established frameworks to finding creative ways to pursue their interests. For instance, a child who follows school rules may do so not out of simple compliance, but as a conscious choice aligned with their own goals or preferences.

This strategic navigation of institutional structures reveals children as thoughtful actors who continuously assess and adjust their approaches based on experience. Rather than evaluating these strategies as either resistance or compliance, we should understand them as demonstrations of children's capacity to make meaningful choices within their educational contexts. This perspective acknowledges children as active participants in their educational experience while recognising the complex interplay between individual agency and institutional structures.

Structured freedom

Understanding how children exercise agency within existing constraints leads us to consider how schools could create environments that support both strategic navigation of structures and their meaningful transformation. The wider context of children's rights in education reveals a persistent tension between recognising these rights in principle and implementing them in practice. This tension becomes particularly significant when considering how educational structures and curriculum frameworks can either enable or constrain children's agency in their learning.

Our new concept of *structured freedom* offers a practical framework for addressing these challenges. At NCS, this approach manifested through their child-led curriculum design and participatory decision-making mechanisms. Children actively shaped their curriculum, but at the same time teachers were able to demonstrate to external agencies that they were meeting national curriculum requirements, demonstrating how structured freedom can work within existing educational frameworks. This practical example illustrates how broader principles of children's rights and participation were realised within the formal curriculum structures that existed at the time. However, the possibility remains that had the policy structures been different the benefits for children and teachers could have been even stronger as the school had to mediate effects that were constraining what they felt and knew from the professional expertise.

In practice, structured freedom manifests at multiple levels within educational settings. At the classroom level, NCS teachers created learning environments that provided clear boundaries while opening spaces for choice. Their approach to lesson design included explicitly communicated learning aims alongside opportunities for children to choose their learning activities. These choices included selecting learning stations, skills, and levels to work at. This classroom-level implementation shows how principles of agency can be translated into daily educational practice.

The school level presents another crucial arena for structured freedom, with our research revealing how different types of schools navigate the balance between structure and agency. SCI demonstrated this through their approach to after-school clubs, offering insights into how institutional structures can support children's agency within formal educational settings. While maintaining clear operational frameworks, such as scheduling and logistical requirements, the school enabled children to initiate new clubs based on their interests and take leadership roles in organising activities alongside peers. Children could propose new clubs, develop activity plans, recruit members, and manage day-to-day operations without teacher direction.

While SCI's independent status and relatively abundant resources facilitated this comprehensive approach, our observations at SCS demonstrated how similar principles can be adapted in state school settings with more constrained resources. At SCS, agency emerged in specific, strategically chosen spaces. Children were given opportunities to exercise choice through carefully structured extracurricular activities, summer projects, and creative curriculum areas. While SCS could not support the same breadth of child-initiated clubs as SCI, it created opportunities for children's agency within existing and innovative activities and interactions, such as Philosophy for Children, cooking, and art activities.

These contrasting examples illustrate that the key elements of structured freedom – genuine child leadership opportunities, clear procedural frameworks, and supportive but non-directive adult guidance – can be implemented across the very wide differences in educational contexts that were a feature of our selection of schools for this research. What matters most is the institutional commitment to creating structured opportunities for children's agency, even if these need to be more focussed or limited in scope due to the different contexts for schools. Through different approaches suited to their specific contexts, SCS and SCI demonstrated how schools can gradually transform their practices to support greater child participation while preserving essential organisational structures.

Structured freedom operates as both a practical framework and a process of institutional change. At both SCI and SCS, the establishment of clear procedures for child participation created opportunities for agency, which in turn led to expanded possibilities as children demonstrated their capacity for responsibility, choice, and leadership. Through this iterative process, both schools' structures evolved to support increasingly meaningful forms of child participation, despite their different starting points and resources.

The implementation of structured freedom requires careful consideration of institutional mechanisms. As our analysis of School Councils demonstrated, formal structures for participation need thoughtful integration across all aspects of school life to be truly effective. Beyond specific mechanisms like School Councils, schools need to develop comprehensive approaches that embed opportunities for agency throughout all of their planning and organisation for children's education.

This involves creating multiple channels for children's participation, from classroom-level decision-making to whole-school governance. Teachers' roles emerge as crucial in this context, bridging the gap between children's rights and educational structures. At NCS, teachers consistently acted as facilitators and co-constructors, helping children navigate between required learning outcomes and their own interests and choices. This shows how educators can effectively mediate between structural requirements and agency-centred approaches to education.

Four key principles underpin successful implementation of structured freedom.

1. Integrate the three domains.

The first principle of structured freedom is alignment across all three domains of reality. Our findings show how misalignment between domains can undermine children's agency. When structural conditions do not translate effectively into daily practices, or when children's experiences do not align with intended opportunities, agency is compromised. Across our schools, we saw how this alignment varied significantly – from cases where structural intentions were successfully realised in practice and meaningfully experienced by children, to instances where disconnects between policy, practice, and experience limited children's agency opportunities.

2. Plan frameworks for choice.

The second principle focuses on the thoughtful design of practical opportunities for agency. Effective choice architecture involves not just creating opportunities for choice but also carefully considering how these opportunities are structured and supported. Our findings revealed how different approaches to structuring choice shaped children's engagement. Success depended on clear frameworks that helped children understand available options, their purpose, and how to navigate them effectively. Where such scaffolding was absent or inconsistent children often struggled to meaningfully engage with choice opportunities, even when these were formally available.

3. Establish systematic mechanisms for agency.

The third principle emphasises the importance of having clear and regular ways for children to influence all areas of school life. Our analysis showed how the reliability of these channels shaped children's opportunities to have a collective voice. Schools may take different approaches to setting up these systems – from comprehensive structures covering many aspects of school life to more limited mechanisms confined to specific areas. These differences in how schools organise opportunities for children's input significantly affect how much children can genuinely participate in shaping their school experience.

4. Build incremental development.

The fourth principle recognises how experiences of agency inform future engagement. Across all three schools, children's prior experiences shaped their recognition and use of subsequent opportunities. When children successfully effected desired changes, this nurtured both their sense of agency and likelihood of exercising agency in the future. Conversely, when attempts to influence their environment proved futile, children disengaged from future opportunities, creating negative cycles of diminishing agency.

These principles work together to create conditions where children's agency can flourish within educational structures. They provide both a theoretical framework for understanding how structured freedom operates in schools and practical guidance for educational reform. Translating these insights into actionable changes requires attention to both policy frameworks that shape educational systems and the everyday practices that bring those systems to life. The principles highlight the need for integrated approaches where policy changes align with classroom-level implementation, creating coherent environments where children's agency can flourish. With this understanding, we can now consider the specific implications of our research for both policy and practice in primary education.

Implications for policy and practice

Our research has significant implications for both educational practice and policy. Drawing on international developments in children's rights and contemporary understanding of curriculum design, these implications centre on the critical alignment between structural conditions, actual practices, and children's lived experiences of agency. The growing global recognition of children's right to participate in decisions affecting them, and the need for children's agency in the complex future world that schools are preparing their students for, points to the need for systematic transformation in how educational policies are conceptualised and implemented, ensuring changes manifest meaningfully at the classroom level.

Implications for policy

At the policy level, several key changes could foster children's agency while maintaining educational standards. First, assessment systems could move beyond heavy reliance on standardised testing to include more diverse forms of evaluation. Portfolio-based assessments incorporating children's self-selected work samples, project presentations where children demonstrate their learning through chosen formats, and structured observations of children's engagement in learning activities all offer promising alternatives that value children's agency while providing robust evidence of learning.

International examples demonstrate how assessment approaches focussed on continuous feedback and children's agency can be effective. For instance, Finland's approach emphasises formative assessment methods, where continuous feedback and self-evaluation replace the emphasis on standardised testing. Finnish educators use observation, peer reviews, and self-assessment tools to help learners understand their progress and set personal goals. This model prioritises personal growth, qualitative feedback, and student well-being over competitive rankings, aiming to develop self-regulation and intrinsic motivation in children (Finnish National Agency for Education, 2019).

Similarly, New Zealand's 'Learning Stories' methodology allows teachers to capture children's learning progress through narrative assessments that include the children's own perspectives. This approach, though initially designed for pre-school settings, has influenced primary education in New Zealand, where some schools adapt its narrative principles for older students. By integrating reflective and formative assessments, primary teachers in certain settings encourage a holistic view of learning that aligns with the participatory and personalised elements found in Learning Stories (New Zealand Ministry of Education, 2020). However, structural changes to the national policies on teaching of literacy in New Zealand that started from 2024 onwards could create barriers to the greater agency advocated in Learning Stories (Wyse & Hacking, 2024).

National curriculum frameworks could evolve to create more space for child-initiated learning while maintaining clear educational goals. This might involve creating flexible curriculum specifications that allow for child-led inquiry while meeting core learning objectives. Explicit requirements for children's input into curriculum planning could be established in new versions of national curricula, supported by clear guidelines for balancing prescribed content with learner-chosen topics. Systems for documenting and evaluating child-led learning would help ensure accountability while preserving agency. At the time of writing this book, England had initiated a review of its national curriculum. Some of the findings of this research were shared with the curriculum review team as part of a call for evidence in November 2024. The Academy of Social Sciences also included reference to the work of members of our research centre, the Helen Hamlyn Centre for Pedagogy, in its submission to the curriculum review.

Resource allocation represents another critical area for policy consideration. Our research indicates the importance of flexible schedules that allow for diverse learning activities and give children choice over aspects of their day. Resources that support agency include open-ended materials that children can use flexibly, technology that enables them to document their own learning, and materials that support different modes of expression. Dedicated time within the school day for meaningful consultation with children is essential, as is maintaining adequate staffing levels to enable more responsive and individualised teaching approaches. Professional development programmes focussing on facilitating children's agency would be essential to help teachers develop necessary skills, while support for schools to learn from successful examples of agency-promoting practices could accelerate positive change.

Implications for practice

At the practice level, our research suggests several key approaches for implementing agency-supporting pedagogy. In the classroom, teachers can create regular opportunities for children's decision-making within clear frameworks. These opportunities include regular meetings where children contribute to learning plans, extending to more complex decision-making about learning pathways and assessment methods. Offering multiple ways to demonstrate learning, combined with regular reflection sessions, enables children to evaluate and shape their learning experiences. The physical environment itself becomes a tool for agency when teachers create flexible learning spaces that children can modify for different purposes.

Assessment practices can support children's agency when thoughtfully designed. Teachers can involve children in creating success criteria and offer choices in assessment methods, moving beyond traditional approaches to include children's self-evaluation alongside teacher assessment. Documentation of learning becomes richer through incorporating children's perspectives via photographs, recordings, and written reflections selected by children themselves, creating a more complete picture of their learning journey.

Collaboration between teachers proves vital for developing agency-supporting practices. Our research showed the value of shared vision and ongoing reflection where teachers share successful strategies, discuss challenges, and plan coordinated approaches to supporting children's agency. This collaborative approach helps ensure consistency across different learning contexts while allowing for adaptation to specific subject areas or age groups. Teachers who regularly share their experiences and insights develop more nuanced and effective strategies for supporting children's agency.

Beyond individual classrooms, whole-school practices create environments conducive to children's agency. Consistent opportunities and clear mechanisms for children to influence school decisions contribute to a culture where agency is valued and supported. Visible evidence of children's impact on their learning environment, from displays of child-led projects to changes made in response to children's suggestions, reinforces the value placed on their agency.

The role of school leadership is crucial in supporting these practices. Leaders create organisational structures that enable teacher collaboration and ensure resources are allocated to support agency-promoting practices. By modelling agency-supporting approaches in their own interactions with staff and children, leaders help establish a school culture that values participation and voice in both theory and practice. The Head Teachers and teachers who featured in our research all showed clear visions about how they conceived agency in their schools.

Conclusion

Our research has shown the fundamental importance of agency in primary education while revealing the complex ways it can operate in practice. The experiences across our study schools demonstrate that creating environments which prioritise children's agency while meeting educational standards was challenging but achievable, even within the systemic constraints of England's National Curriculum of 2014. NCS' success in fostering meaningful agency while maintaining high academic standards demonstrates how competing demands can be reconciled through rigorous institutional design and practice, informed by confident professionals building on their depth of academic study, even in contexts where standardised assessments and prescribed pedagogies have been shown to limit children's experiences of agency.

However, school such as NCS, and all schools in England and other countries and regions, could be so much more effective in supporting children's early education. Our concept of structured freedom provides a practical framework for understanding and supporting children's agency while maintaining necessary educational coherence. However, the contrasting experiences of SCI, SCS, and NCS highlight crucial equity considerations – resource disparities, community expectations, and institutional priorities all shape the opportunities for children's agency. This suggests that fostering agency requires not just pedagogical innovation but attention to broader social and economic factors.

The implications of our research extend beyond immediate educational practice to broader questions of children's role in society. As social, technological, and economic changes accelerate, children's capacity for independent thought and action becomes increasingly crucial. Agency in education develops capabilities and dispositions that extend far beyond the classroom, offering benefits not just for individual children but for schools and society more broadly. Our research demonstrates how children's strategic navigation of institutional structures represents sophisticated engagement with the complexities of modern education.

Looking forward, transforming educational systems to support children's agency requires coordinated change at multiple levels. While current policy contexts present challenges, international developments in children's rights frameworks and curriculum design increasingly recognise children's participation as essential rather than optional. This shift demands new approaches to both policy and practice – from classroom-level strategies to national curriculum frameworks. Success requires moving beyond surface-level acknowledgment of children's rights and agency to creating conditions where meaningful children's input becomes integral to daily educational practice.

Our research demonstrates that such transformation, while challenging, is not only possible and necessary but also very exciting. The examples from our research schools show pathways toward this goal, suggesting that every school, regardless of context or resources, can take meaningful steps toward supporting children's agency. Through careful attention to how agency operates in practice, sustained commitment to supportive environments, and systematic attention to equity, primary education in England needs to evolve to better serve children's needs in the twenty-first century.

References

Bernstein, B. (1975). *Class, codes and control: Volume 3 – Towards a theory of educational transmissions*. Routledge & Kegan Paul.

Bordonaro, L. I., & Payne, R. (2012). The politics and moralities of agency in children's education: The case of the Sierra Leone Civil War. *Children's Geographies, 10*(4), 379–393.

Education Scotland. (2024). *Scotland's curriculum*. https://scotlandscurriculum.scot/4/

Finnish National Agency for Education. (2019). *National core curriculum for basic education*. https://www.oph.fi/en/education-and-qualifications/national-core-curriculum-basic-education

Freire, P. (1970). *Pedagogy of the oppressed*. Seabury Press.

Hart, R. A. (1992). *Children's participation: From tokenism to citizenship*. UNICEF International Child Development Centre.

National Council for Curriculum and Assessment. (2023). *Primary curriculum framework*. NCCA. Retrieved from https://curriculumonline.ie/getmedia/84747851-0581-431b-b4d7-dc6ee850883e/2023-Primary-Framework-ENG-screen.pdf

New Zealand Ministry of Education. (2020, June 14). Learning stories. *New Zealand Curriculum*. https://nzcurriculum.tki.org.nz/Principles/Learning-to-learn-principle/Learning-stories

Wyse, D., Bradbury, A., & Trollope, R. (2022). *The independent commission on assessment in primary education: Final report*. https://www.icape.org.uk

Wyse, D., & Hacking, C. (2024). *The balancing act: An evidence-based approach to teaching phonics, reading and writing*. Routledge.

INDEX

Note: Page numbers in *italics* indicate figures and page numbers in **bold** indicate tables on the corresponding page. Numbers following "n" refer to notes.

ability grouping 37–38, 40, 68, 146–147
Academy of Social Sciences 164
acquaintance knowledge 12; *see also* knowledge
Advisory Panel 19
affordances 39
agency 5, 8, 23, 31–33, 166; ambiguous 159; on children's learning 14; and choices (*see* choices); collective 14, 156–158; competence 35; contextual dimension 36; dimensions in educational settings 35–36; dual nature of 39–40; educational outcomes 5–6, 13; individual 32, 156–158; interpersonal dimension 36; intrapersonal dimension 36; in literacy development 15; practical action 35; in primary schools 153–155; psychological impact 103; and School Councils 122–126; school structures 41; self-determination 35; sense and exercise of 36–39; social dynamics in 119–122, 156–158; socially situated capacity to act 31, 39–41; structure and 32–34, 158–160; and subject hierarchies 114–119; systematic mechanisms for 162; temporal dimension 36; temporally embedded process 35
agents 45
ambiguous agency 159; *see also* agency

Archer, M. S. 32
Art Council 125
assessment 11; formative 11; high-stakes 12, 155–156; impact 155–156; Northern City State (NCS) 146–147; portfolio-based 163; South City Independent (SCI) 142–144; South City State (SCS) 144–145; summative 11
autonomy 14, 81, 148; institutional 83, 98; in learning environments 110; in structured learning environments 113

behaviour management systems 82, 150
behaviour policy: Northern City State (NCS) 96–97; South City Independent (SCI) 71; South City State (SCS) 82–83
Bernstein, B. 10–11, 155
Bhaskar, R. 33
Bordonaro, L. I. 159
Buchanan, D. 24

Cambridge Primary Review 7
Carvalho, R. De 15
causality 44–45; contextual 45–46; cultural context 45; in curriculum 46; historical context 45; institutional context 46
central conflation 32
CHAMP scheme (Calmly and quietly, Hands to yourself, Aware of others,

Move slowly, and Pass on the left) 97, 126
child-centred approach 84–86, 140
child-led curriculum 153; Northern City State (NCS) 86, 97, 138, 157, 160; South City State (SCS) 149
Children's Agency in the National Curriculum (CHANT) Project 2; *see also specific methods*
choices 99–100, 127; independent 14, 109, 110, 113; Northern City State (NCS) 110–114; plan frameworks for 162; in primary schools 153–155; South City Independent (SCI) 100–107; South City State (SCS) 107–110
Chu, P. 14
ClassDojo 150
co-constructed curriculum maps 93, 139–140
collective agency 14, 156–158; *see also* agency
compartmentalised learning 155
contextual causality 45–46; *see also* causality
Convention on the Rights of the Child (CRC) 2
Cook, D. T. 6
core subjects 24, 68, 115–117; national curriculum in 73; structured teaching methods 71; teacher-directed learning in 116
Covid-19 pandemic 2, 50, 67, 70, 73, 145
creative curriculum 72, 83; *see also* curriculum
critical consciousness 159
critical discourse analysis (CDA) 7, 24, 43; critical realism and 44; limitations of 47–48
critical realism 27, 31, 33–35, 57–60; actual domain 33, 38, 40, 47; categories 33; causality (*see* causality); and critical discourse analysis (CDA) 44; domains of 33, 38, 40, 47; empirical domain 33, 38, 40, 47; framework 35; perspectives 38; real domain 33, 38, 40, 47, 156; rigid assessment requirements 33; structural elaboration 34; structural reproduction 33–34; themes and codes **58–59**
cross-curriculum 12, 133
cultural capital 84–85
curriculum 4, 10–11, 26, 136, 164; creative 72, 83; development 132, 148–149;

educational perspective 10; formal 79, 117, 130, 138, 157, 160; foundational skills 2; fundamental aspects 21; inclusive 73; inflexible *vs.* flexible 38; international influences 15–17; and knowledge 12–13; learner-centred 18, 21; limitation of children's agency 25; Northern City State (NCS) 89–93, *90–92*, 137–142; planning 12; in primary education 6–7; requirements 135, 139, 142; restrictive nature 38; sociological perspective 10; South City Independent (SCI) 65–66, 130–133; South City State (SCS) 76–80, 133–137; structured freedom 8, 160–163
Curriculum Council 125
Curriculum for Excellence 23, 157
curriculum making 18, 23
curriculum mapping 86, 126; co-constructed 93, 139

data collection activities 50; *Feelings at School* activity *55*, 55–56; fieldwork activities 56; fieldwork visits/online interviews 50; innovative activities 51–56, 99; *My Agency Timeline* activity 52–53, *53, 54*; *My Ideal School Day* activity 54–55; *My Learning Choice Diary* activity 52, *52*; plan for next visits 51; *The School Tour* activity 51–52; selection 50
decision-making 3, 19, 81; collaborative 105, 148; collective 157; participatory 153, 160
'deep dive' approach 137
Dewey, J. 12–13
Dojo treats 95–96, 150–151
Dong, Y. 15
Draft Primary Curriculum Framework 19
dual coding maps 77–79, 134

Education Act (1880) 6
educational inequality 32
educational policies 1, 3; implications for 163–164
educational practice 33, 40–41, 165
Education Reform Act (1988) 7, 22–23
effective learning 132–133
effect sizes 28n1
11-plus examination 103, 115, 132, 143, 144, 148, 155
Emirbayer, M. 35
emotional economy 37

engagement 140; Ireland primary curriculum 20–21; social 35
England's Early Years Foundation Stage curriculum 22
England's national curriculum 7–8, 24–27, 62; knowledge-based approach 138; systemic constraints 166
England's National Health Service 145
Erdem, C. 14
exercise agency 36–39, 44, 134, 136; Miriam's Learning Choice Diary 108, *108*; *see also* agency
extracurricular activities 108, 130; South City Independent (SCI) 70–71; South City State (SCS) 72

Fairclough, N. 47, 48
Fattore, T. 35
Five Pillars of Islam 135
formal curriculum 79, 117, 130, 138, 157, 160; *see also* curriculum
formative assessment 11, 156, 164; *see also* assessment
foundational skills 2
foundation subjects 24; *see also* core subjects
Francis, B. 37
Freire, P. 159
Frisch, R. 15
Future of Education and Skills 2030 project 16, 17

Gao, X. A. 34–35
Gibb, N. 24, 26
Glasser's Choice Theory 152n2
Gormley, A. 133
Gove, M. 24
Government of Ireland 20

Hargreaves, E. 24
Hart, R. A. 156
Hayward, L. 17
Helen Hamlyn Centre for Pedagogy (HHCP) 4, 27, 164
Helen Hamlyn Trust 9n1
high-stakes assessment 12, 155–156; *see also* assessment
Hong Kong's national curriculum 21–22

implementation gap 155–156
Independent Association of Prep Schools' (IAPS) 49
independent choice 14, 109, 110, 113

Independent Commission on Assessment in Primary Education (ICAPE) 156
individual agency 32, 156–158; *see also* agency
International Primary Curriculum (IPC) 76
Ireland's primary curriculum 19–20, 157; engagement and participation 20–21

Jinling, S. 14

Kaya, M. 14
Ke, Z. 14
knowledge 12; acquaintance 12; curriculum and 12–13; organisers 77–79, *78*, 134; powerful 13; propositional 12; as social construction 138; vocabulary 131

leadership 82; behavioural framework 71; in group activities 158; school (*see* school leadership); senior leadership team (SLT) 49, 57, 82, 130; teacher 14
Leading Out Seminars 19
learner-centred approach: curriculum 18, 21; pedagogy 17
Learning Compass 2030 framework 16–17
'Learning Stories' methodology 164
Lee, C. 15
lesson design: Northern City State (NCS) 94–95; South City Independent (SCI) 68–70; South City State (SCS) 81–82
Leverhulme Trust 9n1, 18
limited agency 107, 109, 110, 152; *see also* agency
literacy development 15, 80
longitudinal in-depth qualitative inquiry 48–49

Maths Mansion 132
Mental Health Assembly 66–67
Ministry of Stories 80, 136
Mische, A. 35
Miseducation (Reay) 37
mixed-ability approach 136
Musical Theatre club 70

National Council for Curriculum and Assessment (NCCA) 19–21
Newly Qualified Teacher (NQT) 85
New Zealand's 'Learning Stories' methodology 164
Northern City State (NCS) 84, 98, 100, 153–154; assessment 146–147; balancing children's agency challenge 87;

behaviour policy 96–97; child-centred approach 84–86; child-led approach 86, 97, 138, 157, 160; curriculum 89–93, *90–92*, 137–142; Dahlia's Agency Timeline 111, *111*, *112*; dyslexia and resilience 89; golden time 95, 150–151; impressive academic abilities 87; lesson design 94–95; My Agency Timeline activity 110; pupil personality 88; Pupil Research Lead 146, 150; reward system 95–96; School Council 93–94; school-society relationships 150–152; social dynamics 121–122; teacher experience 84–87; transition from secondary to primary education 86–87
NVivo 57, 60

Ontario Human Rights Commission 27
Open Futures programme 77, 83, 93
Organisation for Economic Cooperation and Development (OECD) 16–17

Pandya, J. 17
Payne, R. 159
pedagogy 11; 'chalk and talk' 11; child-centred 2; choice in 110; critical 159; experiential learning 11; implications 46; learner-centred 17
People's Republic of China (PRC) 21
Philosophy for Children (P4C) lessons 77, 81, 134
phonics screening check (PSC) 26
policy *see* educational policies
policy makers 18
poverty: and inequity 3; statistics 4
powerful knowledge 13; *see also* knowledge
practices of education 33, 40–41, 165
Priestley, M. 18
Primary Education Curriculum Guide 2024 21
primary education/schools 4; choice and agency in 153–155; curriculum in 6–7, 129; *see also* Northern City State (NCS); South City Independent (SCI); South City State (SCS)
Principles of Learning, Teaching and Assessment 20
professional development 20, 62, 157, 164
Programme for International Student Assessment (PISA) 17, 18, 20, 81
propositional knowledge 12; *see also* knowledge

Quick, L. 24

Reading Champions programme 83
Reay, D. 37; *Miseducation* (2017) 37
Reedy, A. 15
religious education (RE) 135
reward system: Northern City State (NCS) 95–96
Rosen, R. 6
Rubik's Cube club 70, 130

School Council 122–123, 127, 161; collective agency and social dynamics 157; Northern City State (NCS) 93–94, 125–126; South City Independent (SCI) 67–68, 123–125; South City State (SCS) 80–81
school leadership 74; agency-promoting practices 165; choice-based approaches 137; positions 71; *see also* leadership
school selection criteria 48
school-society relationships 147; Northern City State (NCS) 150–152; South City Independent (SCI) 147–149; South City State (SCS) 149–150
school types 48–49
Scotland's Curriculum for Excellence (2024) 23, 157
self-fulfilling prophecy 37–38
self-perception 14
senior leadership team (SLT) 49, 57, 82, 130
sense of agency 36–39, 52, 56; social interactions in 100; South City Independent (SCI) 100–107; *see also* agency
sense of ownership 93, 101, 108, 135
Shen, J. 14
Siry, C. 15
Smart School Councils 81
social dynamics 119, 127; in fostering agency 156–158; Northern City State (NCS) 121–122; South City Independent (SCI) 119–120; South City State (SCS) 120–121
social engagement 35
sociology of childhood 6
South City Independent (SCI) 61, 98, 154, 161; assessment 142–144; behaviour policy 71; choices 100–107; curriculum 65–66; extracurricular programme at 70–71; Feelings at School activity 101, 115; high-stakes assessment

structures 155; lesson design 68–70; Mental Health Assembly 66–67; Musical Theatre club 70; proactive learning behaviours 64; Pupil's Mathematics Exercise Book *69*; School Council 67–68; school-society relationships 147–149; sense of agency 100–107; social dynamics 119–120; Sonia's Learning Choice Diary 100, *101*; student characteristics 63–65; student-led activities 157; student well-being 66–67; teacher experience (2021 to 2023) 62–63

South City State (SCS) 72, 98, 122–123, 154, 161; agency 107–110; assessment 144–145; balanced agency 152; behaviour policy 82–83; child-led learning 149; children's teams of student leaders 80–81; choices 107–110; cross-curricular approach 133; curriculum 76–80, 133–137; dual coding maps 77, 79; experiential learning and enrichment activities 79–80; Feelings at School activity 120; high attaining students 75; high-stakes assessment structures 155; inclusive curriculum 73; knowledge organisers 77, *78*; lesson design 81–82; mayor's education pledge 149; Miriam's Learning Choice Diary *108*, 108–109; My Learning Choice Diary activity 108; project competition 79; Reading Champions 83; School Council 80–81; school-society relationships 149–150; social dynamics 120–121; social experiences 120–121; structural factors affecting 149; student personality and academic abilities 75–76; teacher experiences 72–75; teacher-led choices 105

Spyrou, S. 6

statutory tests (SATs) 142–144, 146

Stoecklin, D. 35

structural determination 32

structural elaboration 34, 156

structural reproduction 33–34

structure-agency dynamics 32–34, 158–160

structured freedom 8, 160, 166; elements 161; implementation 161–163; principles 162–163

subject hierarchies 114, 127; Northern City State (NCS) 118–119; South City Independent (SCI) 115–116; South City State (SCS) 116–118

summative assessment 11; *see also* assessment

synthetic phonics approach 26–27

Tam, V. C. 14

teacher experience: Northern City State (NCS) 84–87; South City Independent (SCI) 62–63; South City State (SCS) 72–75

teacher leadership 14; *see also* leadership

Traffic Light System 82–83

Tsang, V. 14

UK 3–5; national curriculum in 22–24

United Nations Children's Fund (UNICEF) 2; Let Us Learn (LUL) report 2

verbal reasoning 131

vocabulary knowledge 131; *see also* knowledge

Vocabulary Ninja scheme 65, 130–131

Wales' national curriculum 23, 158; *see also* national curriculum

Well-Being Lead 133, 143

Wiliam, D. 37

Wilmes, S. E. 15

Wyse, D. 17

Yousafzai, M. 32

Youth Shadow Panel 7

For Product Safety Concerns and Information please contact our EU representative GPSR@taylorandfrancis.com Taylor & Francis Verlag GmbH, Kaufingerstraße 24, 80331 München, Germany